1.50

MICHAEL JACKSON

MICHAEL JACKSON

The Man in the Mirror

TODD GOLD

SIDGWICK & JACKSON
LONDON

First published in Great Britain in 1989 by Sidgwick & Jackson Limited

Copyright © 1989 by Todd Gold

ISBN 0-283-99799-0

Typeset by Hewer Text Composition Services, Edinburgh
Printed by Billing and Sons, Ltd. Worcester
for Sidgwick & Jackson Limited
1 Tavistock Chambers, Bloomsbury Way,
London WC1A 2SG

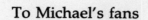

To Michael's fans

ACKNOWLEDGEMENTS

First and foremost, thanks are extended to Michael Jackson and Frank Dileo. Both men made the various times I landed in their company much easier than I expected.

The two individuals who first assigned me to cover the Michael Jackson phenomena, Cutler Durkee and John Saar, deserve thanks. They listened when I found reasons to stay on the case. So do Lisa Russell and Steve Dougherty, friends who helped me complete my stories.

Thanks also to Lee Solters for taking my phone calls, and to Glen Brunman for not going to Japan with me.

I appreciate Madeleine Morel for asking me to write this book, and I was inspired by Jainah Hamann, who never got beyond About the Author in her own book but always wanted to see her name in print.

Finally, my wife, Beth, and my daughter, Abby, showed extraordinary patience throughout this project. They are my superstars.

PREFACE

Tokyo, Japan, September, 1987.

'Six blocks away,' the voice crackles on the walkie-talkie. 'Almost there.'

The big, barrel-chested man relays the message to others. 'They're almost here.'

Several kids on the outside hear them talking.

Word travels fast. With less than a hour before show time at Japan's Yokohama stadium, a nervous horde of teenagers collects in a jittery pack outside the tightly guarded chain-link entrance, growing tense with adrenalin-fuelled excitement. They know they will be close to the legend tonight. They will, at least, see him close up. It is almost too much for them to handle. As they press forward, police try to calm them with the soothing words, *'Sugu, sugu!'* 'Soon, soon!'

Two vans – one blue, one gold – screech up the ramp, eliciting ecstatic screams of recognition. A short distance past the heavily guarded gates, the vehicles stop, the doors are opened, and a lithe young man steps out. In the milliseconds before a phalanx of beefy security guards surround him, the stadium lights catch the silver buckles of his flashy jacket. Then he is whisked away, like a leaf in a strong breeze, disappearing behind a door labelled, in light blue letters, Mr Michael Jackson.

In this second week of what will be a year-long world tour, Michael is a lightning bolt of electricity. His late arrival backstage perks up the crew and band members who've been lazing around his spartan dressing room. Inside, Michael makes his final preparations. He rolls his head to limber up. Gazing in a full-length mirror, he flicks a speck of loose makeup off his cheek. His spindly, five-foot-ten frame seems finely toned, in contrast to the fragile portrait he offers in photographs. 'I'm getting a little worried about my voice getting thin,' says Michael in a more forthright tone than the frail squeak

ix

of his rare public pronouncements. 'But so far things are going good.'

This inner sanctum of solitude is far removed from the frenzy in the stadium. The phenomenon the Japanese press dubbed Typhoon Michael has rolled across this tiny nation with the force of a powerful Pacific storm. All 38,000 seats for tonight's concert sold out weeks ago; and those truly desperate to witness the performer they call My-ke-ru have paid scalpers upwards of $700 for a seat originally priced at $40.

In the calm of his dressing room Michael is oblivious to the raucousness building outside. He pours a cup of hot tea from a tall thermos, lingers over the mug while the rising steam caresses the pores of his burnished ebony skin, and finally sips the brew, ignoring the clamour from the arena and the rising nerves of his fifteen backup musicians and dancers. One last detail: he straps on his heavy belt, its extravagantly large buckle flashing prisms of coloured light in all directions, and then checks himself in the mirror for the final time.

Just behind the stage, in a dark corner illuminated by flickering flashlights, Michael huddles with his cast like a football quaterback and a crew member recites a brief prayer. They clap their hands and stomp their feet. Adrenalin races through their bodies. 'Whatever we play,' yells Michael, his smooth, sculpted features relaxing into an excited grin, 'it's got to be funky!' A moment later, to a wall of lights, shooting lasers and thunderous applause, they jog onstage.

There's no big secret here: the public life of the world's most popular rock star is defined by fame, glitter, standing ovations and immense wealth. His enigmatic private life is a perplexing matter that defies all boundaries governing normal behaviour. By the release in August 1988 of his long-awaited solo LP, *Bad*, his first album in five years, Michael Jackson, at twenty-nine years old, was more than just the most talented entertainer on the globe. He was also regarded as the planet's most celebrated weirdo.

The litany of accusations and denials surrounding Michael plays like a broken record. He has been accused of using chemicals to lighten his skin, of taking female hormones to keep his voice high, of transforming his body with plastic surgery, of refusing to bathe in anything but Evian water, and more. He has uttered no more than a few cryptic sentences in public for six years, the result of a deep-seated distrust of the press' ability to transcribe his words and the public's ability to understand their meaning.

Cynics might argue that the rumours only increased the considerable early sales of *Bad*, that the tall tales flung at the young man are nothing more than the parts of a complicated ploy to generate publicity during the long, dormant stretch between projects. But that wouldn't be correct. Nor would it be fair or compassionate to the very sensitive Michael. 'It's really horrible to have these lies printed about me,' he says in a plaintive voice, his eyes pleading for attention. 'It hurts.'

By all accounts, Michael is the ultimate showbusiness wacko. He's Peter Pan dressed up in belts and leather, flitting around onstage backed by 10,000 watts of amplified rock and roll, leading the terminally bored masses to salvation with his amazing ability to sing and dance. Yet when the lights are off, he becomes the lost boy. The razzle-dazzle turns to dust. Isolation is the price he has to pay for his immense talent. He becomes prisoner of his own quixotic thoughts. His fantasy world turns into a nightmare.

The accusations sting. But Michael has never allowed himself to exhibit the pain. That would be a tacit admission of vulnerability, and much too close a glimpse of the inner life he so carefully protects. But everyone has a limit to the amount of pain they can tolerate, including Michael.

Driven to the brink after the last of three shows in Yokohama, he performs a rare act that reveals a sorely troubled man very different from his magical persona: Late at night, well past midnight, he sat down in the stillness of his empty suite at the Capitol Tokyu Hotel in Tokyo and, on the back of a piece of hotel stationery, wrote what he said would be his only discussion of his private life in response to questions submitted by a journalist. 'Like the old Indian proverb says,' Michael wrote, 'do not judge a man until you've walked two moons in his moccasins.'

Michael's full-page epistle exposes him as a strange combination of man and boy whose personality mirrors the stark contrast in his music – bright, infectious dance tunes laced with foreboding lyrics. The songs express the dark fantasies and hyper-romantic dreams of a frightened individual; the letter uncovers his harsh, unimaginable burdens. In his messy, childlike scrawl, Michael offers forgiveness to the exploitative rumourmongers who have upset him: 'Animals strike, not from malice, but because they want to live. It is the same with those who criticize. They desire our blood, not our pain.'

At the same time, Michael makes it absolutely clear that he has been unfairly punished, misunderstood by all. His piercing shout is that of a desperate child. 'I cry very, very often because it hurts. . .' But he also reveals a superhuman explanation of his life's work. 'But still, I must achieve. I must seek truth in all things. I must endure for the power I was sent forth. For the world. For the children.' In the end, he pleads for compassion. 'But have mercy, for I've been bleeding a long time now.'

1

Michael didn't want to go. Peeking out the second-storey window like a child spying on his parents' dinner guests, he slid the curtain just far enough to let him glimpse the bucolic backyard where sixty invited guests were sipping champagne and strolling the manicured grounds like VIPs at some exclusive outdoor art preview. But he had no choice.

Michael was met at the bottom of the winding staircase by LaToya, his older sister. More outgoing than her brother, LaToya attempted to calm his nerves with chatter of how much she enjoyed parties. 'It's going to be fun,' she said. 'At least, it won't be as bad as you think.'

Michael summoned a half-hearted smile. A week before the release of *Bad*, his much anticipated and long overdue album, Epic records had brought the twenty-five most powerful record retailers in the United States to Los Angeles so they could personally meet the enigmatic superstar on his own turf. The record company felt they needed to be convinced that Michael wasn't the outright wacko of rumour they had been reading about for several years.

After *Bad* was previewed over champagne cocktails at the Beverly Hills Hotel, the group of retailers were ferried by stretch limousines to the fabled Encino where Michael lived. There they encounted the unmistakable imprint of the Gloved One. It was awe-inspiring.

Imagination had served as Michael's blueprint when he created this fantasy land years ago. His name was engraved like an artist's signature on a tiny plaque set next to the front door. A star with his name on it was implanted in the centre of the walkway leading to the entrance. The property glistened in the moonlight. The fountains and turrets, sculpted shrubbery, overflowing gardens, caged birds, swans and endless strands of white Christas lights were all too much and yet just what everyone expected.

With unhindered access everywhere but Michael's upstairs sanctuary, guests took their champagne and caviar hors d'oeuvres and headed off on an eye-popping treasure hunt. They found cavernous rooms furnished with antique clocks (few of which were wound), oil paintings of wide-eyed children, delicate porcelain statues on pedestals and huge sculptures of the likes of Louis XIV on horseback and David killing Goliath. The collections were new and portended to show a cultured taste that bore little relation to the Jackson's storybook rise from the obscurity of middle America.

That more personal story was hinted at in the trophy room. There the walls were plastered with gold and platinum albums. More were stuffed into boxes and hidden under tables and chairs, and still more were just lying on the floor. Yet here too Michael added a prize that was distinctly his own. A large terrarium containing a diorama from *Snow White and the Seven Dwarves* was breathtaking. Actors dressed as characters from Disneyland had even personally delivered the prized possession to Michael.

Behind the formal dining room, guests stumbled into a child's dream: a room crammed with pinball games that didn't require money to play. The tour continued outside, where, above the four-car garage, they visited Michael's personal museum, a virtual warehouse stocked with memorabilia from more than twenty years in show business. Trinkets from every stage of his career were displayed in glass cases: his trademarked white glove, spangled buttons, pins, and his 'Billie Jean' fedora. Two life-size wax replicas of Michael wearing his sequined Bell Man's outfits stood by the door. Hundreds of photographs lined the walls; a few were from Michael's childhood, which showed the pre-cosmetic surgery Jackson as a rascally, pudgy-nosed boy. The rest were more current photos of Michael posing with celebrities including Ronald Reagan, Jimmy Carter, Fred Astaire, Sammy Davis Jr., Elizabeth Taylor, Steven Spielberg and Brooke Shields.

The one glaring omission from this comprehensive testimonial to one of the truly great entertainers in history was more than a slight recognition of Michael's brothers. There were a few photos, nothing more, and absolutely no sense that throughout most of his journey to superstardom Michael had been accompanied by his brothers.

2

'You get an overwhelming sense that Michael adores his own celebrity,' remarked a visitor that evening. 'His image is everywhere, spread across the place like pixie dust. But you also get a sense that it's all been done by Michael to convince himself of his own importance – almost as if he fears that if he isn't acknowledged, he won't be appreciated.'

LaToya, meanwhile, was doing her best to bolster Michael's abhorrence of parties like this one. Never mind mingling over cocktails. The abstemious Michael didn't know how to interact with people. 'I hate to admit it,' he says, 'but I feel strange around everyday people. See, my whole life has been onstage. And the impression I get of people is applause, standing ovations and running after you. In a crowd I'm afraid. If I could, I would sleep on the stage.'

He was serious. The stage was everything and venturing out among the public was a frightening experience. But this evening's event was a command performance of sorts. It was business, probably the only thing that could drag him outside – besides, of course, LaToya's constant tugs on his arm.

Instinct told Michael to run from the party, to run back to his room and lock the door. But that option wasn't a possibility. So while heading for the party, Michael transformed himself like an actor preparing to go onstage. He assumed his public alter-ego: an expressionless observer whose true emotions were concealed beneath a self-controlled, expressionless reserve. It was a mask of resignation and protection, one that seemed to say, 'Okay, I'm going to watch everyone watch me.'

A moment before Michael pushed open the door leading outside, he looked out the window and surveyed the festive scene. He had once designed and hung tiny wooden signs throughout the backyard on which were painted favourite aphorisms. One particular sign, appropriate to the situation, caught his eye. It read, 'Follow your dreams wherever they may lead.'

When Michael released *Thriller* in 1982, he took pop music into a new decade with the confidence of a former child prodigy who was absolutely convinced by age five that 'something special was going on.' *Off the Wall*, his 1979 comming-of-age LP, heralded his emergence as a mature talent, and the unexpected, record-shattering success of *Thriller* underscored it. By 1984, Michael was the biggest thing since chocolate chip cookies, a star of unprecedented proportions. He had followed his boyhood dreams and made them his reality.

3

Three years later, though, he was his own worst enemy. As much as he craved it, success also haunted him. It twisted his thinking, warped his life. The reasons why this happened were beyond anyone's comprehension. And Michael, refusing to be interviewed, offered few clues to the puzzling character of his celebrated life. Musically, he was the baddest dude of all, but no one talked about that. What people asked was, 'Is this guy weird or what?'

That was the question, a question clouded in shades of grey. Michael has purposely shielded his life by an impenetrable mystique. He hasn't given a revealing interview since 1984, and his last major public statement, spoken at a 1986 press conference announcing his $15 million endorsement deal with Pepsi, consisted of three brief sentences. 'This is a great honour. Thank you, Mr Enrico and Pepsi Associates. Ladies and gentlemen, thank you.'

In public Michael rarely deviates from his prepared script, but he showed a surprising, even charming, naturalness at the 1988 American Music Awards. Introduced by comedian Eddie Murphy, Michael stepped forward to accept his honorary awards. The microphone was set too low and Michael was uncomfortable with having to bend as he spoke. Interrupting his prepared speech, he motioned to Murphy and, in a soft aside that was picked up by television, pleaded for the comedian to raise it. 'Come on, Eddie,' he said. 'Help me out.'

Murphy started to the rescue, then caught himself and turned the situation into a joke. 'Hey, this guy thinks I work for him,' he cracked.

Michael laughed at himself as hard as anyone in the audience.

It was a rare performance for someone as rigid as Michael. Few of his associates could recall the last time the performer had ventured so far out of character. After all, through the entire year-and-a-half *Bad* tour, there were, a tour member estimates, less than half a dozen ad libs from Michael. 'He hates doing anything that isn't rehearsed to perfection,' a tour musician says. But there's an explanation for his icy image. Michael, friends and family members say, has an overwhelming insecurity of appearing anything less than perfect. In the grey terrain of his uneasy consciousness, Michael sees perfection as an all or nothing proposition. It's the rule that governs everything he does, from his appearance to his music.

There's no middle ground for Michael. Only success and failure and an overwhelming fear of not being recognized for his accomplishments. He cried uncontrollably when *Off the Wall* captured only one Grammy nomination, and he sunk into a deep depression when he didn't win it. Angry, he vowed that his next album would have to be so successful that no one would be able to ignore it, which *Thriller* was. Even that wasn't enough, though. After having a cleft chiselled in his chin, he reportedly pleaded with executives at Disney to reshoot his scene in *Captain Eo*. And he fumed when his recent *Bad* album, which had already produced a record-breaking five consecutive number one singles, failed to deliver a sixth.

Insiders weren't surprised. Michael, those close to him say, is never satisfied with his accomplishments. 'He is satisfied temporarily,' one of Michael's former publicists says, 'and then he forgets everything. It's as if he has to start from square one again. I've never met anyone of his stature and talent who is as inwardly insecure.'

Director Steven Spielberg called Michael 'one of the last innocents.' That was perhaps too revealing for Michael's comfort for he recently told his friend, actor Corey Feldman, 'You can tell people you know me. That's okay. But don't ever, ever tell anyone what we talk about.'

There's little to indicate that Michael actually enjoys his success. He measures it not from within, but by such fleeting outward signs as record sales, chart position and gate receipts. Years ago he shuddered that someone might surpass the four hit singles, then a record for one LP, produced by *Off the Wall*. 'Nobody broke my record yet, thank God,' he sighed. 'Hall and Oates tried, but they didn't.'

No, Michael did that himself in 1988. But having broken virtually every record in the book, he still battled against himself with punishing ferocity. Nothing was enough to satisfy his hunger. One achievement had to be topped by the next, lest anyone forget who was on top. 'Michael is not happy unless he's number one,' his brother Marlon says. 'The funny thing is, he's already number one, and he still doesn't ever seem happy.'

How could he be happy? Success, insiders observe, only fuels his discontent and failings as a person. 'Michael sometimes thinks buying things will make him happy,' LaToya says. 'But those things don't really help. You have to be happy with yourself from inside.' Michael should heed his sister's advice. For more than a decade, friends observe, Michael has cultivated a personality that's in perpetual conflict with itself.

5

'He's a cross between E.T. and Howard Hughes,' says Frank Dileo, Michael's ex-manager, confidant, friend and protector, 'That's the best way to describe him.' Producer Quincy Jones, a friend since Michael was twelve, says, 'He's the oldest man I know, and he's the youngest kid I know.'

Director Steven Spielberg, also described Michael 'as a man of two personalities.' As expected, the many sides of Michael Jackson are not always compatible. The kid conflicts with the millionaire, the performer argues with the businessman, the performer wars with the insecure person. Michael can be sweet and kind or he can be obstinate, demanding and ruthless. 'I didn't know what to expect when I met him,' an aide to Michael on the *Bad* tour says. 'He called me into his hotel room and I expected to meet this flighty guy who could barely put two words together. But he was amazing. He had this extremely detailed plan of everything he wanted me to do. There was no small talk, no chit-chat. Michael was totally focused on work. Later on, though, I heard that after I left, he and a friend spent the afternoon playing telephone pranks on each other like little kids.'

There is little argument from those who know him that Michael is a perplexing combination of eccentricity and talent. 'He is bright, but also self-destructively brilliant,' a former assistant says. 'He is nice, but he is cold and distant. He makes it impossible to know him.' Without question, Michael is a genuine original, a genius. The effect is both positive and negative. If he was without the disturbing fears and obsessions that make him the weirdo of tabloid headlines, a reviewer once pondered, he might very well be less of a performer. Indeed, his oddball behaviour seems as inseparable from his music as he is from mystery.

The price he pays for being Michael Jackson is steep. As the most successful recording artist in music history, Michael should be the picture of fulfilled ambitions. He should be deliriously happy. His bank account is flush with millions. His homes are plush, filled with everything he's ever dreamed of possessing. He travels in circles reserved for royalty and heads of state. He counts the likes of Elizabeth Taylor, Marlon Brando and Steven Spielberg as friends. People adore him. His name is known throughout the entire world. It's not enough though. Michael says he often feels like the 'loneliest person in the world'.

It's sad. He is charitable beyond the call of duty, but his

lifestyle is hermetic. Rare are the joys of companionship. Mannequins dressed in designer clothing have in the past substituted as friends. His bedrooms, strewn with books and videotapes, serves as a private sanctuary. On the walls are pictures of Albert Einstein, Walt Disney and Peter Pan, the lost boy of Never-Never Land and Michael's self proclaimed alter-ego. Even inside his own house he moves furtively, doing his best to avoid his siblings and parents. 'For a while, it was like a Howard Hughes-type situation,' his father Joe Jackson says. 'Once we hadn't seen him for so long that I had to bust into his room just to make sure he was alive.'

A sumptuous condominium was, his mother says, 'where he went to really work hard and concentrate'. Until he purchased his vast ranch in 1988, Michael rarely left the grounds of his Encino estate. Stepping into the outside world filled him with fear. 'It's something I work on,' he admitted. He is a control freak who insists that everyone with whom he works signs a confidentiality agreement. He makes calls around the clock, whenever inspiration strikes. 'But the odd thing,' says Jeffrey Daniel, a dancer with whom Michael often works, 'is that once the job is completed, he just vanishes from your life. He quits calling and his numbers get changed.'

Michael's daily routine has followed the same basic pattern since boyhood. It's 'day-dreaming most of the time,' he once said. 'I get up early and get ready for whatever I've got to do – songwriting or whatever it is. Planning the future and stuff.' Michael asks himself the same question over and over: 'What next?' He maps his life out in five-year plans, though his everyday life is far less structured. Many days, he has said, he doesn't even get out of his pyjamas. 'Everyday fashion I don't get into,' he said.

Nor does he get into everyday acquaintances. His best friends have always been his animal pals, a private menagerie that includes Bubbles the chimp, Louie the llama, a giraffe, several deer, peacocks, a lion and an Arabian horse. 'He's like a little boy when he runs around and plays with his animals,' says an associate. When he's not involved in musical projects, he's apt to be combing through books on art and medicine. Or he's splayed across the floor in front of the TV watching cartoons. 'Cartoons are unlimited,' he said. 'And when you're unlimited, it's the ultimate.'

Wishful thinking. He might pine for a cartoon-like freedom, but in reality, the world Michael's created for himself

7

is defined by the narrowest parameters. He has sentenced himself to a life at home. Strict spiritual beliefs prevent him from participating in a world he was brought up to view as unjust, sinful and dishonest. His immense personal fortune, estimated in the hundreds of millions, and his celebrity give him an intoxicating sense of power, and yet he's paranoid and distrustful of outsiders. 'Over the years Michael has grown very wary of everything and everybody,' says his brother Jermaine. 'His tactic is to sit back and let everyone come to him so he can see what people are up to.'

Only children, the angels of Michael's imagination, are able to sneak past his matrix of self-protection. 'I guess he feels they aren't going to make any demands on him,' says Marlon. 'He can relax with them.'

If Michael's behaviour is any indication, there is perhaps a reason he seems a prisoner in a gilded cage. For more than a decade, insiders speculate, Michael has suffered from an eating disorder. Though no doctors will comment for the record, not-for-attribution discussions with medical experts and the expressed concern by family members and associates over Michael's eating habits and unorthodox behaviour appear to lead in the direction of what's commonly referred to as anorexia.

The strange process of starvation, or anorexia, experts say, is but an extreme attempt to exert control over a life that appears to be unmanageable. Oddly enough, the unpermissive nature of the disease also satisfies the sufferer's 'urgent desire to be special and outstanding'.

The symptoms of the disease appear to draw a frighteningly accurate parallel to Michael's mysterious character, or at least to the portrait of him that's been sketched in the media. The thinking of an eating disorder sufferer is marked by an obsessive, ruminative preoccupation with diet and health; narcissistic self-absorption; infantile regression; an inability to see oneself realistically; the inexhaustible pursuit of perfection in all aspects of life; and a sense that one's quest can never be understood by anyone else.

Anorexia, a life-threatening illness in its extreme form, generally occurs in consort with some new, life-changing experience. Doctors often point to an impasse with which the person is not prepared to cope. Continuing life as before appears impossible. The sudden concentration on diet, experts explain, interrupts this troubling new development that is perceived as beyond

8

one's control. The sufferer's own body, they say, turns into the only arena where they can exercise control, a symbolic act of rejection that punishes unpleasant physical aspects.

The seeds of an eating disorder, doctors say, are usually planted during the course of a childhood that demands over-conformity. The child is often either expected to play a central role in fulfilling family expectations or else by himself he perceives that role to be his obligation. The pressure is enormous. Yet hanging over them like an ominous storm cloud is the fear that whatever their efforts, nothing will be good enough to alleviate their burdens.

To endure this severe pressure, anorexics typically exhibit great stamina and stubborness. Their tireless determination appears almost superhuman, yet, experts attest, it's nothing more than compensation for their fear of not being respected.

The longer the illness lasts, doctors says, the more the sufferer perceives himself to be special and different. He can no longer live on an ordinary scale of human behaviour and, instead, is driven by a desire to excel beyond all realistic limits. Shouldering enormous burdens, he feels duty bound to make the world better all by himself. Eventually, he can no longer communicate with ordinary people, fearing they can't possibly understand him. Isolation becomes the sufferer's answer, and in the throes of this self-imposed imprisonment, his thinking becomes bizarre, self-imposed and twisted by abnormal ideas.

Information provided by family members and close associates appears to indicate that Michael began displaying the symptoms of an eating disorder when he began to record *Off the Wall*. By the time he made *Thriller*, they appeared to dominate his behaviour. Still, a doctor speculates off-the-record, the groundwork of this illness was probably laid early. From boyhood, Michael played a pivotal role in the Jackson's musical fortune. The harder he worked, he believed, the more successful the group became and the happier his family grew.

For years, his career was an up and down ride, full of high and low points, during which he repeatedly checked personal ambition and individual aspirations for the group's benefit. It was with mixed feelings that he made *Off the Wall*; pressure from his family weighed heavily against his pursuing a solo career. But when *Thriller* finally hit, rocketing Michael into uncharted regions of fame, there was no turning back. 'You can't possibly imagine what it's like to go through something like that,' Dileo says. 'No one, not even Michael, could possibly prepare for that to happen. It's a rare occurrence.'

Seemingly overnight, Michael turned into a phenomenon. He had set what appeared to be a superhuman goal for himself and, realizing it, Michael found himself abruptly cast into a situation for which he wasn't prepared. Quite suddenly, his life was more than even he could handle. What did he do? He withdrew. Literally, and figuratively. He closed the door on the world and his family, turning himself into a reclusive figure who confounded even his siblings and parents. 'I'd have to say we saw him less,' Marlon says. 'He definitely changed. Though he never came right out and said he didn't want to perform with the family any more, I could sense that's how he felt.'

Confusion, those close to him indicate, over what was best for him and his family reigned in his mind. The debate was without solution, and Michael resigned himself to a lonely corner of the world. He no longer granted interviews, something he had done on occasion in the past, sensing himself having become a figure impossible to understand. 'He claims he's always misquoted or misunderstood,' LaToya says. 'He says people never get what he says right. So why bother?'

Exercising control became Michael's objective. He wanted to get his life in order. Map out a plan. He severed his management contract with his father. He hired new people who answered only to him. He began buying up all his old photographs, allowing only his personal photographer to release pictures. He acquired the rights to the old Jackson Five cartoon series. He made employees sign confidentiality agreements. It was a vain attempt to handle a runaway situation.

His fame only increased. No matter how desperately he tried to get a grip, control eluded Michael. Then he hit upon the single place where he could exert his desire at will, where he could realize tangible results of his mastery. His body. Michael admittedly disliked the way he looked. There was little escape from his boyish roundness and pudgey features, reminders of the little cherub who had led his brothers to stardom. In this period of apparent crisis, he decided to change the way he looked.

Everything Micahel abhorred about himself would go. The acne, which he admits left him emotionally scarred for life. The boyish roundness. He changed his diet and followed a self-devised regime. He gave up junk food and all the things he loved as a child, and in their place he substituted a hard

10

macrobiotic diet that gradually stripped every ounce of excess fat from his already sinewy frame. He gobbled vitamins by the handful, sometimes ingesting up to fifty tablets in a single day. He ate, but not with pleasure.

How much did Michael loath mealtime? He once said that if he didn't have to eat to stay alive, he wouldn't. Katherine Jackson says Michael wasn't always like this. As a little boy, Michael loved apple turnovers and sweet potato pies. But he changed, she thinks, for the worse. Sometimes, she frets, her hyper-finicky son skips meals the entire day, and then when he does finally sit down at the table, his portions amount to little more than a nibble. 'I've been concerned about his eating habits for a long time,' she sighs. 'He has his own peculiar ways.'

At restaurants, for instance, Michael's personal chef brings his own organically-grown food and prepares it in the kitchen. The cook even prepares Michael's portions at family gatherings. 'You'll bring him a full meal and he'll eat two teaspoons and send it back,' his mother says. 'He does this all the time. He always says, "Mother, you worry about me, but I'm in excellent condition."'

That's what Michael says. But Mrs Jackson brings up the worrisome incident on the recently completed *Bad* Tour when Michael's strength ebbed to a point where he finally sought medical advice. 'The doctor told him he wasn't eating enough,' his mother says. 'He told Michael that he had to start eating either fish or poutry, and, most important, that he had to start eating more.'

Michael's strict dietary habits, insiders reveal, are based upon pseudo-scientific theories he concocted himself. He eats nothing impure or unnatural. Every Sunday he fasts, a private ritual that includes at least thirty minutes of non-stop dancing as vigorously as possible. The entire day he takes in nothing more than fruit juice. 'It flushes out the system, cleans out the colon,' he offered by way of explanation.

'I think it's great,' he continued, finding no end of interest in the colon and its function. 'To really make it work you have to do it properly. That's the sewer valve of the system. You have to keep that clean like you clean the outside of your body. All these impurities come out of your system because you're not clean inside. It comes out in pimples or disease through big pores. Toxins trying to get out of your system. People should keep themselves clean.'

But Michael's metamorphosis didn't stop with his diet. He

11

wanted to see results, drastic results for a drastic situation. By the time *Thriller* exploded across the airwaves, he had enlisted a plastic surgeon to change his appearance by whittling his bulbous nose – not once but twice – resculpting it until there was nothing more than a tiny, pointed bracket holding his two nostrils in place. No longer could his brothers tease him with their irritating nickname, Big Nose.

Michael wasn't finished, though. Prior to releasing *Bad*, a period rife with anxiety, Michael added a Kirk Douglas-like dimple into the centre of his chin, which rigorous dieting had transformed from the fulcrum of baby fat into a square and bony jut.

His exterior might change, but inside, acquaintances say, Michael was still reeling from private fears. His behaviour became indecipherable. For instance, he was photographed in public with his face covered by a surgical mask. He was pushed around Disneyland in a wheelchair. His only apparent friendships were with children such as Sean Lennon or older women such as Elizabeth Taylor and Sophia Loren.

His eccentricity was translated into crazy thoughts and actions that confused even his closest associates. Michael repeatedly professed his belief in magic. He told an interviewer that he believed man had the ability to actually fly. He reportedly devised a health plan that would enable him to live to 150 years old. He supposedly slept in a hyperbaric oxygen chamber, a high-tech piece of medical equipment used to treat burn patients. He attempted to purchase the remains of the Elephant Man for $1 million. And prior to the release of *Bad*, he reportedly set a preposterous sales goal of 100 million copies, taping the figure to his bathroom mirror as a constant reminder.

Only Michael's closest friends, none of whom spoke openly about him, professed understanding of his whacky ways. Elizabeth Taylor broke their understood code of silence only to reveal Michael's dark side. 'We really do have a lot in common,' Taylor said in explaining their friendship, which was first struck over the telephone. 'Most people don't believe that. I know some of the pain Michael is going through. I have been there and have gone through the same thing myself. But we generally do suffer, and it takes, I think, a fellow sufferer, a fellow survivor, to understand each other.'

The party scene stood before him like a paranoid nightmare. When Michael stepped outside, everything stopped. All eyes were immediately on him. In a tailored suit, he walked slowly, studied by the guests. His body was a loose collection of jangling limbs and joints and seemingly brittle bones bound tightly by a thin coat of muscle and a hypersensitive layer of raw nerves. His skin was smooth and taut, darker than in photos.

'Michael is very sensitive, but he doesn't like to reveal his feelings in public,' LaToya said in his defence.

Rather than mingle, which no one really expected, Michael stepped into a circle of his closest advisors: Dileo, CBS Records chief Walter Yetnikoff, and his own high-powered attorney, John Branca. They closed around him protectively. Standing off to the side, Michael's father, Joe Jackson, watched enviously. He and Michael had been warring for years. His presence was a gesture for the sake of appearances. Dinner commenced shortly. 'But everyone spent their time talking about Michael,' one guest recalls, 'trying to figure out what kind of guy he really is.'

The puzzle is complex, but everyone who spends any time with Michael invariably uses the same four-letter word to describe him – nice. 'He's so grounded and centred and con-nected to his creative soul,' Quincy Jones says. 'He protects his godliness, that sense of God in himself. He realy does. There's a part of him so totally pure, that's connected to his centre.'

It's nearly impossible no to feel Michael's fragility of soul, friends say. 'If you said "shut up" around him,' guitarist David Williams says, 'he'd probably break into tears.' Michael's name means 'in the likeness of God,' and there's little doubt that he envisions himself as a messianic figure. 'I was sent forth for the world, for the children,' he once said attempting to shed light on his misunderstood image. 'I worry about the children, all my children all over the world. I live for them. I must endure for the power I was sent forth.'

Raised a devout Jehovah's Witness, Michael was schooled to believe that life on earth as it now exists will soon end, and it will be followed by a paradise on earth over which Christ – assisted by only the truest saints of God – will rule from heaven for one thousand years. 'So Michael tries to be perfect,' a psychologist, commenting on the condition her name be withheld, says. 'If you're a Witness and you're not perfect, your life is for naught.'

Michael, 'sent forth for the world, for the children,' a divinely touched missionary, appears to interpret the cricitism and gossip directed at him as the cross he must bear for being of this flesh. Rather than speak out, he absorbs the pain and suffers. 'He wants to feel awful when people say things about him more than he wants to correct misconceptions,' the psychologist postulates. 'He views himself as an innocent child, and then projects his own childlike fantasy of himself onto the public.'

'Michael's definitely going through something,' singer Patti Austin, a longtime friend of Michael's, says, alluding to the pressurized life of a child performer. 'And I think he'll be going through it for another ten years before he finally gets it out of his system and grows up. He was never given the opportunity before. He led his life in a goldfish bowl, under a very protective existence.'

'So here's Michael,' Austin continues, 'becoming the biggest thing since candy, and he has no sense of the world. He has to hire a civilian to be his friend. He's isolated. He can't just walk into a Burger King and shake hands with someone. Michael lives a very disciplined life. So the moment he gets the money and the power, he says, Screw you, to his family, and he starts living the childhood he never had. Everybody has to be a kid at some point. It's great to be a kid as an adult, if you realize what you're trying to do. But if you don't realize, that's a problem. And I don't think Michael does realize it.'

Michael's admirers seem able to overlook his eccentricity. 'He's an absolute doll,' Bobby Colomby, former drummer for Blood, Sweat and Tears and the producer of the Jackson's *Destiny* LP, says. 'He's loads of fun to be around. The biggest problem people have with Michael and the reason why he's so fascinating is because none of us can relate to the way he's been brought up. Our problem is that we expect him to do things and relate to things the way we do.

'But Michael comes from such a totally different place, a different focus, that that's impossible. He's spent his entire life in show business. He's been famous practically forever, and somehow he's managed to stay a supernice guy. But who knows what happens when you earn hundreds of millions of dollars? He's now obviously so insulated, protected as well as surrounded by sychophantic types that there's no one who can say, "Hey Mike, don't you think this is a little weird?"'

Michael undoubtedly felt the glare of attention throughout the backyard festivities kicking off his *Bad* album, but he bore them for several hours with professional grace and patience. He didn't like being gawked at, but this was business, and he desperately wanted to succeed in a way that would surpass even his precedent-setting LP, *Thriller*. Few in attendence could ever imagine the self-imposed pressure Michael dealt with. Few probably would ever want to.

Michael's own escape came later in the evening. After the guests had long disappeared, after the caterers had cleaned up the yard and peace had settled over the estate like a comfortable blanket, Michael returned to the privacy of his bedroom and sought tranquility and solace the only way he knew how – by dancing.

He turned the music up to full volume and disappeared in a flurry of whirling, turning, stutter-stepping moves that seemed to lift him off the ground and out of this world. Moments like these, he once said, were beautiful, serene and distinctly his own, a private escape into his unique brand of genius. Moments like this recalled the chilling comparison Michael once made between himself and E.T., the alien who was so full of love and so misunderstood.

'His story is the story of my life in so many ways,' Michael said. 'He's in a strange place and wants to be accepted . . . he's most comfortable with children . . . He gives love and wants love in return, which is me. And he has that super power which lets him lift off and fly whenever he wants to get away from things on earth, and I can identify with that.'

2

'Well, maybe it *is* in the blood.'

Or so Katherine Jackson, the gracious, soft-spoken, deeply religious Jackson matriarch, ponders in those quiet moments when she reflects on all the good fortune that music has brought to her family after more than twenty years in showbusiness.

Told of his wife's meditation, Joe Jackson, the tenacious and brooding father of the nine Jackson offspring, offers a slight chuckle and then settles into a sly, knowing grin that reflects years of struggle. 'Maybe so,' he says. 'But it took a whole lot of sweat, too.'

Katherine and Joseph Jackson have been married for thirty-nine years and are polar opposites.

She was born in 1931 in Russell County, Alabama, a rural farming settlement that had been home to her family for generations. Her father was a farmer, as was his father, who tilled the land just as his father had done. Her sister, who died in 1979, was named Hattie. As a child Katherine was better known to everyone as Katie. She was four years old when her family left the South and resettled in East Chicago, Indiana.

As a girl, she was told that her great-great-grandfather, a slave for an Alabama family named Scruse, whose name he eventually adopted as his own, sang every Sunday in the Russell County church. He possessed such a fine and powerful voice that it would rise above all the other parishioners, and on warm days when the church windows were open it would carry throughout the entire valley.

Katherine's own voice is a soft, lilting soprano. She refuses to show it off in public, though her children often say, 'Mother, you have such a beautiful voice, you sing so well.' But as a young girl, she dreamed of being in showbusiness. She and her sister were quite involved with music. They belonged to their high school orchestra, the church junior band and the

16

school choir. Their father played Country and Western music on the radio, and they grew up listening to *Suppertime Frolic* and the *Grand Ole Opry* programmes. Ernest Tubb, Hank Snow, Hank Williams and comedian Minnie Pearl were their favourite performers.

Katherine modestly accepts some credit for her children's fine singing voices, but says they didn't inherit any dancing skills from her. She came down with polio when she was eighteen months old. From then on, she either wore a brace or used crutches, and she was in and out of hospitals for operations on her foot until she was sixteen. While bedridden she learned to draw quite well, a talent she passed on to Michael, who's an accomplished artist and constant doodler.

Like his wife, Joseph comes from the South, but there the similarity ends. He was born in 1929 in Arkansas. His father was a high school teacher who married one of his students. They had two boys and one daughter. Both Joe and his brother were big, strapping men like their father, who separated from his wife when Joe was eight. She moved to Gary, Indiana, and he took his boys to Oakland. Always the restless type, Joe left home as soon as he was old enough to travel on his own and moved to Gary, where he found work in one of the local steel mills.

He and Katherine met soon after. She used to pedal her bicycle in front of his house. 'I used to see her all the time, riding by and never stopping,' he says. 'Then, one day, I stopped her.'

They wed in 1949 and set up home in Gary. He was twenty, and she was eighteen. The next year Maureen (better known as Rebbie) was born, and the other children followed right behind: Jackie, Tito, Jermaine, LaToya, Marlon (whose twin brother lived less than twenty-four hours), Michael, Randy and Janet. Says Katherine, 'I was having children so fast, and they were mostly boys, that my mother said, "Katie, one day you're going to be very proud of those boys."'

Michael, the seventh of the nine children, was born on a late summer night, 29 August 1958. The impish rascal of the bunch, his memories of Gary are vague: mostly singing, dancing and working 'too hard for a child'. He recalled, 'I just remember little things like the corner store or certain people in the neighbourhood. The high school behind us always had a big band with trumpets and trombones and drums coming down the street – like a parade. That's all I remember.'

17

Actually, there is little about Gary, a grim industrial town, worth remembering. A brief jaunt down Route 80 from Chicago, Gary is the picture of blue collar economic hardship. At night giant smokestacks spewing flame and pollution tower above buildings that in the daytime reflect the struggle and decay of the poor working class. Once known as 'Sin City', a place where people in trouble could escape, it's become a town where dreams are hatched, but few are realized.

Joe worked as a crane operator, and he would often have to take a second job at night as a welder to help support his fast-growing family. On good days, he brought home thirty dollars; in a good year he'd make about five thousand dollars. 'We didn't have much money,' says Katherine. 'Raising nine children isn't an easy task. We weren't able to provide them with the material things that we would have liked to. For a while we had Rebbie and Jackie taking dance and piano lessons, but then as more children came, we couldn't afford it.

'Later, with all those children around the house, we had to entertain them in some way, and music is what we had. We always had instruments around the house – a saxophone, a guitar, a trombone – and the kids would help themselves, or sometimes they would sing with us. My husband and I used to sing to ourselves even before the children were born, just sit in our living room on a cold winter night and sing harmony on Christmas carols and popular songs.'

As parents, Joe and Katherine fostered traditional, midwestern values of love, family unity, God, and hard work. She was generous; nurturing and kind; he was an iron-fisted disciplinarian who brooked no nonsense. They worked hard and made sure there was always food on the table. 'Mother was a great provider,' Michael recalls. 'The lessons she taught us were invaluable. Kindness, love, and consideration for other people headed her list.' He says his father 'has always been something of a mystery to me and he knows it'.

Michael is a composite of both his parents: sensitive, gentle and pious like his mother and determined and stubborn like his dad. 'He definitely has his father's perseverence,' says publicist Steve Manning, a family friend who once headed the Jackson Five fan club.

The Jacksons lived in a small, white, two-bedroom clapboard house at 2300 Jackson Street, a neighbourhood of low-income housing with neat lawns. They were a disciplined and close-knit family. Though Joe and Katherine both worked, they made certain one of them was always home with the children. The older boys played Little League in the expansive park behind the house, while Marlon and Michael ran in the fenced-in front yard where Katherine could keep an eye on them.

'They were a nice, religious family,' says Johnny Jackson, the Jackson Five's original drummer. Every Sunday Katherine, a devout Jehovah's Witness, dressed her children up and walked them to the Kingdom Hall. 'It was a pleasant walk,' says Marlon. 'My father even went in the early days. But it was so boring.' Not to Michael, who, like his mother, took the Bible teachings to heart. 'He and LaToya and Rebbie were the most serious about all that,' says Marlon.

Especially Michael, who, according to his mother, came alive during services and always asked her questions about God. 'I believe in the Bible and I try to follow the Bible,' he said as a teenager. 'I don't just pray at night. I pray at different times during the day. Whenever I see something beautiful, I say, "Oh God, that's beautiful." I say little prayers like that all through the day.'

From early childhood until his break with the Witnesses in 1987, religion was a special bond between Michael and his pious mother. It's hard not to wonder what effect the Witnesses' gloomy prediction of world destruction had on the young, impressionable boy, who was taught that only a limited number of God's truest servants would survive. If the world ended, he must have wondered, would he be spared? Would his mother? Taken literally, such notions would certainly have frightened a little boy who loved his mother dearly. Perhaps Michael believed if he were extra good, he could ensure that both he and his mother would survive.

Years later, after his was one of the most recognizable faces in the world, Michael gave his mother great joy by dutifully continuing his weekly 'field service', delivering the Witnesses' apocalyptic message door-to-door. 'I once asked him how he went out and did that without people recognizing him,' says Katherine. 'And he said, "I disguise myself, Mother."' Once, she saw him in the kitchen before he left with a stack of *Watchtower* and couldn't believe her eyes. 'He had on a suit that made him look fat, a brown hat, a moustache and some different teeth,' she laughs. 'I didn't even recognize him.'

With nine children crammed into the tiny house, everyone had chores. 'Lots of them,' says Jermaine. 'We scrubbed and waxed the floors, did the windows inside and out, stacked bricks and did the gardening. Tito did the dinner dishes and I would dry them. Also, each of the four oldest had an ironing board. We'd have a big bag of clothes to iron and our parents would say we couldn't go outside until we finished the bag.'

In those days, there was little that distinguished the Jacksons from other steel workers' struggling families. 'Times were hard back then,' says Katherine. 'There were times when my husband was laid off and we were down to our last penny. We were all workers.'

At night, the boys piled into their triple-tiered bunk beds – Michael on the bottom, Marlon in the middle and Jermaine on top – and talked about growing up. 'We'd lay there in the dark and dream about all sorts of things,' says Marlon. 'Like what kind of car we wanted to drive when we got older or about being some famous athlete.' Privacy was in short supply, but crammed quarters made for wild times. 'We were always having pillow fights or getting into some kind of mischief,' he says. 'We'd have lots of fun all packed in together, but then my father would come in and tell us to be quiet.'

Although Joseph's imposing size, and gruff, domineering manner commanded respect, there was a lighter side to him, too. Before all the children were born, he had secretly harboured dreams of a showbiz career, which he never completely relinquished. At weekends, he sang and played guitar with a band called the Falcons. 'It was a local group, out of Chicago,' he says. 'We played mostly colleges and bars. It was a blues thing, which is what everybody was getting into.'

Michael, then a spry three-year-old, was too young to remember the Falcons. But they often rehearsed in the Jacksons' living room, a treat Jackie, Tito and Jermaine relished. They watched closely as Joe took his cherished guitar out from the closet and plugged it into the tiny amp he stored in the basement. The older boys regarded that closet as a sacred shrine and Joe made it clear to them that his guitar was off limits. No one was to touch it when he was away. 'When my father made rules,' says Marlon, 'you didn't question him.'

But after Joe left for work, Tito, Jackie and Jermaine would wait for Katherine to disappear with the babies and then carefully remove the instrument from the closet and sneak it back to their bedroom, where they would play along with the popular songs on the radio. If Michael promised not to tell, he was allowed to watch. Katherine eventually discovered their secret, but promised not to tell her husband as long as they were careful. 'She knew that guitar was keeping them from running with a bad crowd,' says Michael. 'She wasn't about to take away anything that kept them within arms' reach.'

Then one day the unthinkable happened – a string broke. Tito put the guitar back in the closet and pretended like nothing had happened. But when his father discovered the mishap, he erupted in a furious rage. 'After Joe found out, he whipped Tito pretty good,' recalls Johnny Jackson, the Jackson Five's drummer. LaToya advised Michael to keep his mouth shut and stay far away. Later, though, after Joe's anger cooled, he called Tito out and said, 'Let me see what you can do.' According to Michael, 'Tito picked up the guitar and started really playing. My father was shocked because he saw some talent there. He was really surprised.'

Katherine wasn't. Once, during a particularly frightening tornado alert, she calmed frayed nerves by leading everyone in 'Cotton Fields' and 'You Are My Sunshine', and knew the quality of their voices. After the guitar incident, she voiced her enthusiasm to Joe and persuaded him to listen to the children sing. Impressed, he went out and bought a red electric guitar, a smaller version of his own, for Tito, and a bass guitar for Jermaine, who also started to sing. With Jackie playing shakers and Johnny Jackson on drums, they christened themselves the Jacksons and began rehearsing. 'The Beatles "Twist and Shout" was the very first song we learned,' says Johnny.

Joe, sensing a second opportunity at the showbusiness career that had eluded him earlier, backed out of the Falcons and turned his attention to the music his boys were making at home. 'I went overboard,' he says. 'My wife and I would fight, because I invested in new instruments that cost so much money. When a woman's a good mother and finds all the money going into instruments, she doesn't like it.' But Joe had big time plans, which he eventually confided to Katherine, and pretty soon, recalls Michael, 'Our bedroom and living room began to look like a music store.'

Three years later:
Gordon Keith stood outside the door at 2300 Jackson Street, took a deep breath, and hoped he wasn't wasting his time with this audition.

A gravelly-voiced, religious man, Keith was possessed by an ambition that took him well beyond the unforgiving, grey smokestacks of the Gary steel mills where he laboured each day. With four other men and a shoestring budget, he owned and operated a small music company called Steeltown Records, which had released singles by several undistinguished local acts, with little success beyond the city limits.

Keith was searching for a talented, well-disciplined act he could produce by himself, and for the past few months he had seen a rash of posters and placards all around Gary advertising a kiddie group called the Jackson Five.

The year was 1967, and the world was rife with change. U.S. sentiment was turning increasingly against the Vietnam War; boxing champion Muhammad Ali was stripped of his world heavyweight title for refusing the draft; the Beatles released their psychedelic masterwork *Sergeant Pepper's Lonely Hearts Club Band*; and the Japanese began marketing their latest product: the microwave oven.

In Gary people were beginning to notice the Jackson Five, which now included Marlon, who joined his older brothers when he was six, and Michael, the Jacksons' pint-size James Brown impersonator, who was admitted when he turned four. Even then, Michael possessed a voice that inspired awe. He had stunned his kindergarten class with a stirring rendition of 'Climb Every Mountain' from *The Sound of Music*, and because he was also so short and cute, with those big eyes and cherubic dimples, as well as a nimble dancer, Joe stuck him out in front and let him alternate lead vocals with Jermaine.

They first performed as the Jackson Five 'with Johnny', at a local hospital. 'They had a big Santa Claus,' recalled Michael. Another early show was at the Big Top, a Gary shopping centre. It was in 1964 that they got their first paying gig at a nearby nightclub called Mr Lucky's, and the next year, when Michael was seven, they won top prize in a citywide talent contest at Roosevelt High, Jackie's school, with rousing renditions of 'My Girl' and 'Shake It Baby'.

They quickly acquired the polish and discipline of veteran performers, but only as a result of hard work. Joe was a merciless taskmaster who entered his children in as many talent contests as he could locate. Usually, they walked away with the first prize trophy. When they didn't, he drilled them harder. Indeed, when they weren't performing, the kids were rehearsing under his critical eye. 'Every morning before school he had us rehearsing,' says Johnny Jackson. 'We'd be up at six a.m. And then we'd do it again after school. Joe was strict.'

Strict is an understatement. Says Marlon, 'We'd break for

Batman, and later, for our favourite programme, the *Green Hornet*. Then it was back to rehearsal, until it was time for homework and bed. We barked, but not that loud. Nobody wanted to work that hard, but we had no choice.'

When it came to practice, Joe ruled like a dictator. 'You know how some movies are rated triple X?' says Marlon. 'Well, my father was triple strict.' No kidding. During practices, he was liable to blow up in anger and lash out at the slightest error. Michael, in his book *Moonwalk*, remembered, 'If you messed up, you got hit, sometimes with a belt, sometimes with a switch.' And he added, 'I'd get beaten for things that happened mostly outside rehearsal.'

Joe denies dishing out beatings. 'I don't remember hitting the kids,' he says. 'But if I did, I guess they deserved 'em.'

Perhaps. For despite his goody-goody image today, Michael was then a fleet-footed rapscallion, who often begged for trouble. 'He was very fresh, almost bratty, as a child,' says Steve Manning, the one-time Jackson aide. Once when his grandparents were visiting, Michael, then five, refused to follow his parents' instructions. 'I think he also threw something at my dad,' says Marlon. 'And my father grabbed him, held him upside down by one leg and gave him a whoopin'. But he deserved it.'

Likewise, there is only one other time anyone can recall Michael getting hit. 'It was during rehearsal, and he didn't want to do something Joseph told him to do,' says Johnny Jackson. 'So Joseph hit him, and Michael turned around and told him that if he ever touched him again, he'd quit singing forever.'

Joe makes no apologies for his stern actions. He was extra tough, and he believed in strict discipline. Though his boys were the ones onstage, it was Joe who really yearned for stardom, for what the Falcons had never achieved. 'I had a vision that my boys would be the number one talent in the world,' he says. 'That was my aim. I wanted to make them superstars.' In addition to practice, they watched performers on TV. 'I thought that would give them an idea that it was worthwhile.' It did. 'Pretty soon,' he says 'after maybe a year-and-a-half, they began to dream themselves.'

Shirley Cartman, the orchestra teacher at Beckman Junior High, had misgivings about the Jackson Five competing in Beckman's talent show. She had Tito in class, and though he was an excellent student, his brothers were in different schools. Allowing them to appear at Beckman would be against the rules. However, after Tito protested, Joe went to school after work to talk to Mrs Cartman, and she agreed to audition them at their home.

The evening Cartman came over, Joe introduced his nervous family. There was Jackie, the star athlete. Tito, whom she already knew, was the master mechanic. LaToya was 'the second little mother'. Jermaine was the most serious and sensitive child, and Marlon was the devilish prankster. Katherine, standing off to the side, cradled baby Janet in her arms. 'That's Michael, our little showman,' said Joe, 'and Randy, his shadow.'

They were polite, well-dressed boys, Cartman recalls, but when they played, 'Suddenly the room came alive . . . and the once-shy little boys were soon lost in the magic of their music.'

Several weeks later, the Jackson Five took first prize at Beckman's talent contest, but even more important, Shirley Cartman brought news of a talented local group to Gordon Keith, the owner of Gary's only record label. Having already seen their posters all over town, he acted on her recommendation and made an appointment to hear them play.

Joe answered the door before Keith could knock and ushered him inside. The two men talked briefly. Keith remembers the house as small and crowded, the living room jammed with equipment. 'Joe had the boys all come into the living room and hook up their instruments,' he says. 'He said, "Let's go, boys," and without a moment's hesitation, they began playing for me right there.'

The tiny, cramped room reverberated with amplified music, the walls rattling from the pulsing drums and guitar, the floor vibrating while Michael, Marlon and Jermaine were gliding and shaking in their best James Brown imitation. Rough around the edges, remembers Keith, but for kids they were a relatively tight, smooth unit. Jermaine played bass and sang; Johnny was on drums; Tito played guitar; Jackie was on shakers; Marlon kept time with a tambourine; and the smallest of the bunch, Michael, sang and danced. 'Basically, that was it,' he says. 'They just played a couple of songs that were big then.'

But even back then, it was obvious the group's small lead singer had a magical spark. From the moment he saw Michael enter the room and position himself in front of the microphone, the sceptical producer knew the nine-year-old had the poise and showmanship of a gifted performer mature beyond his age. 'The boy walked out and went right up to this guitar cord that was stretched between Tito's guitar and the amp,' he says. 'It was between waist and chest high, and Michael just jumped right over it, no problem. I thought that was a superhuman feat and right then I knew he was superbad.' That sold Keith. 'I just about signed them there,' he says. 'But it took a few days to draw up the papers.' Joe was ecstatic.

The next step was to make a record. In the late winter of 1967 Keith booked studio time in Chicago and the Jacksons recorded several songs. The most memorable tune, a hastily written rhythm and blues ballad called 'Big Boy', features a playful, call-and-response vocal between Michael and his brothers. Michael's voice is deeper than his usual boyishly ripe tenor-soprano, which returns to normal on the B-side, a song called 'You've Changed'.

In the studio the Jacksons were well-behaved and professional, exactly the way Joe had trained them to be, not to mention appropriately excited. 'But I had to bring in some older guys to help them cut on instrumentation and background vocals,' says Keith. 'I'm even singing on the background.'

'Big Boy', which Michael recalls having a 'killer' bass line, was released at the end of January 1968, and by the end of the first week of April, the song was a minor hit, hovering near the top of the local charts in Gary as well as a few neighbouring cities. Michael and his brothers were overwhelmed. The few occasions they heard themselves sing on the radio were thrilling. 'It was no different from the stars we were trying to imitate,' says Marlon.

The single's popularity led to the Jacksons' first regular gig at Mr Lucky's, a well-known Gary nightclub. The boys were booked there every week night. Katherine objected to the atmosphere and the hard work, but her argument paled when Joe countered with how the extra income was beneficial to the entire family. It was hard to dispute paid bills.

Joe's ambitions raged like a wildfire. Inching closer to the big time, he worked his children harder and harder. At weekends, they hit the road. Joe packed the boys, who now included keyboard player Ronnie Rancifer, and their equipment into the back of a rickety Volkswagen minibus, which he had purchased from his brother. He painted 'The Jackson Five' on the side like TV's Partridge Family. In the bus they covered vast stretches of highway driving to smoke-filled, whiskey and blues clubs all over the East and Midwest, like Chicago's Capitol Theatre, Joe Green's Club Woodlawn, and the Regal, where the Jackson Five became regulars, opening for slick pros such as Gladys Knight, the Temptations, and the O'Jays.

All this sweat, toil and discomfort was not without dividends. The Jacksons were acquiring a valuable stage maturity to accompany the smooth moves and sugar-coated soul warbling they practised in their living room at home. The results were evidence enough. Like when they won amateur night at the Regal three times in a row. Michael, hailed as a rubber-legged prodigy, was already hearing himself rumoured by rival bands to be 'a thirty-year-old midget'.

Not quite. He was a tadpole, a scrawny nine-year-old who was devoted to his favourite Saturday morning cartoon characters, Bugs Bunny and the Road Runner. But Michael was also fiercely dedicated to becoming a first class entertainer. At what cost, though? No one asked that question. No one saw that he was sacrificing a normal youth. He knew his place: in front of the microphone. And he knew not to question that role. Still, he admits, he often ached to be with the kids playing outside while he laboured under his father's tyrannical tutelage. 'I'd just stare at them in wonder – I couldn't imagine such freedom, such a carefree life – and wish more than anything that I had that kind of freedom, that I could walk away and be like them,' he wrote. 'So there were sad moments in my childhood.'

Adding to the anguish, Michael was regularly harassed by neighbourhood children, the very ones whose freedom he envied. They taunted him for the time he spent practising. 'The kids eating candy and popcorn would come around while we were inside rehearsing,' he said. 'This would get us mad. Rocks would come in through the window, and people would tease us, saying we were wasting our time.' Yet Michael handled the worst of all criticism, the jeers of his contemporaries, the same way he would handle bad press twenty years later: by telling himself that his musical endeavours set him apart from other kids, that he was different, and that made everything okay.

If this wasn't enough, Michael was reassured of his special place in life by audiences who could hardly believe a pint-size child was capable of delivering such commanding vocals and dazzling stage theatrics. Michael already knew how to work a crowd. During the Jacksons' rendition of Joe Tex's 'Skinny Legs and All', he would go out in the audience, lift up the girls' skirts

26

and look under. He's embarrassed by that now, but back then the place would go crazy. People would throw money, which Michael learned to equate with success. Taking in up to fifty dollars on a good night, he 'remembers my pockets being so full of money that I couldn't keep my pants up'.

But what kind of child was Michael becoming? Back home Katherine, tending to LaToya and the babies, Janet and Randy, fretted about the influences her sensitive, impressionable nine-year-old son was being exposed to. The exhausting grind of performing six shows a day, seven days a week, subjected Michael to a sweatshop-type work ethic outlawed decades earlier by child labour laws. He was also exposed to a world of swearing and drinking. Even worse, thought Katherine, in light of his strict religious upbringing, he stood in the wings and watched men whoop and holler as strippers shimmied down to their altogether. 'That to me was awful,' he later remembered.

Still, the road provided Michael with a worldliness young boys found difficult to shun. At the Peppermint Lounge in Chicago, the Jacksons' dressing room had a peephole that looked right in to the ladies' bathroom. 'We all fought to look in there,' says Marlon. 'We learned everything there was to know about ladies.' A decade later, when the Jackson Five were in London for a Royal Command Performance, Michael and Marlon found another inviting peephole in their dressing room. This one looked directly into the room next door, which was occupied by stage actress Carol Channing. 'Michael and I took turns looking and laughing,' chuckles Marlon. 'We saw Carol without anything on, including her wig.'

Without question, these frenetic early days were an education – if not scholarly, then relevant to a budding career in pop music. Watching every move from the wings, Michael was tutored by the masters: the grand-daddy of soul James Brown, Sam and Dave, and Jackie Wilson. 'I might've learned more by watching Jackie Wilson than from anyone or anything else,' he says. Michael absorbed every nuance and then practised until he was a breathtaking imitation in miniature. 'Some musicians – Springsteen and U2, for example – may feel they got their education from the streets,' says Michael in his book. 'I'm a performer at heart. I got mine from the stage.'

Michael's skills improved, but he still wasn't old enough to be privy to Joe's and Keith's late-night plotting. They sold the distribution rights to 'Big Boy' to Atlantic Records. Then Keith took the Jackson Five back into the studio to cut a follow-up single. Unfortunately, side A's 'You Don't Have To Be Over 21 (To Fall In Love)', was saddled with amateur instrumentation and wafer-thin vocals that evidenced the group's tender age. And the flip side's 'Jam Session', notable only because Michael plays bongos and Joe strums his precious electric guitar, his only recorded performance, fared no better. Neither sold well.

They didn't worry. They had a distribution deal. Their house was full of first place trophies. Their name was recognized on the 'chitlin' circuit' as a quality act. They sensed the promised land beyond the not-too-distant horizon. Gladys Knight had already approached them about signing with Motown, but Joe declined because other record companies were also beginning to make overtures, and he was intent on waiting for the best offer, not the first.

The last hurdle on the way to big time recognition and money, they felt, was the famous Wednesday night competition at Harlem's legendary Apollo Theater. If they won, they were a sure bet to attract a lucrative offer from record companies. Ella Fitzgerald, Billie Holliday and Joe Tex were only a few of the famous entertainers who had found the hallowed Apollo a launching pad to prosperous careers. In May 1968, the Jacksons finally got the chance.

For the special occasion, they took an airplane, arriving in New York the day before their show. The line-up at the Apollo that steamy summer night included blues singer Etta James, the Vibrations and newcomers the Jackson Five. Before the show, Michael prowled the fabled halls, taking in the smells and sounds of the theatre, gazing at the rows of framed pictures of Jackie Wilson, Sam and Dave and the Godfather of Soul himself, James Brown. Excited, the nine-year-old had no problem imagining himself in their shiny, patent leather dancing shoes.

Michael got his chance when the emcee introduced the Jackson Five. 'There was this object just offstage which resembled a tree trunk which was supposed to bring good luck to first-time entertainers if you touched it just before going on,' says Joe. Each boy touched the object as they ran to their place onstage. From the crowd, it was impossible to tell that everyone from big Tito to little Michael was nervous. But they had heard terrifying stories about how rough the Apollo audiences could be on acts they did not like. It was not unusual for bottles, cans, and food to be chucked at unpopular performers. 'The kids were more afraid of that than anything else,' says Joe.

'We weren't afraid of losing the contest; we knew we had it. We just wanted people to like us.'

Call it destiny – that combined with hard work, plenty of dues paying and luck won the Jackson Five the Apollo's amateur night competition that evening. 'We got a standing ovation,' says Joe. 'And from that point on we got invitations to come back to the Apollo Theater and perform for money.' Naturally, fate did not escape the very perceptive Michael either. 'I certainly sensed that we wouldn't be doing talent shows and strip joints much longer,' he says.

3

Gary, Indiana. 1969.

At this time, Michael's everyday life was not that different from other boys his age. He awoke early in the morning and happily skipped off to school, where he excelled in most subjects. After class he played on various athletic teams. At night, he did his homework and then went to sleep. In spare time he delivered newspapers in the neighbourhood to earn extra spending money. He was also a Cub Scout. And when he could, he dutifully helped his mother care for the littlest Jacksons, Randy and Janet.

If this sounds too good to be true, it is. The entire preceding paragraph is false, written only to show how unusual Michael's life at the time actually was.

At ten years old, the young man, a skinny wisp, was already certain he was different from the other children his age. He already knew what he wanted to do with his life. He knew he possessed something the others didn't: talent. An immense dose of it. He had the innate ability to stand in front of an audience of adult strangers and charge the crowd with his electrified singing and dancing. However, away from the lights, in the company of contemporaries, he disappeared into the background and withdrew into himself. He was shy, unsure of how to relate to others. He didn't have the interests of a normal kid.

His waking hours were already strictly regimented. There were rehearsals, school, more rehearsals, and little else in between except meals and sleep.

In these formative years Michael was being shaped by forces beyond his control. He naturally gravitated to music, sure, but Joe's unrelenting coaching, fraught with criticism and punishment, taught him that his best was never good enough. He could hit his marks perfectly in rehearsal, but still Joe would

30

find reason to erupt. As a result Michael found his father confusing and unpredictable, a problem that would eventually lead to their estrangement. But for now, he only wanted to do good so Joe would not yell at him; the better he did, the more peaceful his homelife would be.

Similarly, his quest for perfection was only reinforced by the Witnesses' ominous prediction of the world's end. He took the words to heart. If only the truest of God's servants were to survive, Michael had to prove himself through good works. Consequently, in matters of piety or performance, he made certain he was not only the best he could be, but also better than everyone else. Why? Failure would mean separation from his beloved mother, whom Michael knew to be pure and good, and not being with her was too frightening for a little boy to imagine.

Aside from these psycho-dramas, Michael was like most children his age. He had an infectious, ready laugh, inquisitive eyes and a mind that was sharp and quick. He pored over his school books during the week, and on Saturday mornings he raced to the television to watch his favourite cartoons. He occasionally played basketball with his brothers in the park behind the house, but mostly he shied away from sports. He preferred more prankish delights. He loved to play practical jokes on his mother and his brothers and sisters, and he especially liked to scare his sisters with plastic bugs and spiders.

Michael learned to steer clear of his father when he was in these playful moods. He was always wary of upsetting Joe's hair-trigger temper. But he respected his dad for the effort he put into the group. When Joe travelled to Chicago to scout music acts for new moves and songs, Michael waited anxiously for him to return, knowing that his father would teach them the newest dance moves and songs.

On the other hand, it was impossible for Michael to share a close bond with his father. The problem was religion. Joe, raised a Lutheran by his mother, made a game effort to accompany Katherine and the children to the Kingdom Hall every Sunday. But sometime in the late sixties – 'I can't recall when,' he says – his participation in the family's spiritual observances waned. When Katherine led the family to services, he stayed at home. This caused strain between Joe and his wife – at least until they came to an understanding. But Michael didn't comprehend it. Why wouldn't his father want salvation with the rest of the family? Joe's decision made an indelible impression on

31

Michael, drawing him away from his father and ever closer to his mother.

Meanwhile, Joe was busy manoeuvring for the Jackson Five's leap into the record business. In New York he met attorney Richard Arons, a musicians' union employee who helped with paperwork prior to the Apollo show. Joe offered him half-interest in managing the group, a move that provided the backroom business expertise he needed to negotiate with record companies. Joe also got Keith to cancel his distribution deal with Atlantic records, and then he made it clear to the minor-league producer that he was no longer going to be involved with the Jackson Five.

Still revelling in their Apollo victory, the Jackson Five performed one of their regular stints at Chicago's Regal Theater. Bobby Taylor and the Vancouvers, a second-string Motown act with whom Joe had become friendly, were also on the bill. Taylor, like Gladys Knight, had been speaking to Joe previously about auditioning with Motown in Detroit. But this time, when he raised the subject, Joe was receptive to the offer.

There was only one small problem. Earlier, Joe had accepted a call from a talent agent who caught their winning act in New York and booked them on the *David Frost Show*. They were supposed to go back to New York.

The guys were beside themselves with excitement – first over their scheduled appearance on national television, and then over their unplanned excursion to Detroit. Joe had cancelled one trip for another. Katherine, though, was home in Gary with no idea of the change in plans – and fortune. As far as she knew, Joe and the boys were supposed to leave Chicago after their Regal dates and go to New York for their appearance on the *David Frost Show*. Instead, they headed for Detroit. 'I didn't know where they were,' says Katherine. 'Finally, I called Chicago and was told, "No, Joe and the boys didn't go to New York."'

'Well, where are they?' she asked.

'They went to Detroit.'

'Detroit?' she said, puzzled. 'You mean to tell me he gave up that television show just to go to Detroit? What for?'

'Motown.'

Although future Motown press releases would portray the Jacksons as a model American family, clean-cut, loving, and problem-free, their home was not the harmonious den depicted by corporate image-makers. Music was fast becoming the family business, but their rapid ascent raised issues that could not help but affect Michael.

Joe made no secret of his master plan. He envisioned his entire brood, all nine children, eventually working in the family's act. His reasoning was simple. The more who worked, the more money came in. 'And a man can't never have too much money,' he liked to say.

However, just before their departure for Motor City, Rebbie (aka Maureen), the oldest of the Jackson offspring, upset this carefully laid blueprint by announcing her engagement to Nathanial Brown, a staunch Jehovah's Witness like herself. If her brothers were offered a contract, which would probably require them relocating to Los Angeles, Rebbie and her new husband were going to move to Kentucky to start a life of their own. Katherine gave her blessings, but Joe disapproved. 'It was all cooked up by Maureen and her mother,' he says. 'I wasn't happy about it at all.'

Joe took his daughter's strike at independence as a personal affront. He believed Rebbie was too young at eighteen to marry and too immature to be making decisions on her own. There were many nights he railed against the whole idea of marriage. As the ceremony grew closer and closer he threatened to boycott it entirely. Joe's voice boomed through the small, crowded house as he and Katherine argued constantly. But by the wedding day, Joe's roar had turned into a silent protest. His wife had won – mostly. 'I didn't stand in Maureen's way,' he says. But he did manage a protest. 'I didn't give her away like a father's supposed to do, that's what I wouldn't do.'

At the root of the issue was Rebbie's unwillingness to follow Joe's dictates. She didn't want to perform with the rest of her siblings. 'If I could've worked with her a little more,' he says, 'she could've been a bigger star than she is now, instead of being a housewife and raising a family.'

However, the drama of Rebbie's wedding was overshadowed by the Motown audition. It was the break upon which years of perspiration and sacrifice hinged. Joe, more than anyone, recognized that this the was family's future, not to mention fortune, staring them straight in the eyes, and he responded by lecturing his sons on the seriousness of this opportunity. Michael recalls being fixed by his dad's dark eyes and told, 'I'd like to see my ten-year-old singer make it to eleven.'

By the time they arrived in Detroit, late at night, and checked into the Gotham Hotel, Tito, Jackie, Jermaine, Marlon and Michael had caught their father's earnest mood. Adrenalin tickled their nerves, pumping them up with excitement. 'We always did the best we could,' says Marlon. 'But we knew we had to work extra hard for the tryout.'

Not only did Joe tell the children how important their Motown audition was, they knew how vital a recording contract was from overheard discussions between their parents. With a legitimate contract practically a sure bet, Joe wanted to devote himself to the group full-time. He talked more and more about quitting his job at the steel mill, almost as if he had to convince himself that such a big move was right.

But the thought frightened Katherine. She had taken on a part-time sales clerk's position at Sears to help defray the extra costs of her children's burgeoning career. This was in addition to night school, where she was earning her high school diploma. She could not imagine a greater risk than Joe leaving work.

Michael picked up on these concerns. Silently, he shouldered the worry. By the time the old VW bus was chugging its way to Detroit, he could feel a change in himself. His sense of purpose was expanding to gigantic proportions – well beyond the responsibilities of a ten-year-old.

Despite the apparent happiness of the Jacksons' home, Michael perceived the strain that was simmering below the surface of his family's once-uncomplicated life. It stemmed directly from the music that had become his sole focus. His father was upset over Rebbie's marriage. His mother was concerned about money and security. Everyone was poised for something to break with the group. Aware of the stress and pressure, Michael, like so many bright and talented children who in later years focus attention on diet and appearance, felt obliged to shoulder these burdens by himself.

It made perfect sense. Sizing up the situation in his ten-year-old mind, the charismatic frontman, who knew full well his commanding power over an audience, found a simple solution. He would work harder. If money was what mattered most, he would simply work harder. Yes, Michael would work harder, and everything would be okay.

The morning of the Motown audition, Michael was more than ready for the challenge, having concentrated for the entire trip on his newfound determination as if it were a mantra to be chanted. Joe woke everyone up early for their ten a.m. appointment and then drove them the short distance to Motown's headquarters, Hitsville, U.S.A. When the greyish van pulled into the parking lot, hardly a person noticed the hand-painted logo on the side that read 'The Jackson Five'.

They entered a dingy studio rehearsal hall, and found instruments and microphones already set up. They waited as the room filled with Motown personnel. Many of the veteran Motown musicians saw the kids ushered in and thought it was pretty funny that they were being passed off as pros. 'Jackson Jive,' they chortled. When the two most important members of the audience arrived, Berry Gordy and his label's star, Diana Ross, the room took on an air of seriousness. 'They whispered and talked among themselves and then we played,' says Marlon.

When the Jackson Five finished their last song, they were met by the strangest reaction they had ever encountered. Silence. No one applauded. No one cheered. No one even said 'nice job'. Just a few hushed whispers and an eerie, business-like quiet. Gordy and Ross conferred some more and left the room. Michael was confused. His brothers were perplexed. Joe Jackson was neither pleased nor displeased. 'Thanks for coming,' they were told. And that was it. They climbed aboard the van, then hit the old asphalt rope, I–94, and returned to Gary.

In 1969 Motown impresario Berry Gordy, fed up with the isolation of his midwest location, was in the midst of moving his incredibly successful operation to Los Angeles, where he could exercise his increasing clout in the entertainment industry by branching off into feature films.

Gordy, a hardened ex-prizefighter, retailer and songwriter, was a rebel whose own career frustrations led him to found Motown in 1959. Despite the enormous odds against him, he turned the fledgling black label into a multimillion-dollar powerhouse whose trademarked party-time sound became the most important influence on early sixties pop music. Motown mainstays like the Temptations, Diana Ross and the Supremes, Stevie Wonder and Smokey Robinson became heroes to generations of music fans.

Legend and years of hype have clouded the Jacksons' discovery so much it's difficult to say exactly how Gordy first learned about the budding group. The official Motown version had Diana Ross finding them in 1968 at a campaign rally for Richard Hatcher, who was running for mayor of Gary. 'Michael won me over the first moment I saw him,' she told *Newsweek* in 1970. 'I saw so much of myself as a child in Michael. He was performing all the time. That's the way I was. He could be my son.'

However, it is more likely that it happened at the Motown audition. The silence that followed the Jackson Five's tryout was misleading. The Motown honcho was impressed. In the youngsters Gordy's keen eye spotted a means of marketing sixties innocence with the infectious, dance-till-you-drop sound his Motown songwriters were manufacturing for the next decade. A few days later he called Joe and offered his kids a contract. 'We were ecstatic,' recalls Marlon. 'We knew we were going to have to work very hard, and that our lives were going to change.' After Gordy eventually made a deal with Joe and the contract was signed, he gathered the boys together and gave them an inspiring pep talk in which he assured them the Jackson Five would hit the charts at number one. 'I'm gonna make you the biggest thing in the world,' Michael recalls Gordy saying, 'and you're gonna be written about in history books.'

The decision to move to Los Angeles from Gary was an easy one to make. Joe and the boys would leave immediately. The difficult part was that Katherine was going to stay behind in Gary with Janet and Randy. Michael, the youngest in the group and most attached to his mother, was not pleased with the arrangement, but he accepted it. If he worked hard enough, the family would be reunited and everything would be okay. 'We discussed it,' says Joe, 'and decided we had to get established before bringing the rest of the family out.'

Once in Los Angeles, the Jacksons moved around the city like the rootless troubadours they were. Motown took care of their accommodation, which was initially much seedier than they were used to. First, they stayed at the old Tropicana Hotel on a rundown section of Santa Monica Boulevard in Hollywood. Michael, Marlon, Jermaine and a friend named David Wilson all shared a room. Tito and Jackie took another room. 'Every day Motown had someone pick us up and take us to the studio,' says Marlon. 'We were really working hard.'

After a few months, Motown moved the Jacksons to the Hollywood Motel, a neglected hostelry across from Hollywood High School favoured by prostitutes and junkies. It was closer to the studios and the various music schools the Jacksons were shuttling in and out of during the course of long, arduous work days. The Jacksons did not complain. 'It wasn't a great neighbourhood,' says Marlon, 'but we were so busy that our heads hit the pillow and we were out.'

The group was practising one afternoon at the Sound Factory on Selma Avenue in Hollywood the first time Hal Davis, the chief of Motown's West Coast office, heard them perform. 'Berry Gordy called me one evening and said I want you to meet a group I signed,' recalls Davis. 'The next day I walked in and saw five little guys. They played a few songs and they were good. I was interested, but I knew I had a lot of work to do.'

Likewise, Michael was intrigued by the veteran producer, who had picked the Jacksons up from the airport when they arrived in Los Angeles for a year of intense polishing and grooming. 'I used to wear really dark shades all the time, and he'd always ask me why. He'd say, "I want to see your eyes." '

Right off, Davis realized Michael's precociousness. 'Among themselves, they didn't really have a leader,' he says. 'Jackie and Marlon were the dance guys, really into the moves, and Jermaine and Tito were really involved with their instruments. As for Michael, he was already super shy, but you could see he had his own thing going. The way he moved, the way he sang, the way he was always thinking. He was a natural.'

It was summer when the Jacksons moved, and Motown was able to get a full schedule of work from the boys without the interruption of school. Their first project was, 'I Want You Back', a new tune by Freddie Perren and Fonce Mizell, a couple of untested songwriters whose work had been sent to Motown staff producer Deke Richards. 'He liked our stuff and said he'd like to work with us,' says Perren. 'He said one way to get the spotlight on you right away is to find someone who's cold and write a hit on them.'

One afternoon Perren and Mizell, who had just moved to California, were sitting around Richards' Hollywood apartment and they came up with a little song they called 'I Want to be Free'. Intended for Gladys Knight, the track turned out so well they thought it might be perfect for Diana Ross. But Gordy had a different idea. 'We just signed these five brothers out of Gary, Indiana, and this sounds like a lively track,' he said to Perren. 'Why don't you rewrite the song for them?'

This was not Perren's first encounter with the Jackson Five.

He had been playing piano for Jerry Butler at Chicago's Regal Theatre when the group, riding the regional success of their 'Big Boy' single, was the opening act. 'Michael was tiny,' he recalls. 'I felt so sorry for him, because it was a nightclub. I said the little kid's gonna go out and they're gonna murder him. [But] Michael went out there and brought the house down.'

After much tinkering on the rewrite, the threesome came up with a finished version that was ready to record. Their only worry: could the bashful little kid reach the high notes? 'Michael didn't say much at all,' remembers Perren. 'He wasn't as outgoing or playful as the other guys. He would just stand there. We were singing the song, and all the time we were showing it to him, I was thinking, "Can he reach those notes?" Finally, we took a try at it – and he just reached it the first time with no effort at all.'

When Gordy, ever the perfectionist, heard what his production crew thought was a perfect version, he shook his head with displeasure. 'Oh, man, you guys are getting ready to blow a hit,' he said. 'Get the fellas back and go do some more rehearsing.' Gordy's eye for detail made a big impression on Michael, who observed every part of the boss' meticulous supervision. 'I'll never forget his persistence,' says Michael in *Moonwalk*. 'This was his genius. To this day, I use the same principles.'

The lessons Michael was learning at Motown would endure. Outside the studio, the Jacksons underwent a complete image makeover, a repackaging in which they could actually watch stylists tinker with Colorform models of how they would soon look. They were told how to dress. They were given new hairstyles: oversized Afros that were trimmed and rounded to appear hip but inoffensive. They were chauffeured to music and dance lessons. They were given strict instruction in everything from table etiquette to grammar. Told what to expect from the press, they were questioned in mock interviews and they studied answers prepared for them by Motown publicists. Even then, their interviews were handled by publicists; the boys stood silently in the background – not unlike the way Michael's publicists now serve him.

In a short time they were transformed from cute, unsophisticated kids plucked out of a struggling steel town to a superslick, freshly-scrubbed and highly marketable pop group. They were symbols of a new era at Motown, and their public debut was a Hollywood event. Invitations signed by the label's reigning diva, Diana Ross, went out via telegram to every opinion-maker in tinseltown. 'Please join me in welcoming a brilliant musical group, the Jackson Five, on Monday, August 11th, 6:30 to 9:30 p.m. at The Daisy, 326 North Rodeo Drive, Beverly Hills,' they said. 'The Jackson Five featuring sensational eight-year-old Michael Jackson will perform live at the party. Please come and listen to this fabulous new Motown group.'

It did not matter that Michael was little more than two weeks shy of his eleventh birthday. Motown liked him younger than he actually was, all the better to sell as a grammar school prodigy. However, Michael was always uneasy perpetuating publicity stories he knew to be fabrications. 'People always used to ask him about Diana Ross discovering the Jackson Five,' says one of the group's early publicists. 'He would squirm and turn quiet. So finally, one day he asked if it was okay if he didn't talk about it any more. I told him yes.'

There was no way to gauge how much Michael missed his mother, who was still in Gary, but by the time the Jackson Five finished cutting their first single, he had found a surrogate mom in Diana Ross. The boys had once again changed their residence – this time for the better – alternating between Gordy's and Diana's sumptuous mansions. Both happened to live on the same street in the Hollywood Hills. 'We could stay wherever we wanted,' says Marlon. 'It was great. There were cooks and games and we could swim whenever we felt like it.'

For Michael, this life was, to use his favourite word, 'magic'. Diana ushered him into a sophisticated world of culture. He says that she sparked a lifelong appreciation of art, introducing him to the works of great painters, taking him to museums and encouraging him to draw and paint. More important, Ross awed the impressionable youngster with her glamour. She became a role model who would serve him into adulthood. He was impressed by her mystique. He admired the sylphlike manner in which Diana seemed to float through rooms without delivering anything more of herself than her weighty celebrity. And he loved the way she chatted knowledgeably on so many different subjects. They talked endlessly about music, fashion and other entertainers whom Michael had only heard about. Diana nurtured the young performer in a way his own mother could not and he drew close to her. 'She was my mother, my lover and my sister all combined in one amazing person,' waxes Michael in *Moonwalk*.

Two months after their public unveiling, Motown released 'I Want You Back', the Jackson Five's first single. 'It was a

39

very nervous time for us,' says Marlon. 'We were all excited, wondering how it would do.' The song entered *Billboard*'s Hot 100, a list of the 100 most popular tunes, in mid-November at number ninety and began to soar. On 31 January 1970 it hit the top and the Jackson Five had their first number one record.

More significant, perhaps, is that the success gave Joe enough confidence to finally send for Katherine and the three children – LaToya, Randy and Janet – who were still back in Gary. Michael could not have been more delighted. His private resolve was confirmed: hard work was once again providing the reward he most desired and delivering exactly what was lacking in his family.

His mother.

4

Gary, Indiana. 31 January 1971.

Jackson Five Day. Elaborate ceremonies were planned in the dingy, industrial city the Jacksons once called home. The programme included a helicopter ride to town and a parade past their old house on the corner of 23rd and Jackson Streets. But because of cold, blustery winds and a snow storm, the outdoor festivities were cancelled, including the helicopter ride, which disappointed the two youngest Jacksons, Michael and Marlon.

Instead, the party proceeded directly to City Hall, where hundreds of excited fans crammed into a high-ceilinged chamber for a glimpse at the fabulous fivesome.

It was as much a political event as anything, a chance for the Jacksons to acknowledge their roots and say thanks to old friends like Gary's Mayor Richard Hatcher, who was up for re-election in this predominantly black city. Four years earlier the Jackson Five, unknowns, had played at a Hatcher-for-Mayor fundraiser starring Ross. This time the Jacksons returned as stars themselves. They were headlining their own sold-out performance later in the evening.

With the crowd straining to get the best views of their favourites, the Jacksons, in their suits and sport coats, dutifully posed for pictures. They exchanged soul handshakes with winners of a poster contest who earned the enviable chance to leap onstage and actually meet the hometown heroes. In addition to a state flag and a plaque from Indiana University, Mayor Hatcher presented them with keys to the city, and said he was honoured 'that the Jackson Five has carried the name of Gary throughout the country and the world, and made it a name to be proud of.'

Less than two years after leaving Gary, the wholesome, family were welcome symbols of a new hope and opportunity for a black America whose leading spokespeople had been the more militant Angela Davis and Mohammad Ali.

On the podium Joe Jackson, all dewey-eyed and gracious, his demure wife Katherine smiling in the background, appeared outwardly moved as he bestowed a heartfelt thanks upon the crowd. Each of his boys then said a few words. Michael uttered a soft-spoken thank you and then melted back into the ranks of his older, more outgoing brothers. Tito, acting as the group's spokesman, finished. 'We're glad to be home,' he said. 'There's no place like home.'

Despite Tito's exclamation, life in no way resembled the simple days of old. It had happened quickly. The next release after 'I Want You Back' was 'ABC'. Writer-producer Freddie Perren admitted that it was nothing more than the chorus of their initial hit song with a few embellishments. Released in the middle of March 1971, it took over the number one spot six weeks later from the Beatles' 'Let It Be'. But after two platinum singles, Gordy, who really wanted three in a row, posed a tough question to his crew: 'What about the follow-up?'

Next up was 'The Love You Save', another irresistible pop gem. It was previewed by the Motown chief before it was completed. 'He stayed fifteen minutes,' recalls Perren, 'and half-way through said, "You guys got it. I'm not worried any more."'

Indeed not. The Jackson Five's hot streak continued uninterrupted. Two months later, for the third time in a row, their single shot to number one, toppling the Lennon/McCartney composition, 'The Long and Winding Road/For You Blue'. It gave the Jackson Five the distinction of being the first group of the rock era to have their first three songs each go to number one.

Each new smash release only increased the pressure on the boys. Success had to be maintained. 'We didn't really feel the pressure that much,' Marlon says. 'There was time to kid around. But we had to work very hard. We knew the stakes were getting bigger all the time.'

Sensing the change, Michael dived head first into the work. He became a studio rat. Entranced by the creative process, he spent as much time as possible absorbing the knowledge of the more experienced musicians. More than willing to offer instruction, they were impressed by his determination to always improve. The studio became his classroom, the musicians his tutors. It was, and remains, the only place he truly feels comfortable.

Motown's veteran producers couldn't help but marvel at the

42

youngster's tireless dedication to perfection. He would repeat entire songs over and over, never satisfied with the result. He'd re-do passages, alter his phrasing, but most important, he always showed improvement. 'This would go on and on,' recalls Perren. 'With every take he got better.'

Little did any of these studio professionals realize that Michael gave himself no other choice. He was compelled to do his best – for his mother, for his God, to please his father, to please the powers at Motown. Ingrained in his mind was a simple notion: he *had* to outdo himself. The charts and sales figures were now ways of calculating his success.

Michael didn't let up. Sessions began for the Jacksons' fourth single, and writer-producer Hal Davis remembers Michael as a pre-teen workaholic, albeit one blessed with an abundance of talent. 'Whatever it took to get the song done right, he was willing to go the distance,' he says. 'And that was impressive, since he was still just a little kid.'

The song Davis had them record, 'I'll Be There', was a beautiful, soulful ballad. It was a risky change from their three previous hits, and not what anyone would expect from the young popsters, who had become known for their up-beat bubblegum groove. But the ballad, which had been kicking around for a while, was one of Davis' favourites. 'This particular tune was a natural,' he says. 'I first heard it on just the keyboards. I loved the melody – the title was "I'll Be There", and I thought it needed some lyric help.'

With the help of some slick penmanship from Gordy, the song was quickly finished and the instrumental tracks laid down. 'The next thing you know,' says Davis, 'we're in the studio with Michael and the kids.' Michael liked the tune instantly. 'I put it in a high key,' says Davis. 'I wanted his tenor voice to sound really sweet.' When the song was finally completed, 'there were a lot of people saying it wouldn't go, that these guys were bubblegum and no one would buy them singing a ballad,' says the producer.

In early October Motown released the group's fourth single. 'Berry called at five a.m. and, needless to say, woke me up,' recalls Davis. 'He said, "I've been hearing some comments about the new song." I said, "Like what?" and Berry said, "Oh, people are saying he sounds so high." Then I said, "But how's the record doing?" Berry kind of laughed and said, "We're already over two-and-a-half million." This was from Tuesday to Thursday, just three days. After he hung up, I went and sat in my car in my pyjamas and listened to the radio.'

On 17 October, 'I'll Be There' knocked Neil Diamond's 'Cracklin' Rosie' out of the pole position, making the Jackson Five the only group ever whose first four singles each soared to *Billboard*'s number one.

Following Gordy's exacting plans, the Jackson Five's first album sparked a nationwide phenomenon dubbed Jackson-mania. At the centre of it all was the four-and-a-half-foot tall firecracker. 'Fronted by the exuberant Michael Jackson, who dipped, spun and moved like a miniature James Brown,' said the *Rolling Stone Illustrated History of Rock and Roll*, 'the Jackson Five transcended all barriers of race and age in their appeal.'

Stardom was a mixed blessing for Michael. 'He never had a normal childhood,' says older brother Jermaine.

From the start, nothing was more important to the pre-pubescent prodigy than the reunion of his splintered family, which hinged on their success. Michael was ecstatic when Katherine packed up their Gary household and brought LaToya, Janet and Randy to Los Angeles. The move confirmed his belief in the benefits of successful work. 'Michael was very excited,' Katherine recalls. 'After all, he was the youngest of all the children out in California and it was difficult for him. But we were all excited to be coming out, excited that everything was going so well,' she says. 'The boys really seemed to be doing something very good.'

The reunited Jacksons settled in a comfortable home in the Hollywood Hills, a substantial improvement over their Gary residence. Liberace lived down the street and Davey Jones, the Monkees' lead singer, was one block away. But the Jacksons were the neighbourhood's primary attraction. Their address was on the Map to the Stars' Homes, and fans by the busload streamed by at all hours.

If overzealous groupies weren't attempting to sneak past the guards and into the house, others more docile but no less crazed waited politely outside, hoping to meet or see their favourite Jackson. From the earliest days, Michael's fans were the most devoted and crazed. Many of them camped out overnight, refusing to leave until they saw him. 'I always feel so sorry for those kids,' says Katherine, who still occasionally takes in a stray child and attempts to talk sense into them.

There was no respite from Jacksonmania. Every day brought

its own hysteria. The family was forced to adopt a kind of siege mentality for their own protection. 'We never knew what to expect,' LaToya says. 'I remember finding girls hiding in the bedrooms or the bathrooms, looking for one of my brothers. I once discovered a girl in the bathtub who said she was waiting for Michael.'

The older Jackson boys revelled in the attention. Already in their late teens, they had discovered the appeal of their celebrity to members of the opposite sex. 'All we had to do to meet girls was say we were Jacksons,' Johnny Jackson recalls. 'It was magic.' It was also hard to find a star-studded event that didn't boast either Jackie, Tito or Jermaine on its guest list.

Michael, unlike his brothers, loathed the fuss. He shied away from excursions beyond his home or the studio. The bedroom he shared with Marlon and Randy was his sanctuary. The backyard where he sheltered his pets was his refuge. These were the only spots where he could escape from outsiders. It wasn't that he disliked people. He just didn't know how to deal with them, and his family made no demands that he learn how.

His isolation became a matter of self-preservation. The moments were rare, but when he was at home, free of the tremendous pressure he put on himself in the studio, Michael could shed his burdens and just be a child. 'Michael was the kind of kid you wanted to kill all the time,' LaToya says. 'He'd jerk the hat off your head and run and hide it. Or if you were eating something, he'd pop it out of your hand. Worst of all, he was so fast you couldn't catch him.'

But his solitary lifestyle restricted his development. Michael had so little contact with the outside world that his solitude began to hinder the development of ordinary interests and social skills. 'He'd sometimes kid us or play hide and seek,' says Johnny, who lived with his adoptive family until the mid-seventies. 'But mostly when we'd play sports or go out and fool around, he was happy staying at home with his pets or his drawing. Even at home, he was always pretty much quiet and shy.'

He amused himself easily. He was a skilled mimic, he worshipped cartoons, and he showed himself to be a budding artist, who spoke about one day attending art school. His room was papered with his drawings of Mickey Mouse, Diana Ross and even Richard Nixon. He also thought he might like to act, he 'liked the kinds of things Sidney Poitier does'. He listened to

45

classic music and was a big fan of Copeland's Peter and the Wolf. His taste in music was eclectic. 'Sometimes I sit and listen to soft stuff like Johnny Mathis,' he said. 'I like Ray Charles. And most of the time I listen to Three Dog Night.'

Michael found school a difficult adjustment. He attended sixth grade at Gardner Street Elementary. The next year he joined Marlon at Emerson Junior High. They lasted there just two weeks. 'It got so crazy there we had to leave,' Marlon recalls. 'There were mobs of people standing in the halls, just looking into the classroom. It was embarrassing.'

It was dangerous, too. Towards the end of those two weeks, an unidentified caller telephoned with a death threat against Michael. The incident, which turned out to be a hoax, prompted Katherine and Joe to yank their kids out of public school. 'Nothing ever came of the threat,' Katherine says. 'But it was frightening. We were ordinary people and not used to the way everyone was reacting around the kids.'

As a result, Katherine arranged for Michael to enter a private school. He went to Walton Academy and then to Montclair for ninth grade. His report card there showed three As, a B+ in grammar and a B− in French. Also an 'excellent' in work habits. The next year he attended California Prep, where Marlon, LaToya, Jermaine and Tito were also enrolled. There were just five classrooms and twenty-nine students. Yet even in the comfort of the intimate, uncrowded classrooms, alongside children of stars, Michael assumed an attitude of disinterest. 'He was a good student, but he didn't make all As,' says LaToya, who stuck close to her brother in school. 'We did everything together. Michael already knew what he wanted to do in life, so school wasn't important to him.'

Not that he lacked the necessary skills to achieve. 'He had the ability to do well,' she says. 'He could answer or do anything he wanted to. And he knew he didn't really have to study hard to appear knowledgeable.' However, when it came time to buckle down and do school work, Michael bore no relation to the determined workaholic of the recording studio. 'The teacher would ask why he didn't do his homework,' LaToya recalls, 'and he'd say, "Well, it was boring." Just like that.'

If the teacher insisted he complete his assignment, Michael usually obliged, though it was clear school wasn't his top priority. 'In class Michael was always drawing pictures, little sketches of animals and monsters. Or he'd daydream,' LaToya laughs. 'Sometimes he'd get so involved he wouldn't pay attention to what was going on in class. When the teacher would call on him and he didn't know the answer, I'd feel bad. After all, he is my brother and I didn't want him to be embarrassed in front of everybody. But Michael didn't ever seem to care. He was always so sure of where he was going. School just wasn't as important to him as the work he did in the studio.'

When it came to music Michael was an honour student working several grades ahead. From the start, he impressed everyone at Motown with his intelligence and quickness. 'He had an unbelievable memory,' Motown staff producer Hal Davis recalls. 'When he was only nine or ten, Michael could memorize three songs in less than thirty minutes, which is pretty amazing. The kid knew how to work.'

Work – that was the key. Motown's carefully orchestrated handling of the press won the Jacksons a just-plain-folks image that had as wide an appeal as their music. To reporters, Jackie spoke about studying business, Tito came across as the family's most serious musician and Jermaine, a smiling, outgoing teenager, relished his role of sensitive pinup idol and target of adoring teenage girls. As for Marlon, always described as a smooth dancer as 'polished as a diamond', he was forever lurking in the shadows of his bunkmate, Michael.

In 1971 the Jackson Five's first U.S. tour, which stopped in over ninety cities, underscored Michael's critical importance to the family's fortune. The other brothers might've been flanking him onstage, but everyone shared an understanding: it was Michael's whirling onstage wizardry that set the group apart from all comers. 'Needless to say, he was the star,' says Bob Jones, the former Motown publicist who now heads MJJ Communications. 'There was no doubt about that from Jump Street. And everything sort of centred around that. He was the key to the J-five and everyone just sort of over-protected him.'

Meanwhile, his talent was mass-marketed like any other product. It was amped on the radio, hyped in the press and spread on the street. At twelve years old, Michael was enjoying a rapid ascent to stardom, that most performers sweat for their entire careers. 'Here you have the chief child, the new model, the successor to James Brown and the Temps and Sly, the cherubic incarnation of their sum,' wrote Ben Fong Torres in a *Rolling Stone* cover story. 'Colour, flash and a mayfield of

47

messengers, drumming, pounding, screeching, blowing out the word. The Jackson Five are this and more.'

The 'more' was Michael. Onstage, he was drawn to the spotlight as if he were possessed, magnetized by the attention, hypnotized by the power he had over the crowd. He stormed the front line with hands flailing, sweat flying, hips twirling, legs kicking, slipping to his knees, popping up on his toes, down and up, moving this way and that, grabbing the mike with one hand, flinging it into the other, bringing it in tight, doing a little James Brown and more, which had been his routine since he was four years old anyway, so it was all second nature. 'It was amazing,' says Suzanne DePasse, chief of Motown films and the former creative director of the Jacksons' stage show. 'He had it down to a T.'

Offstage, Michael bore no resemblance to the performer. Minus an audience, background music and scripted lines, he shrank into an invisible cocoon. As soon as the Jacksons left the stage, he disappeared within himself, evaporating from the tinsel and huzzahs that surrounded the group at each stop. His amusements were simple: card tricks, afterhours hijinks – pillow fights and water balloon tosses – with his brothers back at the hotel, pets and telephone calls back to his mother.

After performances, he was already weary enough to grimace when much older interviewers sidled up to him and said, 'Hey man, I heard you really were a midget, that you're actually thirty years old.' No, he was just a kid and as capable of mischief as anyone. 'He was a little brat during the early days,' Bob Jones remembers. 'He loved to play games, loved to pull tricks on the rest of us when we were on the road.'

Michael was studious in his workplace. 'He was very inquisitive as to what you were doing, what was happening and all that,' Jones says. 'But first and foremost, he was concerned about his performance and his career.' This brought out his quiet side. As lively as Michael was onstage, he grew remote off it. 'He was an introvert,' Jones adds. 'Once he came off the stage, he would come back to the hotel, put on his robe and relax in his room.'

When the others went out to explore whatever city they were in, Michael usually stayed behind. He loved ordering room service, eating in bed and watching TV, cartoons especially. 'They also carried a big easel, with a big sheet of paper on it for him to draw,' Jones says. 'He spent most of his spare time drawing or reading. The rest of the guys spent their time playing backgammon or going out sightseeing or playing ball. He was very much into doing something more creative.'

Michael's memories of road trips read like notes from summer camp. Fast-walk races down hotel corridors, pillow fights, wrestling matches, shaving cream wars, water balloon battles and ordering room service for other people's rooms. A tutor travelled with them. In each city, they'd try to shop in the trendiest stores, though eventually going out in public became too much of a hassle. 'Being mobbed by near hysterical girls was one of the most terrifying experiences for me in those days,' Michael writes in *Moonwalk*. 'It was rough.'

Road trips offered plenty of tutelage in matters of sex – both innocent and not so innocent. In hotels Michael and Marlon roomed with their older, more worldly brother Jermaine, who used to wait for the chief of security, Bill Bray, to nod off before sneaking downstairs and flirting with the girls who waited in the lobby. Occasionally, he brought them back to the room. 'He'd tell us to "play sleep", Marlon laughs. 'We used to play sleep for Jermaine all the time. He'd sneak in girls and Michael and I would keep our heads tucked way under the covers.'

Curfew was eleven o'clock – sharp. The boys had to be in bed, the lights out, ready for bedcheck. 'Every once in a while Jermaine would get caught,' Marlon says. But the same rules didn't apply to their father. With his wife back home, Joe stayed out late and caroused with the other men on the crew, picking up young ladies by boasting that he was the father of the world famous Jackson Five. 'My father would knock on the door,' Marlon recalls. 'We'd let him in and he'd have maybe three or four girls with him. We'd have on our pyjamas and they'd laugh at us and then disappear. He thought it was funny, but we'd get very upset.'

In his book, Michael makes only the slightest mention of this. He recalls it as one of 'the meanest things'. 'Listen,' an old family acquaintance says, 'those boys knew exactly what their father was doing and what that meant to their mother. They were mortified, angry and pained.'

Privately, Michael seethed from the embarrassment. He filed away the implications of Joe's philandering in his memory, recalling it years later when his mother required his aid and protection. Back then, it was enough merely to recognize that his father was a shadow of the man who preached family values. Not only was Joe falling prey to the enticements of rock and roll – fast money and easy women – he was parading it in front of his kids.

The warning bell sounded. Michael began to realize that his dad was someone of whom he should be wary. Unconsciously, he began erecting a wall between them that was every bit as forbidding as the one that prevented intruders from entering their home. 'This is really the beginning of Michael and Joe's poor relationship,' a family insider offers. 'He never got over the way Joe was humiliating his mother.'

5

Encino, California. August 1973.

When Michael lay back in bed at night and counted his heroes, several names immediately came to mind. In music James Brown, Jackie Wilson and Sly Stone headed his list. Outside of music, it was physicist Albert Einstein. His portrait was tacked to the bedroom wall. Michael might not have understood the physicist's work but he appreciated the spirit of the scientist's originality.

Michael was also intrigued by the genius of both Thomas Edison and John Lennon. Their ingenuity and determination to achieve moved him. He stencilled inspirational quotations from their work onto the wall of the Jacksons' backyard studio in Encino. Edison's aphorism concerns the three essentials of achievement – hard work, drive and common sense. Lennon's has to do with being a conduit for a power greater than oneself. 'When the real music comes to me – the music of the spheres, the music that surpasseth understanding – that has nothing to do with me cause I'm just the channel.'

Michael took both to heart. He attributed his gift for song to the Almighty. 'I've been doing this since I was five years old onstage and I feel it's something that God gave me to do,' he said. Later, Michael articulated similar feelings when questioned about his compositions. Rather than accept individual credit, he claimed that he was simply one of God's chosen scribes, a translator for the great spirit, delivering music that was sent to him through a force he couldn't control. A friend joked that Michael should be careful about making such statements, since pesky reporters would no doubt want God's phone number in order to verify his claim.

When it came to his biggest influences one name topped all others – Walt Disney, the creator of the Magic Kingdom and Michael's favourite cartoon characters. Disney's creativity

51

reflected all that Michael deemed important – the entertainment of children, originality, the realization of dreams. Uncle Walt had also constructed Disneyland, the only place besides home where Michael could completely unburden himself and leap freely into childhood. The name Disney, all by itself, implied magic – which Michael adopted as his favourite word.

'He always liked Walt Disney,' Katherine says of her son. 'Michael is a dreamer. He's always enjoyed sitting back and letting his mind go, cooking up all sorts of ideas. Some of them are really crazy and some are wonderful. Walt Disney was a dreamer, too. What Michael likes so much about him is that Walt Disney made his dreams come true.'

Michael set about doing the same thing for himself. By age four, his dreams were clear cut. He would become a singer. 'When he was very young, Michael knew what he wanted in life,' LaToya says. 'And that was it. He was that determined to achieve exactly what he wanted.' Not only did Michael define his destiny, he also mapped out a particular destination. Number one. 'He liked to be number one,' his father says. 'He liked to do things first.'

With such lofty goals, though, disappointment was always lurking around the corner, like a whisper he didn't want to hear or footsteps that haunted him at every bend. No matter what Michael accomplished, he had to ask himself if it was good enough. If he couldn't do better. And Michael was constantly asking himself those questions. So often that they echoed in his ears. 'Am I good enough? Am I doing the best I can? Am I number one?'

In the beginning, there were few reasons for him to worry. The pop charts gave Michael a convenient way to measure his success. When each of the Jackson Five's first four singles shot to number one, he could ask himself if he was doing his best and reply without a doubt, yes, he was. However, his contentment was not long-lasting.

The mid-seventies were not kind to the Jacksons. In 1971 Gordy decided to cash further on the Jackson Five's impressive commercial clout. They hosted their own TV special, 'Goin' Back to Indiana', and made guest appearances on numerous variety shows. Gordy also urged Michael, his most valuable property – er, prodigy – to record his first solo record, 'Got To Be There', which peaked in the charts at number four. Motown's head honcho then did a deal that led to the aptly titled Saturday morning cartoon show *The Jackson Five*. Michael loved seeing himself as an animated character, and every Saturday morning he'd race to the TV to watch himself. 'It was like a fantasy come true for all of us,' he says.

But except for the cartoon series, the group was struggling where it once dominated. After 'I'll Be There', they never again had a number one song. Their next two singles, 'Mama's Pearl' and 'Never Can Say Goodbye', went only as high as second place, while the little known 'Sugar Daddy', released in 1972, stopped at number ten. Otherwise, each new Jackson Five release seemed to sizzle and then sink, doing a slow, uneasy tumble down the charts, stalling someplace in the top twenty, but nowhere near the top.

Michael, at the mercy of Motown's omnipotent decision makers, who selected, wrote and produced his material, seemed to be groping for a formula that would work. His solo follow up, 'Rockin' Robin', a playful tune that highlighted his still boyish enthusiasm, fared better than his initial outing, reaching number two. His third attempt, 'I Wanna Be Where You Are', pulled up lame at sixteen, and his next recording, 'Ain't No Sunshine', didn't even chart. Needless to say, he was worried.

Miserable is more like it. What was wrong? What could be so upsetting as to turn a world famous pop star sullen? The same thing that irritates most teenagers – adolescence. When Michael studied himself in the mirror, he discovered a new person staring back. His body was in the midst of an overhaul. Seemingly overnight, he'd shot up like a beansprout. No longer a squat, dimpled cutie, he was now a tall, skinny, lanky young man. When he introduced himself, he found people not only incredulous but also disappointed.

He was fourteen when he discovered these confusing alterations of character, though they'd been apparent to others close to him for more than a year. Besides the obvious physical differences, there was a definite change in his demeanour. 'Michael changed when he was about thirteen,' LaToya says. 'He got more quiet, more serious and he kept to himself even more than before. I think Michael was just trying to find himself at a time that wasn't easy for him.'

The period Michael was passing through was agonizing. His skin broke out in a terrible case of acne, he says, and seemed to sprout a pimple in every pore. The damage he suffered was irreversible. 'I became subconsciously scarred by this experience with my skin,' he admits. His shyness was exaggerated even more. He turned inward even more than before and avoided meeting other people as much as possible. He became depressed. His self-esteem plummeted. He didn't want to go outside. He just wanted to hibernate and wake up one day realizing it was all a bad dream. 'The effect on me was so bad that it messed up my whole personality,' he says. 'I couldn't look at people when I talked to them. I felt I didn't have anything to be proud of.'

But his skin wasn't solely responsible for the depth of his despair. Without a hit single, his delicately balanced world was in jeopardy. 'Michael worried constantly about his career,' says Marlon. He had good cause; the numbers didn't lie. If he wasn't number one, who was he? When Michael asked himself, 'Am I doing my best?' he couldn't provide the right answer. When he asked, 'Am I good enough?' it was impossible to say yes without the proof. He *had* to be the best. He gave himself no other options.

In 1972 Michael rose up from his depression when he recorded 'Ben', the theme to an odd, low-budget horror movie about a boy who raises rats to carry out his schemes of revenge. From the moment he heard the beautiful ballad, which celebrates the boy's relationship to a very intelligent rat, he was, recalls Don Black, one of the song's composers, 'very anxious to do it'. In October Michael's fifth solo recording went to number one, providing him a much sought-after hit as well as succour for his tender psyche.

The horror film served as Michael's introduction to movie-making, which he augmented with excursions to the set of 'Lady Sings the Blues', which Berry Gordy was financing, where his old mentor Diana Ross was creating her smouldering portrayal of blues diva Billie Holliday. Watching Diana, Michael became entranced by acting, which seemed a way to flee from his own life. 'With acting, it's like becoming another person,' he said. 'I think that's neat, especially when you totally forget. If you totally forget, which I love to do, that's when it's magic.'

What could Michael want to forget? Plenty. Although a world tour that literally spanned the entire globe, stopping in Japan, Australia and Africa, proved a rich window into other cultures, the Jackson Five were stuck in a rut back home, which frustrated Michael. Because he was the group's acknowledged power source, if he didn't gel, they didn't either. Only one of the two Jackson Five singles released in 1973, 'Hallelujah Day', charted, and then it sputtered at number twenty-eight before disappearing.

54

There was trouble afoot. It didn't take a detective to figure that. The magic spontaneity that had marked their first year at Motown, those kinetic hours in the studio, the cocksureness of being on the cutting edge of new music, the ability to spin out hit after hit; all of it, which they had so confidently had, somehow escaped them. Michael didn't yet have the insight to see what was happening, although he sensed something was wrong when Jackson Five studio sessions were crammed with more advisers than musicians and no one could agree on anything.

The family was well aware that Joe was having difficulty dealing with Gordy, whose hands-on interest in the Jacksons (as well as other Motown groups) was dissipated more and more by his company's rapid expansion and diversification. 'There were differences between the brothers and Berry,' Joe says. 'More and more we weren't seeing things concerning the group in the same way, but we weren't having major disagreements yet.'

On the surface, things couldn't have appeared more solid. In December 1973, Jermaine married Gordy's nineteen-year-old daughter, Hazel, who had first met the entire Jackson clan when they moved to Los Angeles. A few years later, she invited him to get a hamburger, their first date, an offer he at first declined. 'But she sort of knew I liked her because I kind of kidded with her,' says Jermaine, who owned a Rolls-Royce and a Bel Air mansion by the time he turned nineteen.

After a five-year courtship, Jermaine won the heart of the mogul's daughter, who 'never thought she would get involved with somebody in the music business', he says. 'But she told me I had a certain innocence.' Papa Gordy pulled out all stops for the star-studded ceremony, lavishing nearly a quarter of a million dollars on an all-white, winter-themed wedding, featuring mountains of snow, live doves, inscribed napkin rings and mugs, thousands of dollars' worth of white camellias, and an original tune, 'The Wedding Song', sung by Smokey Robinson.

Back in the studio the Jackson Five worked on what would be their last Motown hit, 'Dancing Machine'. By 1974, disco had usurped the airwaves and was pulsating in clubs everywhere. 'Dancing Machine', with its blasting horns and sci-fi synthesizer noises, fit right in. A sixteen-bar intro, on which Michael coos a romantic monologue to a space lady, was edited out. But a great hook and a smooth-as-ice performance by Michael on *Soul Train*, where he unleashed his superlimber limbs in the Robot, the latest street dance, gave the tune a boost. Like the old days, it rose up the charts, climbing all the way to number two.

But things weren't the same.

6

New York City, July 1975.

Ten plain, high-backed black chairs were set behind a long boardroom table in the centre of a raised dais inside Manhattan's fancy Rainbow Grill. They held the promise of an important event. Dozens more chairs were arranged to face the dais. The setting was informal, the mood businesslike. Then a phalanx of reporters was let in. They struggled for seats and good camera positions and then waited for something to happen.

Music blared. Jackson Five tunes alternated with songs by LaBelle, and Harold Melvin and the Blue Notes. Sure-fire dance cuts, only no one danced. Then a frizzy-haired publicist from the record company paraded in front of the newsmen, her high-heels clicking on the linoleum floor as she moved across the crowded room, opened a side door and ushered eleven members of the Jackson family, single file, towards the high-backed chairs. Their faces were serious. No one smiled.

Joe, dressed in a slick black suit, sat at one end. He was followed by his wife, Katherine and LaToya, Janet, Randy, and Rebbie, who held her own daughter, Stacy; and then Jackie, Tito, Marlon and Michael. Conspicuously absent was Jermaine, long the group's sex symbol, who was back in L.A. with his wife, Hazel Gordy. But the purpose of the press conference shed light on the missing Jackson. According to the stern, sombre patriarch, speaking in a slow, measured tone, music's number one family had signed a contract with Epic Records and would leave Motown on the expiration of their contract, in March 1976.

Why, a reporter asked?

'We left Motown because we look forward to selling a lot of albums,' Tito answered.

'Motown sells a lot of singles,' Joe added, 'but Epic sells a lot of albums.'

57

Michael, sixteen, the real star of the group, who was wearing a black velvet jacket and plaid waistcoat, was then asked how he thought the move would affect him.

'I'm sure the promotion will be stronger,' he said.

Joe and his oldest sons, now fully-grown men, exuded a proud bravado. On the dais, they held their heads high, their chests forward, and their comments, optimistic and confident, resonated an 'anything's possible' attitude. Michael was just the opposite. Painfully shy, awkward in front of people, uncomfortable, he looked as if he wanted to disappear. His eyes fluttered downward, locking on the tabletop. Only occasionally did he glance up and then, it appeared, only to see if the conference was over yet.

Someone asked if the Jacksons had tried to renegotiate their contract with Motown.

'Sure, we tried to renegotiate with Motown,' Jackie snapped. 'But the figures were just Mickey Mouse.'

It was a shallow answer to a deep problem. A problem that had been brewing over time. A problem that was aggravated by the increasing maturity of the Jacksons themselves. A problem that only got worse when the Jackson Five's last few Motown albums failed to produce a substantial hit single. A problem rooted in two very stubborn men; Berry Gordy, Jr and Joe Jackson. A problem that caused a deep, unsightly rift in the intensely loyal and closeknit Jackson family. 'It didn't have to be that way,' Joe says. 'No, I don't think it did.'

The schism between the Jacksons and Motown, particularly Gordy, came to a boil when the Jacksons recorded their *Dancing Machine* album. Basically, the guys wanted more creative control over their sound. They felt they were lagging behind contemporary trends, so far behind, in fact, that Michael felt they were in danger of becoming a 'nostalgia' band – and this before his eighteenth birthday. The Jacksons wanted more input in the writing and producing. Not unreasonable requests, especially by artists of their stature. But Motown disagreed. Their answer was firm: no.

Also on the table were a spate of accusations that Motown had unjustly withheld money owed the Jacksons. But money wasn't the main issue here.

'I wanted to stay with Motown,' Joe maintains. 'The boys wanted to stay with Motown. The only reason we left was that the label wasn't giving the boys a chance to do what I knew they could do, and that's write their own material. It showed they didn't have any confidence in us. If they would've let them write just one song on the next album, it would've made the boys feel much better.'

Michael was asked to confront Gordy directly, and their one-on-one discussion brought the bitter negotiations to a head. The faceoff required the teenager to summon every last ounce of courage and fortitude in his spindly frame. But Gordy didn't agree – or wouldn't – and the summit between the two superpowers amounted to nothing. 'Being at a record company is like being at school,' Michael explained later. 'If you're not happy with the principal or the school, you go to another. At Motown we wanted to do our own writing, but that wasn't in our contract and they wouldn't give it to us. We didn't have publishing rights, either, and we had trouble getting a proper accounting of our money.'

In a brief period of time Michael had acquired the equivalent of a college-level business degree. Using himself as an example, he had studied first-hand the creation of a product, its packaging and marketing. He had learned about management and quality maintenance. And he realized that everything boiled down to one basic ingredient: control – an idea that quickly became basic to his way of thinking.

Michael knew that success depended on him controlling the reins to his own career. He just wasn't in a position to exercise that sort of power – yet. 'Michael always had his own idea of how things should be done,' Marlon says. 'But the Jackson Five was a group, not his special project, and his was just one vote.'

If nothing else, the Jacksons have always been egalitarian. To this day, they make most major decisions in family meetings. In these conclaves, held over simple dinners at one of their homes, they all voice opinions, engage in debate and then decide a particular matter by vote. One vote per person, no matter who has sold the most records.

In the early summer of 1975, they gathered in the living room of their recently-purchased Encino estate to decide their future. Everyone in the family was present, except Jermaine. 'If he would've been there, it would've caused an explosion,' a family associate says.

There was little discussion, family members recall. Michael, who kept his thoughts to a few words, felt in his heart a loyalty to the label that had shepherded them to fame and fortune. But when it came time to vote, all hands were raised in unison in favour of leaving Motown.

Several days later Joe telephoned his third oldest son and asked him to stop by the family's house – without his wife, please. When he arrived Jermaine didn't have a clue about the latest developments and he strolled inside the large house as if nothing were wrong. Joe's face told a different story. He ushered his son into an empty bedroom where a pile of contracts were spread out. There were four signatures on each one: Jackie, Tito, Michael and Marlon. All they needed was Jermaine's.

'They saved me for last because they knew I'd be trouble,' he says.

He was shocked. Quickly, Joe attempted to explain as well as to persuade his son to go along with the plan. Epic, he said, was part of CBS, the biggest record company in the world. The executives at CBS had told Joe they'd make the Jacksons 'the next Beatles'. There was also a lot of money involved, including publishing interests, as well as Epic's enormous marketing machinery, which would be at their disposal. According to Joe, the offer dwarfed Motown's.

It didn't matter to Jermaine. He recoiled in absolute horror and ran out of the house without saying a word. His Rolls-Royce screeched out of the driveway and stopped up the street at the nearest pay telephone, where he called his father-in-law. Gordy, who was also hearing about the group's decision for the first time, was equally shocked by the dramatic news. 'Well, how about you?' he asked his son-in-law. 'What are you going to do?'

'I didn't sign,' Jermaine replied. 'And I won't sign.'

In the midst of this tumult the family, including Jermaine, flew to Las Vegas, where the Jackson Five were headlining at the MGM Grand. Their act, a combination of rock, nostalgia and middle-brow comedy, now included Randy on Bongos, a song or two by LaToya, and an hilarious Mae West impersonation by an eight-year-old Janet, who showed a natural stage flair by slinking out in high heels and a tight-fitting, sequinned dress and winning howls from the audience. Onstage, they looked a seamless unit.

Offstage, however, the Jacksons were a family divided by conflicting loyalties. Their dressing rooms simmered with hostility. Several times Jermaine and Jackie lit into each other in heated disputes over the merits of one record company versus the other. Their biggest fight was over publishing. Jackie felt the group deserved their own while Jermaine toed Motown's draconian line. Jermaine felt more and more ostracized, an enemy within his own family. 'I never knew my family would take it so hard and show that towards me,' he says. 'That's when it really hurt.'

The dispute reached a nasty conclusion one night only minutes before the Jacksons took the stage. Gordy telephoned backstage and told Jermaine not to go on with his family. He was finished with them, the Motown chief said, and he should pack up and leave. 'We were surprised,' Marlon says, 'really in shock. But we had a show to do. We really didn't talk about it. We knew what we had to do.'

Michael didn't say a word. For him, the situation was utterly frightening. Everything for which he and his family had worked so hard for so many years had suddenly been put in jeopardy. But his place was well defined. He had long ago accepted the responsibility for providing whatever the family lacked. When their dreams hinged on signing a record contract, he worked harder. When he wanted his mother to join the family in Los Angeles, he worked harder. Michael's solution now was exactly what it had always been.

'We worked harder,' he says.

At the end of their performance, the Jacksons earned – and received – three standing ovations.

The Jacksons filled the brief period of transition between Motown and Epic with their own network television show. Michael hated doing the show. 'I don't know why,' Joe ponders. 'It helped him a lot. It told the world he was a good entertainer and let everybody see him. I had all the children on the show. I thought it was a good thing to do – not forever, but for that time.'

Despite strong misgivings, Michael was outvoted by the rest of his family and he agreed to go along with the show. He believed the series would only overexpose the Jacksons as well as damage whatever musical credibility they retained. He also loathed the costumes they had to wear and the short sketches they had to perform. Though Michael has a good sense of humour, he's never considered himself a comedian. Even so, when it came time to work, he performed like a pro. 'I never knew Michael hated the show,' comedian Biff Manard, one of the show's writers, says. 'If he did, he disguised it well.'

Michael would usually slip into the studio by himself. 'He'd sometimes come into my office,' says Manard, 'and ask, "Did you write anything funny today, Biff?"' The only segment of the programme taped live was the musical performance and it was the only time when Michael seemed to spark. 'Nothing went down musically without him,' Manard recalls. 'It was a trip. He was pure magic. The kid did a three-hundred-sixty-degree turn and became a whole other guy. Otherwise, he was very shy.'

True to form, Michael exhibited his Dr Jekyll and Mr Hyde act. 'With the family, he was always alone,' Manard says. 'Michael would wander around the hallways by himself. Or if he was with the brothers, he always stayed in the background. But once they started with the music, from the opening note, Michael was in the front. Even in the wings, he was downcast and shy. I'd say, "Gee, you really look good tonight," and he'd barely say, "Thank you." But then, onstage, forget it, the pot boiled over.'

Fortunately – at least for Michael – the TV series lasted just one season. Then it was back to business. The group, rechristened the Jacksons since Motown retained ownership of the moniker Jackson Five, began recording their first album for Epic. Production chores went to Kenny Gamble and Leon Huff, who had created the soulful Philadelphia sound of the early seventies with steamy dance tunes like the O'Jays' 'Backstabbers' and the Three Degrees' 'When Will I See You Again'.

Listening to and watching experienced pros like Gamble and Huff pound out their demos on the piano and then stitch together the songs on vinyl taught Michael advanced lessons in songwriting. Structure. Melody. Production. The process was all beginning to come together. In their backyard studio, the guys had started writing and producing their own songs and demos. As a result, the jazzy 'Blues Away', written by Michael, and the hard jamming 'Style of Life', co-written by Michael and Tito, became the first two Jackson originals to make it onto an album.

In 1976 Epic released their first Jackson album, *The Jacksons*. Two singles, 'Enjoy Yourself', which hiked up to six on the charts, and 'Show You The Way To Go', which only went as high as twenty-eight, carried enough punch to power the disc to gold record status. The following year the Jacksons turned out their second Epic album, *Going Places*, which included two more Jackson originals. However, the album, a carbon copy of the first, showed little growth and took them nowhere.

'The CBS people didn't really understand the mechanisms of how to promote a young group,' Joe grouses. 'That was

62

the reason. Things began to open up a little when they got the boys more involved.'

In 1977 Michael planned a special outing for the fourth of July. There's not much a nineteen-year-old superstar can do without attracting attention. But with Janet, his constant companion, and their pal Kim Fields, then eight years old, the effervescent actress from TV's *Facts of Life*, Michael arranged a trip to Disneyland. Infused with childish excitement, he thought of everything. 'At five a.m. up pulls this Rolls-Royce,' Fields remembers. 'My aunt and my mother were breaking their necks looking at the car. Then out jumps Michael wearing a safari hat, sunglasses, jeans and a shirt.'

He was smiling, eager. This wasn't the man-child who harboured worries of sales figures and future projects. No, today he was carefree, a kid going out to play. He had reserved a room at the Disneyland Hotel so he and his pals could rest during the long, hot day. But Michael bounded from ride to ride, a bundle of unreleased energy. He rode the Pirates of the Caribbean, his favourite, over and over again. 'People hardly recognized us at all,' Fields says.

Such happy-go-lucky days were few and far between, though. His face was still broken out and he worried about his appearance. His brothers, detecting his sensitivity, chided him by calling him 'Big Nose'. He hated the nickname. And when he wasn't nursing these psychological wounds, Michael fretted over the wreckage the Jacksons called a career and wondered how to go about salvaging it. He spent countless hours with his brothers in their backyard studio, writing songs. 'He was always working on a song,' Joe recalls. 'Or he had his nose in a book.'

Michael had always been a voracious reader, and once compiled a list of his ten favourite books. His choice revealed a restless character searching for something to satisfy an emptiness in his soul. His choices ranged from the pseudo-spiritual *Jonathan Livingstone Seagull* to the sweet *The Red Balloon* to the surprises of O. Henry short stories. All are simple reads.

Yet the first two titles on his list, *The Greatest Salesman in the World* and *The Gift of Acabar*, both odd, inspirational, and obscure Horatio Alger-like novels written by a former Metropolitan Life insurance salesman named Og Mandino, testified to Michael's compulsive, do-or-die drive for success. The worries in his mind never eased.

63

By his late teens Michael's personal development was on hold. He had long ago turned inward. His own mother had even yielded to his insistent will, suppressing her instinctive alarm when he refused to eat on a daily basis. But he hadn't yet shut himself completely off from the world. There was, for instance, an early teenage crush on one of Smokey Robinson's nieces. 'He called her a girlfriend,' Marlon says. 'We used to talk about her all the time, but it was just giggle time, really.'

The drug culture didn't escape him, either. Despite his insulated upbringing, simply by being in the music business Michael couldn't help but come into contact with drugs like marijuana and cocaine. 'We were offered drugs all the time,' Marlon says. 'But we never took them.' Tito, for instance, hosted a wild rock and roll party at his sprawling Encino house and a famous performer was in the back room snorting coke. When Michael and Marlon strolled in to investigate what was going on he didn't make any attempt to cover up his illegal activities, but smiled kind of sheepishly and warned the brothers, 'Stay away from this. It's bad for you.'

However, there were things Michael couldn't avoid. His bashful nature, high voice and gossamer physique gave rise to a slew of unsavoury rumours. The most talked about tale pegged Michael as a homosexual. Skuttlebutt linked him with songwriter Clifton Davis. 'Do you believe that magazines have been writing that he and I are getting married?' Michael told an interviewer, revealing his naïve astonishment. 'I know it's not true, so it doesn't bother me.'

Another hot rumour making the rounds at that time had Michael in seclusion in order to undergo a sex change operation. 'I was in a Sears store buying some records while on tour when I first heard about it,' he told *Soul* magazine. 'This one girl came up to me, saying, "It isn't true, it isn't true!" I said, "What isn't true?" and she said, "You're not a girl!" I said, "What? Where did you read that?"' The mean-spirited fabrication was even printed in *Jet* magazine. 'I felt like I knew who I was at that moment,' Michael explained. 'But things like that are a sign of success.'

The truth is, Michael was greatly disturbed by the underground rumblings concerning his sexuality and the startling fact they had made it into print. 'When I first heard the rumours that he was gay, I thought I'd go crazy,' Katherine Jackson said. 'He's my son and I know the truth. He knows the truth, too. We both talked about it and cried about it. Michael was very hurt by the rumours. He was young and he didn't want anyone else to be hurt.'

How did this affect Michael? Aside from intensifying his already phobic relationship with the outside world, he developed a distrust of the press that continued to grow for several years until he finally stopped communicating with them altogether. 'He developed an on-guard behaviour about the press,' former Motown publicist Gene Shelton says. Weird is more like it. He started taking Janet with him to press conferences and using her as his mouthpiece. Michael just stood in front of reporters with his head bowed or gazing off into space and refused to make any eye contact.

'How are you?' he'd be asked.

Then Janet would ask him, 'How are you, Michael?'

He would whisper in her ear, and Janet would answer, 'Fine.'

The charade was a disquieting spectacle. 'It was unbelievable,' Shelton says. 'I couldn't believe that was really going on. I would have to sit through several of these sessions. It was unreal. Maybe he was trying to be a star, but the behaviour was absolutely ludicrous.'

Aside from Janet and LaToya, Michael had few people to whom he could confide his secrets. In terms of experience, he was an untainted child swimming in a sea of adults. On the outside, he sparkled, sure. And the sounds he made were giddy, joyous, upbeat ones. Inside, though, Michael was an empty barrel, a nineteen-year-old bundle of Type A stress and anxiety. On the cusp of adulthood, his life had no clear direction and this discouraged him. Without a hit record, upon which his whole identity and self-worth hinged, Michael floundered in a quagmire of confusion. His credo remained the same as always – hard work. But on what?

That was the question burning in Michael's mind when the opportunity arose to audition for the part of the nimble, acutely insecure Scarecrow in *The Wiz*. Although the $20 million production was financed by Berry Gordy, the big-time power broker didn't harbour a grudge against his former protegé when director Sidney Lumet cast him opposite Diana Ross, who was Dorothy. The film also featured Richard Pryor and Lena Horne.

Michael was thrilled and more than ready to tackle something other than music. He had been mulling over various options, he admits. In analysing his choices, he worried about 'repercussions', which suggests that he was already considering leaving his brothers in favour of the solo career interviewers were constantly pestering him about. *The Wiz* offered him an alternative, without encroaching on his musical career. Essentially, it bought him time as well as a change of scenery.

An all-black, contemporary send-up of the fantasy classic, *The Wizard of Oz, The Wiz* was filmed in Manhattan. Michael, who hadn't lived apart from his parents since he and his brothers had alternated bunk beds at Ross' and Gordy's Hollywood mansions, moved into a plush, high-rise apartment in the exclusive Sutton Place area that cost two thousand dollars per month.

LaToya accompanied Michael to prevent the hermit-like teenager from leading too solitary a life away from the set. He couldn't be left alone, and he didn't want to be. After all, here was a young man past voting age who still tucked his napkin in his shirt collar, didn't know what quiche was, didn't yet possess his driving licence and scolded himself when informed that vice-president Gerald Ford had, in fact, become president after the Watergate scandal forced Richard Nixon to resign. 'Boy, I gotta keep up on these things,' he reproached himself.

For his movie debut, Michael received 'lots of good tips' from superstar thespians Sidney Poitier and Ryan O'Neal, the father of his first serious girlfriend, Tatum O'Neal. He had met her shortly before leaving Los Angeles in On the Rox, a private club on Sunset Strip. The evening had been a typical, laid-back Hollywood party; the guest list fast lane. In addition to Michael, his brother Randy and two publicists from Epic, Susan Blond and Steve Manning, the revellers included actors George Hamilton and Tony Curtis, George's ex-wife, Alana Hamilton Stewart, who had remarried rock star Rod Stewart, Ryan O'Neal and his daughter Tatum, a child performer like Michael who had won an Academy Award at the age of seven for her work in *Paper Moon*.

Michael was sitting at a table when he felt a small, soft hand take hold of his. He looked up and saw it was Tatum's. When it came to socializing, Michael had not yet come of age. His voice was still high. His face was still broken out. And he still cringed when his brothers called him Big Nose. He was accustomed to being grabbed by girls on tour. When the Jacksons had played in London in 1972, nearly ten thousand fans were waiting for them on the airport tarmac and Michael had escaped by standing on top of a Rolls-Royce until the police cleared the area. But he wasn't used to being touched in a romantic way by pretty young ladies, and when Tatum's gentle hand rested upon his, Michael's heart melted.

On their first official date they went to Hugh Hefner's Playboy Mansion, an enormous stone castle in Holmby Hills, with a reputation for being an orgiastic playground. Inside, the rooms were generally dark and full of leather furniture. The rambling backyard was home to Hef's envious collection of exotic animals, not the least of which were the many shapely young women who regularly lounged topless poolside in all their pneumatic splendour.

Halfway through the movie they were watching, Tatum, then fifteen years old and light years ahead of Michael in sophistication, led her more innocent date outside for some fun and relaxation in the backyard. Discarding their clothes, they slipped into the roiling hot tub. In recounting the incident, Michael says they had their swimming suits on, but mansion insiders say they were indeed skinny-dipping.

Consequently, the bare facts remain buried in a frothy sea of bubbles but Michael's sexual preference seemed clear. 'I can't tell the details of that evening since I wasn't there,' Marlon says. 'But Michael definitely isn't gay. He's not as innocent as people think. When it came to girls in the early days, he and Jermaine were something to keep up with. Michael definitely isn't a virgin.'

With Michael in New York, this relationship with Tatum continued through long distance telephone calls. Most of Michael's time was spent on the set. It took five hours every day just to apply his Scarecrow makeup. Despite the tedious process, he loved watching himself disappear under layers of clownish paint and then slipping into funny-looking, baggy clothes that were stuffed with garbage instead of straw. This is why he embraced acting. He no longer had to endure the shoulder-bending pressure of being Michael Jackson. 'I got to be somebody else and escape through my character,' he admits.

The truth is, Michael as the fretful Scarecrow was truly inspired casting that struck a chord within the performer himself. 'My character knows that something is wrong with the way he sees things, but he can't quite put his finger on it,' he said.

At the end of many of the long days of shooting, Michael had to be persuaded to step out of costume. Only begrudgingly did he return to his own identity. Why? He didn't want to look in the mirror and see ol' Big Nose. He didn't want to tote the burdensome baggage of being a lonely, confused, pimply twenty-year-old who had just completed another record album that failed to fulfil expectations. Finally skipping down the yellow brick road towards a career separate from his brothers, he didn't want to be reminded of all that he was running from.

All in all, New York provided Michael with an education he couldn't have got back home. At dinner one night at the Rainbow Grill, he met Jackie Onassis. Later, he appeared at the Robert Kennedy Tennis Tournament, along with Muhammad Ali, Lauren Bacall and Bruce Jenner, where he was introduced to two of his fans, Caroline and John Kennedy. 'They talked to him for a long time about music and his dancing,' publicist Steve Manning says. He also spent many wild nights at Studio 54, then the Mecca of New York's socialites, where he partied and danced with such late night luminaries as Liza Minnelli, Halston, Mick Jagger and Andy Warhol.

When *The Wiz* came out later in 1978, and flopped at the box office, critics lambasted Ross for being too old at thirty-four to play the teenage Dorothy, but everyone agreed that Michael's rubber-legged dancing and satiny tenor provided the film with its most electrifying moments. But in addition to acting, the movie aided him in two ways. It served as valuable preparation for his groundbreaking music videos five years later. And it also introduced him to an important new acquaintance in his life.

Quincy Jones, the highly acclaimed record producer and musician, was music director on *The Wiz*. He had been intro-duced to Michael years earlier by Sammy Davis Jr, a mutual acquaintance, who was enthusiastically touting Jackson as a future superstar. Jones listened, but he didn't think anything more about the comments until Michael tentatively approached him one day on the movie set and, in his own meek but formidable manner, asked, 'Do you think you could find me a producer?'

Jones, saddled with the enormous task of scoring the movie, didn't give the question attention immediately. 'I said some-thing like "Don't bother me, I'm doing a movie,"' he laughs. 'But I didn't really talk that way. You don't talk that way to Michael. He's too sweet. But he was serious.'

Jones had no trouble picking up on that. From watching Michael on the set, the veteran producer gained enough insight to realize that if the younger man was bold enough to crack his protective façade of silence and ask a question, he was serious. 'So I started to watch how he dealt with the picture,' he says.

'He'd show up for work at five and be at attention the moment he was ready, waiting to work. Never complaining. Knew all his lines.'

Michael drilled himself until everything was second nature, and the more Jones watched him, the more he was convinced that the kid was a unique performer. 'At first, I admit, I thought he was just a talented bubblegum singer,' says Jones. 'But I saw another side. Watching him in the context of being an actor, I saw a lot of things about him as a singer that rang a lot of bells. I saw a depth that was never apparent and a commitment. I saw that Michael was growing up. Finally, I decided that if we could find some great things deep down inside him, I'd produce him.'

7

Encino, California. 4 July 1977.

On a perfect summer afternoon Michael Jackson was enjoying a holiday weekend at Jermaine's beachfront home on an exclusive strip of Malibu coastline. The hot orange sun hung straight overhead, painting the wavetops with shards of shimmering light. Michael was frolicking in the shallow white water of the broken surf, just down the beach from where Tatum lived with her father.

Suddenly, he couldn't breathe. Fighting off panic, struggling for oxygen, he sprinted back to his brother's house. Jermaine rushed him to the hospital. Doctors examined him immediately and found that a blood vessel had burst in his lung. It was painful, but not life-threatening. Michael's doctor suggested that he slow down. It was good advice, but not realistic. Michael's crammed schedule was like a rollercoaster going downhill, picking up more and more speed. 'Hard work continued to be the name of the game,' he writes in his autobiography.

Michael returned from New York invigorated by his new accomplishments. As Quincy Jones observed, he appeared to have grown up. He hung out with Farrah Fawcett, Liza Minnelli, and Caroline and John Kennedy. For his twentieth birthday, he gave himself a $60,000 black Rolls-Royce. When his parents forced him to learn to drive, Tatum became his driving instructor. He almost seemed to be enjoying himself. But old habits die hard. No sooner did he return home than Michael fell back into the same, stress-filled life from which he had fled.

The anxiety attack at the beach, which triggered the broken blood vessel, was the outward sign of all the pressures that weighed down his thoughts. The Jacksons were ready to begin work on their third Epic album. They needed a hit to reestablish themselves. The record company once again pencilled in Gamble and Huff as producers. The brothers were disappointed.

The Philly team had failed to produce hits, and with their backs against the wall, the Jacksons were itching to show their stuff.

As always, whenever they needed a spokesman they turned to Michael. It had been this way ever since he was little. He'd been the one to confront the powerful, intimidating Gordy while the rest of his family stayed in the background, waiting for him to determine their fate. This was one of those situations that beckoned him, and Michael accepted the responsibility. He felt it was his duty.

Michael and his father met CBS executives and told them that, in light of Gamble and Huff's two previous Jackson LPs, neither of which met expectations, the group wanted to write and produce their own record. The conference, Michael says, boiled down to an ultimatum – either they got creative control or they didn't make an album. Given two flop albums in a row, the Jacksons had little real negotiating power. Realistically, their ultimatum to the corporate decision makers was probably more of a suggestion.

It was a moot point. Unbeknown to the Jacksons, their future at Epic was in jeopardy. The decision had already been made, though not yet executed, to drop them from the label. 'That's right,' Bobby Colomby, then the head of Epic's West Coast artist relations and the ex-drummer for Blood, Sweat and Tears, says. 'The execs didn't want them on the label any more. Neither of their albums had done anything. They had lost their credibility. They were over. Under normal circumstances, my job would've been to try to get them the right producer and make a record,' Colomby continues. 'But the people I was working with at CBS really wanted me to get out of the deal. They wanted me to try to buy them out. But the fact is, having been an artist myself, I felt so bad for these poor guys – and I liked them, they were so sweet and innocent – I said to myself, "My God, if I give these people $100,000 to go away, they're going to pay their bills and they're out of the business forever." I also felt like they hadn't gotten a decent shot at CBS yet. All their lives, they'd never gotten the opportunity to see who they really were and to test themselves. That's basically what I thought they needed to do.'

Acting without concern for boardroom decisions, Colomby followed his instincts and attempted to hire a frontline producer. He went to David Foster. Then Jerry Peters. And then others. Everyone turned him down. 'Nobody wanted to touch the Jacksons,' he says. 'A producer has to look out for his own career, and at that time doing a Jacksons album would've been similar to having just done a Bay City Rollers record. They really had been sold out. There was no career.'

After several weeks, they had a turnaround in fortune. Barry Blue, who'd produced the group Heat Wave, agreed to pilot the floundering project. The Jacksons met the prospective producer and told him they wanted to co-produce the album. 'Blue said, "Forget it,"' recalls Colomby, who then called a brief meeting with the Jacksons and told them, 'Look, I'll do it with you. Don't even worry.'

The busy A&R man was also producing another group, Pages, which later evolved into Mister Mister, but at the time he decided the Jacksons were well worth adding to his schedule. 'I liked these kids a lot,' he says. 'Especially Michael. He was like a little brother to me, and I didn't want to see them dropped. I didn't want to see anything bad happen to them.'

Before work got underway, Colomby interviewed the brothers and discovered a shipwrecked crew who needed only to learn how to use their navigational equipment to set themselves on the proper course. So Colomby hired a talented young keyboard player named Greg Phillinganes, a veteran of Stevie Wonder's band, sat him down in his office and told the skinny, bespectacled musician that he was to do all the rhythm tracks for the new Jacksons' album.

'What?' Phillinganes replied, startled. 'I've never arranged before.'

'You can do it,' Colomby said.

'But . . . but . . .'

Colomby had already prepared his argument. 'You have eighty-eight instruments in front of you every time you sit down and play,' he said. 'And you're telling me you can't arrange a rhythm section?'

Phillinganes smiled. He was defeated and convinced at the same time.

'You're right, I can do it,' he said.

Colomby then introduced the new arranger to the Jacksons. 'I went out to the house in Encino to work with the guys and was fairly surprised at how much music they had in them,' Phillinganes said. 'They were real enthusiastic and excited because this was the first time in their entire careers that they controlled the music. All of them could write, but I thought Michael and Randy were probably the strongest writers in the family.'

72

During preproduction, everything seemed to gel. Ideas hummed in the Jacksons' home studio. When they finally got down to recording the album, they quickly knocked off two songs. One was called 'Blame It on the Boogie' and the other 'Push Me Away'. After that, though, the brothers held an impromptu meeting that turned into a confrontation with Colomby. 'Okay, what is it?' he asked.

'Bobby,' Jackie said, 'you told us that we could be involved in this project.'

'Ah-huh,' he nodded.

'But you're doing everything.'

'You're right,' Colomby said. At this point, he was guiding the project. 'I'll let you guys get more involved. I just wanted to make sure we had a hit or two here, before we just went crazy.'

That settled, the Jackson brothers took over the *Destiny* LP, though Colomby continued to supervise the appropriately titled venture. But Michael, he recalls, didn't really seem to care who was in charge. 'He was too busy having fun recording,' he says. Michael was, in fact, so consumed by the passion of creating the music that at times he lost control of himself. For instance, while laying down the vocals for the album's biggest hit, 'Blame It on the Boogie', he suddenly stopped singing in mid-sentence, and then just as suddenly threw down his headphones and ran out of the studio.

Another CBS executive, followed him into the hall.

'What's the matter?' he asked, understandably perplexed.

'I can't stand still,' answered Michael, who was spinning, twitching and shuffling his feet as he spoke. 'I just want to dance.'

Moments earlier, Michael had been singing the rapid-fire lines, 'I just can't . . . I just can't control my feet.' He had simply lost control and yielded to what came naturally. 'Michael wanted to dance so badly he couldn't stand in that one spot and sing,' Colomby laughs. 'So he ran out and started dancing up a storm in the hall.'

The closer Colomby worked with Michael, the more the older, experienced musician realized how totally consumed by music the younger man was. 'He was a dreamer and he lived in a fantasy world,' Colomby says. 'But there was one overriding constant to his life.' He liked music. He listened to everything he could get a hold of. He danced at all hours of the day. He focused his thoughts on music. He studied books and pictures of performers.

73

Michael was, indeed, possessed. 'Every waking hour, at least of what I saw,' Colomby says, 'was dedicated to music. The kid didn't give himself any other options. But that's how you get really good, so good that you can do everything better than everyone else.'

In the studio, Colomby would witness that firsthand. Like the other Jacksons, he didn't have to be convinced of Michael's extraordinary talent. 'There was one point where he sang a lick and I screamed, "Oh my God!"' he remembers. 'I turned to Marlon and said, "Did you hear what he just did?" Marlon just smiled. "Man," he said, "Michael's been doing that since he's been five years old."'

'Oh, the brothers knew, absolutely, that Michael was different,' says Colomby, who sensed the delicate balance of egos composing the Jackson enterprise. 'I didn't see any jealousy.' The brothers might not have acknowledged it, but Michael had been the leader since childhood.

There were not yet any obvious signals that the stressful responsibility was beginning to overburden Michael's tender psyche. Co-workers found him extremely likable. 'In all of his innocence, he was a charming, charismatic, terrifically gentle soul,' Colomby says.

Outside the studio, Michael existed in an isolated world of fantasies, pet animals, television and movies. His closest companions were his sisters. But the outsiders with whom he came into contact found the superstar's strange personality innocent and friendly. Michael, an acknowledged phone freak, called Colomby nearly every day. 'I never knew if it was a woman or Michael,' he laughs. 'He would say, "We had fun yesterday," and I would pause and go, "Fuck, who is this? Who'd I have fun with yesterday? I don't remember." Then I'd realize who it was and say, "Michael. Sorry about that."'

Michael's ability to laugh at himself allowed him to chuckle on those frequent occasions when he stumbled over his own ungainly naïvety. One night Colomby was having dinner at the Jackson household when Michael raised a touchy subject. 'Bobby, you know one thing that makes me so sad?' he said. 'When kids come up to me after a show and ask if I'm a homosexual, it makes me so sad,' he answered.

'You know, Michael, there is a solution,' Colomby offered.
'What?'
'Be one. Dress up like a woman.'

74

'Bite your tongue,' Michael managed to say before doubling over in convulsions of laughter. 'Bite your tongue, Bobby.'

The subject of sex was a continual source of entertainment for the two. In the studio several days after their dinner together, Colomby asked Michael if he knew that there were many gays in the music industry. 'No, there aren't,' Michael said.

'Yes, it's true,' replied Colomby, who remembers the singer continuing to shake his head. He mentioned a certain industry executive. 'He's gay,' Colomby said.

'No, he's not,' Michael argued.

Michael then went back to recording vocals. Colomby left the studio and returned a few moments later. 'Michael, you have a phone call . . . from . . .' Then he mentioned the man's name.

'No, no,' Michael pleaded. 'I don't believe you. Bobby, leave me alone.'

Michael, on the other hand, was utterly infatuated with the woman whom Colomby was then living with, actress Pam Grier, the tall, sexy star of low-budget black exploitation films like *Foxy Brown*. 'When he found out I was living with her, he just flipped out,' Colomby recalls. 'She'd walk into the studio and he'd squeal and run out and hide.' When Grier called, Michael felt tongue-tied. 'She'd want to have him over for dinner. I'd say, "Hey Michael, it's Pam," and I'd hand him the phone. He couldn't handle it. It'd just drop in his lap and he'd stare at it. He wouldn't even talk.'

But Michael's curiosity was like an open floodgate and he couldn't stop talking about Grier. 'What does she do with you, Bobby?' he asked.

'What do you mean?' Colomby replied.

'She must hit you with skillets,' Michael laughed. 'I think when you come home, she throws a skillet at you. She bops you over the head.'

Michael's gullibility about sex worried Colomby so much that one day he took him upstairs to one of the small, second-storey offices at Cherokee Studios for a man-to-man talk. 'Michael,' he started in, 'you're a young man. You're about to get out there in the world and meet a lot of people – a lot of women. And you might run into some interesting situations. Sometimes it's difficult for you to go to your parents or your brothers and talk about those kinds of things. But I want you to know that I'm there for you. That any time you need a friend, in any kind of situation, I'll help you.'

Michael smiled. He was touched. 'God, that is so sweet of

you,' he said. 'But I already have someone I confide in like that.'

'Oh, great,' Colomby replied, mildly surprised. 'Can I ask who?'

'Diana Ross.'

When Michael approached a record company executive or a movie producer, he commanded their respect. But the same couldn't always be said for the way his siblings treated him at home. Many times, LaToya declares, Michael deserved far worse for his practical jokes. For years she felt duty-bound to keep her gentle doe-eyes focused on her famous brother. 'Michael is very mysterious,' she murmurs in the family's trademarked feathery voice. 'I look at him as my brother, of course. But I see more to him than that. He comes up with some pretty amazing things, which makes me wonder, "Where did he get that talent from?" It must be a gift from God.'

The real godsend, according to LaToya, was having her bedroom just down the hall from Michael's. 'He always made so much noise,' she laughs. 'He'd have been impossible to live right next door to. You'd hear music in his room when he was trying to create. Or you'd hear the Three Stooges on TV and he'd be up all night laughing real loud. His light was always on, since Michael is forever reading books. Even today, you can't get in his room for books. And there's junk! He still collects everything. He's a pack rat. I felt sorry for the housekeeper having to go in there and wade through that garbage.'

Her sympathy didn't extend to Michael, though. The day finally arrived when LaToya decided to seek revenge on her sneaky brother for all his pranks. Late one warm, lazy afternoon, she checked on Michael. He was up in his room, paging through magazines and books, listening to the radio. LaToya hurried into her room, shut the door and called Michael on the house telephone line. In a high, squeaky voice she pretended to be a secretary calling for Sidney Lumet, who'd directed *The Wiz*.

'He'd like to have dinner with you tonight,' she said.

'He would?' Michael gushed. 'What time? Where?'

'He's in the neighbourhood,' she said, 'and said for you to be ready in about ten minutes.'

'Hold on,' said a very excited Michael, who then barged into his sister's bedroom. 'Toya! Sidney Lumet just called me. He wants to have dinner . . . tonight . . . now.'

She slid the phone receiver under a pillow. 'Really?' she said, looking up, surprised.

'What should I wear, Toya? Help me pick out something.'

'Michael never acts like that,' LaToya says. 'He couldn't care less about what he wears. But I said, "Jeans. Anything. Don't be crazy."'

Michael dashed back to his room, picked up the phone, made arrangements, and then hung up. LaToya followed and watched him prepare as he whirled around getting dressed while asking her question after nervous question. He then sprinted through the house until he found his mother. 'Get dressed!' he told her. 'Sidney Lumet is coming over.' Finally, Michael went outside to wait.

'When Sidney didn't show up, Michael started wondering what was going on,' recalls LaToya. She asked whom he had spoken to.

'His secretary.'

'Did she sound like this?' LaToya asked, mimicking the high, screeching voice she had used on the phone.

'Oh, you rat, you were listening on the phone,' Michael cried. 'How could you?'

'No, I wasn't,' she said. 'That was me on the phone.'

With that confession, Michael snatched a hose from a nearby gardener and sprayed his hysterical sister.

As a rule, though, Michael wasn't so easily taken advantage of. Whether he was in a restaurant or in the studio, he was guarded. He was as skittish as a bird. He didn't want to make a mistake. He abhorred the notion of being vulnerable. Which is why he was full of scepticism about the *Destiny* album.

Except for Michael, the brothers, their fragile egos at stake, backed the family's patriarch. 'It was always easier doing what he wanted,' Michael said. But this time he risked disagreement with his father by supporting the A&R man's claim. There was a meeting. Lawyers were brought in. Colomby handed Joe and his attorney a pile of signed affidavits from the album's engineers and arrangers, testifying that despite the liner notes Colomby and not the Jacksons actually served as producer.

'The father and his lawyer saw that,' he recalls, 'and said, "You got to get paid. Goodbye."'

The incident tripped off alarms inside Michael. Was this a sign that *Destiny* would fare no better than the previous Jackson LP, *Goin' Places*? Did it signal the need for Michael to make the leap into the solo career everyone predicted for him? Publicly, he declared all was well and he had no intention of breaking from his brothers. 'My brothers and I get along fine,' he said. 'Right now we feel that the Jacksons are in evolution. It's just not the time to make any drastic change.'

When pressed about his future, Michael offered a glimpse of the mysterious inner landscape where he retreated when faced with important decisions. 'I don't do very many things until a certain force tells me to do them,' he said. 'The force tells me when, and then I make my move.'

Certain natural forces were altering the picture of his family. His older brothers had all married, moved out and started families. Even younger brother Randy was itching to find his own apartment. Of course, these worldly concerns weren't likely to interest Michael. 'Separated from the tools and terrain of his expertise,' journalist Timothy White, who interviewed Michael around this period, writes, 'he had little sense of himself.' He was 'a phantom, a formless creature who cast no reflection, left no worthy trace'.

No, Michael didn't worry about independence and growth in the personal sense. Not when it concerned girlfriends, wives, or getting his own place to live. But he did debate the issue of professional independence. He had been thinking about it for some time. It was his private war, an age-old conflict that pitted duty to his family against duty to himself. The struggle was never more apparent than in lyrics of the song, 'Bless His Soul', which he penned for the *Destiny* album and admitted was about him:

> Sometimes I cry cause I'm confused
> Is this a fact of being used?
> There is no life for me at all
> Cause I give myself at beck and call

The frustration he had felt during the recording of the group's latest album, which he had kept to himself, and the arguments afterwards sparked off a thorough, intense evaluation of his career. The force to which he listened was calling out, asking him to make that change. 'I had always shouldered a lot of responsibility, but it suddenly seemed that everyone wanted a piece of me,' he writes. 'There wasn't that much to go around, and I needed to be responsible to myself. I had to take stock of my life . . .'

8

Encino, California. 1979.

When Michael returned from the Jacksons' *Destiny* tour, a disaster during which he lost his voice and his desire to perform, he was plagued by grave doubts about his career. There was too much pressure on him to carry the group and too little satisfaction resulting from the work. Sure, he had a starry showbusiness history and the Jacksons had sold tens of millions of albums, but the new songs he was forced to perform paled in comparison to the oldies-but-goodies the group had recorded more than a decade earlier. The music was stale. While the ambition burned inside him, he felt no sense of growth. Who wouldn't feel stifled?

At home, Michael retreated into his bedroom, where his mood settled somewhere between sullen and depressed. 'He must've started having some ideas about branching out on his own,' Marlon says. 'But he never told anyone about them.' No, he was intensely secretive about his individual endeavours. Since the family was used to his inaccessibility, they didn't wonder about his strangely quiet behaviour.

Around his brothers, Michael's lips were practically a locked safe when discussion turned to future Jackson projects. He was Mr Noncommittal. Yes, he still went into their backyard studio every day with Randy and Tito to write songs – that routine was unquestioned. But his priorities were changing rapidly. In fact, while recording the group's last LP, Michael had begun collecting ideas for songs that he felt would work better on his own solo effort. In matters of debate, he found himself giving into his brothers a lot sooner than he would have done if he hadn't been plotting a course that didn't include them.

In his heart, Michael was preparing for a much-needed severing of ties. The need to please himself welled inescapably inside him with an unrelenting determination, the mysterious 'force' he often spoke about. And now, with his last major commitment to the Jacksons completed, at least for the year, the prospect of emerging from the Jackson Five's broad shadow and longtime sales slump greatly excited him. 'I hear an ideal record in my mind, maybe with Quincy,' he mused to an interviewer. 'We'll see.'

On the threshold of such a monumental change, the anxious singer and his brothers made a striking contrast. From Jackie, the oldest, to Randy, the youngest, they were calm, confident and content, resigned to their status, willing to work as hard as required, churn out records, and fulfil contract obligations, spending their money on nice homes, fancy cars and their families. They would've enjoyed being number one again, but their egos didn't require it. Michael's did, though. He not only required it, he craved it. By comparison, he was nervous, unfulfilled by past accomplishments, concerned that he wasn't living up to the incredibly high expectations he set for himself as a child. His brothers had all let their ties to the Witnesses dissolve. They sought peace and contentment in their families. However, Michael looked in the only direction that made sense to him – to God. His spiritual pursuits, Katherine recalls, were at an all-time high. 'He was very serious about his Bible studies,' she says. 'After services at the Kingdom Hall, we'd often talk about God and his expectations and being a faithful servant.'

Which, of course, to Michael, meant being perfect. A daunting task. And when he considered it, Michael knew that it was something he could accomplish only by himself. Other people couldn't possibly entertain his same vision. They couldn't possibly work as hard as him. They couldn't possibly be good enough. Or as true. It wasn't their fault. He was simply answering God's call. He was going to be his *truest* servant. He would show everyone else – lead the way, in fact.

He started by firing his manager, who just happened to be his father: another difficult task. Michael, like his other brothers, didn't like the way Joe was running things. Their *Destiny* tour had not done as well, financially, as expected. Joe's relationship with the record label was also on the thin side of dismal. Company executives had long ago tired of his constant harping for more money. In addition, he was spending less time at home and more time at his Hollywood office.

When Joe's management contract with his sons expired in early 1979, they chose not to renew it. 'We had different opinions,' Marlon says. 'A father will always feel he knows more than his kids, but it got to the point where we were grown men with interests of our own.' But the move crushed Joe emotionally. He launched a major yelling fit, letting his sons know that if it wasn't for his sacrifices they never would've reached the top. 'I was very upset,' he says. 'I felt they weren't going to be treated fairly.'

More likely, an associate of Michael's says, the grumbling patriarch feared his seemingly limitless supply of cash, which outside pursuits were eating up, would suddenly vanish when his children handed management chores to the flashy but proven industry heavyweights, Freddie DeMann and Ron Weisner. However, almost as an after-thought, in an attempt to placate Joe, they made him a co-manager with the new team, a decision that would cause Michael extreme embarrassment three years later when he fired his father once again.

Michael's next step was to begin work with Quincy Jones on the album that would become *Off the Wall*. The accomplished producer found his charge 'very, very introverted, shy and nonassertive'. Michael approached his first solo album in five years tentatively. 'He wasn't at all sure that he could make a name for himself on his own,' Jones recalls. 'And me, too. I had my doubts.' They were short-lived. In control of a project for the first time in his fifteen-year career, Michael impressed everyone as a quick, bright study whose talent had been tapped but not yet fully tested. 'He was like a sponge,' the producer says. 'Michael showed a curiosity for everything. It was unbelievable in someone so young. I appreciated watching it work.'

Michael made just one hard and fast request to his seasoned producer, a simple one that underscored his desire to distance himself from the past. 'I said to Quincy I didn't want it to sound like a Jacksons' album at all,' he says. No, indeed not. This one had to fly where the others had sputtered along the runway without ever taking off. This one had to capture that intense flame that burned within Michael's soul. It had to justify his belief in himself. It had to fulfil his desire to produce something that was great.

The timing was perfect for Michael. After more than a decade of wild, mind-boggling success, the music industry, geared towards excess, was just beginning to slip into a protracted slump, the result of changing audience demographics, fluctuating tastes and a muddle of clashing trends as rock, disco

81

and punk all collided at once. Now his brothers had all moved out of the house, Michael had plenty of time to isolate himself in the studio and plumb the depths of his creative soul. He no longer had to worry about compromising ideas. He could try whatever he wanted, experiment. There was no image to fit into, no sound to conform to. He had room to move. His mind could drift, his senses float, his heart pound. This project was his long-awaited coming of age.

Michael devoted all his energy to work, dived into it like a zealot in pursuit of a higher purpose only he understands, and the result was nothing short of magical. In this period of self-discovery, he worked all hours of the day and night. Not a skilled musician, he slowly plucked out rhythms and melodies on keyboards and drum machines, pulling brand new tunes out of thin air like a magician. 'He hears just as many notes and chords as a trained musician, only his voice is his instrument,' says guitarist David Williams, one of the highly-respected session players Michael invited to his house, along with Phillinganes, to fill in the blanks. 'I learned very early that if he doesn't start dancing while I'm playing, it's not right,' Williams says. 'When the groove is right, Michael can't control himself, can't stop his feet from moving. He just slides across the floor.'

From the start, the chemistry between Michael and Jones clicked, a match made easy by their similarly low-key temperaments and high standards. 'They compliment each other perfectly,' Phillinganes says. 'They're both very positive people, very talented, with an innate sense of what makes a good song great.' Paul McCartney and his wife, Linda, whom Michael had met years earlier at a party for McCartney's band, Wings, provided a song entitled 'Girlfriends', which they had written especially for Jackson.

Jones then asked Rod Temperton, the eccentric keyboardist for the British soul band Heatwave, to write several songs. 'I said it was impossible,' Temperton said. Or so it seemed. He was committed to his own group's third album, but Jones convinced Temperton to fly to Los Angeles with a sole composition and he ended up working through the entire production and writing three songs for the record: 'Rock With You', 'Burn This Disco Out', and the title track, 'Off the Wall'.

However, the biggest surprise turned out to be Michael's own original composition, 'Don't Stop 'Til You Get Enough', the LP's first single, which entered the charts at eighty-seven, made a steady climb, and arrived unceremoniously eleven weeks later at the highly coveted number one position. 'I just came up with the melody,' remembers Michael, who made the feat look far too easy. 'It's about forces and the power of love. Walking around the house, I started singing it and kept singing it. I went into the twenty-four track studio we have at home. I told Randy what to play on the piano. I did percussion and piano, and when I played it for Quincy, he loved it.'

Forces. Power. Michael was answering the call. Nothing had changed since he was a little boy. He had to be tops. It was the way he qualified his existence. Michael's was a highly personal, individual mission, and he knew only one method of gauging his success – chart position, record sales. Filled with lofty expectations, his next single, 'Rock With You', an elegant, dreamy ballad, reached the first spot in mid-January 1980. Another number one! Vindication. God smiled. Michael smiled. Then the next two singles, 'Off the Wall' and 'She's Out of My Life', each cracked the top ten, making Michael the first solo artist to have four top ten singles from one album. History! Sales soared past eight million. Further proof!

Michael knew he was different and *Off the Wall* only confirmed it. But the rewards were fleeting. Record sales and chart positions were variables beyond his control. They were as unpredictable and elusive as unadultered happiness. Reaching the top only generated insecurity about whether he could get there again. One success only cast suspicion over the next attempt. There was no real satisfaction, no resting on laurels, no chest-thumping confidence. No matter what Michael attained, he heard disappointment hissing in the background like a grouchy relative, quicker to criticize than compliment.

For this reason, Michael searched. Months before his album was released, he knew he needed to exercise complete mastery over something that would provide him with happiness. He had to conquer something other than music to dislodge the ever-present pall of self-defeat that hung over him. But what could he exercise absolute power over? What bothered him most, brayed at him like a cranky old mule, chafed at the surface of a life that should have glistened like a polished gem?

Michael hated the way he looked. He despised his reflection. Onstage, he could be anyone he wanted, but in real life, well, let's say he wasn't exactly enamoured of himself in general, anyway. How could he have been? He set himself such incredibly difficult goals that he was constantly falling short, deluding himself into believing that he was a failure. When he looked in the mirror, he shuddered at the sight. His face was broken out. His body clung greedily to rolls of cuddly baby fat. His childlike voice refused to acknowledge the passing of puberty. Worst of all, though, was the round, bulbous honker that had inspired his brothers' slanderous sobriquet, Big Nose.

His body, Michael learned from reading dozens of magazine articles and health books, was something he could alter. The body could be changed through diet, exercise, and plastic surgery. He could, if desired, effectively remake whatever part of himself he considered to be a genetic goof. But what to do first?

His brother Jermaine, whose romantic swagger and handsome carriage Michael had always admired, was a longtime vegetarian. This was a start. Then one afternoon superstar model Beverly Johnson and her husband were visiting the Jackson spread in Encino. She was a stunning beauty whom Michael greatly respected and they got into an involved discussion about diet, skin and body care. 'Michael told her that he wasn't real happy with the way he was feeling,' publicist Steve Manning, also present that afternoon, says. 'He was looking to make some kind of change.' Johnson, a vegetarian herself, convinced Michael to follow a similar diet, which, Katherine Jackson says, he took to like a religious convert. 'If he's interested in something, Michael pursues it all the way,' she says. 'He doesn't do anything half way.'

Though his embrace of the new diet was serious, he didn't then have the fanaticism he would develop in later years. Nonetheless, Michael realized results in a short time. The chunky handles of baby fat around his waist disappeared and the roundness in his face vanished. Suddenly, he had cheekbones. The padded, oval curves of his youth were pared into clearly defined lines and a face in the process of maturing was revealed. For someone as appearance-obsessed as Michael, this was a positive step, but, as it turned out, only a precursor to future leaps.

In the meantime, he was slogging his way through murky layers of self-awareness. Plagued by uncertainty in all areas of intellect, Michael struggled to shore up his weaknesses. He picked up art, history and science books by the bundle and ploughed through them. Painfully aware, when he was around more educated and sophisticated people, of the academic sacrifices he made as a child in favour of performing

Left: Michael was a budding artist on canvas as well as vinyl. *(Neal Preston)*

Below: Michael's bedroom wall showed off some of his early masterpieces. *(Neal Preston)*

Above: The recording studio served as the classroom where Michael learned (and sang) his ABCs. *(Neal Preston)*

Left: The Jackson brothers rarely had time to hang around their backyard. *(Neal Preston)*

Above: Michael capped off a long day at the studio with a carefree smile. *(Neal Preston)*

Right: He wore a formal tuxedo and a curious look to Jermaine's wedding to ex-wife Hazel Gordy. *(Neal Preston)*

Left: By the age of 15, Michael was a dancing (and singing) machine. *(Neal Preston)*

Above: Michael threw an over-the-shoulder glance to the camera but never to his competition. *(Neal Preston)*

Left: Michael prior to cutting *Off the Wall* and before he was bobbed, clefted and gloved. *(Neal Preston)*

Above: Jane Fonda helps her pal Michael handle a few of the many gold albums racked up by *Thriller*. *(Neal Preston)*

Right: Michael stood out on the Jackson's Victory Tour, which he wanted to call 'The Final Curtain'. *(Neal Preston)*

Michael's older sister LaToya before she was influenced by her brother's beauty tips . . . *(Neal Preston)*

. . . and after *(RCA Records)*

On stage Michael sang, 'Don't stop . . .
(Neal Preston)

. . . don't stop . . . *(Neal Preston)*

. . . till you get enough.' *(Neal Preston)*

Michael was determined to rectify his shortcomings. As usual, his method was extreme. 'He was heavily into his notebook stage,' singer Patti Austin, a close friend of Jackson's, says. 'He'd always walk around with a notebook, scribbling notes on whatever he heard that seemed interesting. If you mentioned a book, he would write it down. If you mentioned a movie, he'd question you about it and write down your answer. He was trying to absorb everything about everything.'

Adulthood hung on Michael's narrow shoulders like a baggy suit several sizes too large. Occasionally, even the most mundane tasks caused him to react with uncertainty. For instance, Austin once caught him walking up the street to a party at Jones' Bel Air home. 'He had parked his car a block away because he didn't think he could manoeuvre it into the gates of the house,' she laughs. 'So he parked his Rolls on the streets of Bel Air.'

She told him to hand over the keys. Michael looked bewildered. 'I know you think you're in Bel Air and everything's going to be okay, but people whip around these corners at ninety miles per hour in their Porsches,' she said. 'Let me move the car for you.'

'Okay,' he said.

She returned laughing. 'If you don't think you can get it through the gates of this house, what in the world are you doing driving such an enormous boat of a car?' she asked.

Michael rolled his eyes and smiled sheepishly. 'Oh, Patti,' he sighed.

He liked the smart, effervescent singer. She knew Michael from the studio, where he operated with the confidence of someone who'd grown up there. 'He was shy but extremely knowledgeable,' says Austin, who duetted with Jackson on the tune 'It's the Falling in Love', which was slated to be the seventh single from 'Off the Wall'. 'Our voices sound very similar on the tune, so no one knows it's me singing with him.'

They worked together again several months later when he was producing Diana Ross' single, 'Muscles'. Michael summoned Austin into the studio for vocal chores. 'This was the first time he was producing on his own,' she says. 'He was a very hard taskmaster, a total perfectionist. Naturally, he made me do the silliest thing I've ever done in my life, which was to sing through a thin plastic tube so that he could get a specific sound. I was in hysterics and he was very serious. But of course, it worked.'

The party at Jones' house, a classy afternoon affair, was the first time Austin encountered Michael in a social setting. 'There were lots of bigshots there, people like Spielberg, Springsteen, and Streisand,' she says. 'Michael could've cared less. You never would've known he was also a big star. He wasn't that comfortable. He just walked around with his notebook, and after a little while he drifted outside and played with Quincy's kids.'

At one point during the fete, Austin found herself alone with Michael in Jones' downstairs studios, which didn't exactly strike her as a choice opportunity for scintillating conversation. 'Here I was, sitting with the shiest person in the world, the quietest and the shiest,' she recalls. 'I thought, "Great, this is perfect."' But one-on-one, Michael opened up – at least to her. 'He just broke into this conversation and started talking about his mom and dad and family,' she says. 'It was amazing.'

Truly amazing. However, Michael desperately needed someone to whom he could pour out his heart, open up and reveal his gut feelings, even if what he offered was really only the tip of an emotional iceberg on the verge of cracking. The Jackson family was in a uproar, a state of chaos they had never imagined. In the middle of October 1980, Katherine found out that Joe was having a torrid, not-so-secret affair with his secretary, Gina Sprague.

Now, if this had been his only sin, who knows what would've happened. But he was guilty of more than one indiscretion. Katherine discovered that the nine children she had borne him had an illegitimate little half-sister whom Joe was also supporting. Either she had never known about her husband's numerous dalliances with other women or she just quietly averted her eyes, but this time Katherine exploded in a fuming rage so alien to her calm, gentle nature that it frightened everyone around her.

Joe's office was in a high-rise building on Sunset Strip. The door was always locked. Visitors were screened through a tiny peephole before entering. When the receptionist saw Katherine, Janet and Randy standing outside the door late one afternoon, she buzzed them in, completely unaware of their intentions. Joe wasn't there at the time. All the better.

Without a moment's hesitation, the threesome stalked down the short corridor. They were the picture of contained anger – their jaws tensed, muscles taut, hands clenched, movements sharp. They pulled up in front of Sprague, who drew back in fright. Harsh words were exchanged. They then grabbed the secretary, pulled her out into the hallway and began hitting her. 'They beat her up, right there, just started pounding her,' a man from an adjoining office recalls. 'After a few minutes, they let up and left. But someone had called the cops and the fire department and right away, it seemed, there were so many sirens people thought the building was on fire.'

No, the fire was just Katherine's hot temper. The matter might appear to have been settled, at least to Katherine, but the incident merely revealed the surface pain of a deep wound the likes of which a self-respecting, Godfearing, righteous woman like herself couldn't tolerate. Sprague was the wrong woman. True, she was having an affair with Joe, which, the boys explained, was nothing new. He had fooled around with lots of women on the road for years. The boys had endured his numerous nighttime surprise appearances, those embarrassing moments when he would burst in with several women and snicker at the little pyjama-clad Jacksons.

This time, though, it was different. This time, Katherine knew and the truth couldn't be concealed any longer. The child's mother, Cheryle Terrell, twenty years younger than Joe, had begun hanging around the Jacksons in the early seventies, hoping to strike up something with Jackie, whom she had a crush on. When he didn't show any interest, Joe did. By the end of 1973, Terrell was pregnant, and on 30 August 1974 a little girl, Joh Vonnie, was born. The birth certificate, filled out at Centinela Valley Hospital, listed Joe as the father. His occupation: manager. His business: entertainment.

Yet there was nothing entertaining about this startling revelation that was uprooting the family's once solid foundations. The battle lines were quickly drawn. On the one side, Katherine and all of her children. On the other, Joe stood all alone. Within the course of a very long, tense and dramatic confrontation with his irate family, Joe confessed that he had been leading a secret double life for nearly six years. From the beginning, he had supported his out-of-wedlock daughter and her mother. He had bought them a secluded $100,000 home set behind security gates, a new car and had arranged a job for Terrell. He paid support money and set up a trust for the child.

He was dutiful in his attention to both mother and daughter. 'Joe is over there practically every weekend, and he stays over,' a neighbour once confided. 'Sometimes he takes her [Cheryle] out for the evening. And he plays with Cheryle's daughter.

87

She's a very pretty little girl, and she and Joe obviously love each other.'

Several years later, the furtive relationship cooled, Joe hosted a showcase performance at the Roxy for a young female singer, one of his managerial charges with whom he was rumoured to be romantically involved. To ensure that the show received press coverage, he somehow persuaded Michael and Janet to attend. But Cheryle also showed up, along with Joh Vonnie and an ulterior motive. 'It was so sad,' a reporter recalls. 'She dressed the little girl in clothes that were very similar in style to what Janet wore, hoping that Michael and Janet would recognize their sister.' They didn't.

In January 1983, Sprague filed a million dollar lawsuit against Joe, Katherine, Randy and Janet, charging that the Jackson matriarch and her children had beaten her so severely that she wasn't able to work or pay her huge medical bills. As for Joe, she claimed he had failed to warn her about the 'dangerous and violent propensities' of his wife. The case was quickly and quietly settled out of court and the secretary was never heard from again.

Meanwhile, Joe and Katherine agreed to a separation of undetermined length. She threatened divorce and he hurled threats of his own. But only one thing was clear: tempers needed to cool before their future could be discussed. Besides, a family insider says, 'they weren't talking to each other'. The children left no doubt about whom they favoured; they lent their emotionally crippled mother their unconditional support. Their father moved into a nearby West Los Angeles townhouse they'd purchased as an investment years earlier.

'Michael's next move should've been to follow up his album with either a tour or another solo album,' a longtime Jackson co-worker, demanding anonymity, says. 'He has a very shrewd business sense and I'm sure he realized that. But he had family obligations to fulfil.'

Fulfilling family obligations. The pattern was a familiar one in Michael's life, one that greatly contributed to his unhappiness. Instead of pursuing his own interests, he shucked his individuality in favour of compliance with the group. The family. Indeed, when he should've been working on his own LP, for reasons of good business and sanity, following up his *Off the Wall* success and grappling with his family's internal upheaval, he set to work with his brothers on the next Jacksons album, *Triumph*.

It was a period during which Michael avoided dealing with his strife-ridden family. For him, work was an easy and available escape, though not a satisfying one. Writing sessions for the album resulted in one of his finest tunes to date, 'Heartbreak Hotel', a fright-filled tale about menacing creatures that scare innocent souls. It's the first of Michael's compositions to reveal his macabre, dark side, a glimpse at how he perceived his relationship to the clamouring public. A thirty-six city tour supporting the record in 1981 netted the Jacksons more than $5 million.

However, Michael isn't motivated by money. He looks inward for inspiration, and this time around it was sadly lacking.

'After we got back from that tour, Michael was real quiet,' Marlon says. 'He wasn't committing to anything. He didn't really get involved in business discussions. And you know, that was fine with us. We didn't think anything of it. We still saw him pretty often. Like he'd come swimming over at my house and he'd play with my kids. But as far as work went, Michael didn't seem ready to get into any projects.'

For good reason. What could he say to his folks? To his brothers? 'I don't want to do this any more'?

It isn't that easy to quit a family group that's relied upon you, that's raked in millions of dollars by sticking you out in front of audiences. It isn't that easy to just dismiss burdens that have been shouldered since childhood, habits ingrained so deeply in the mind there's never been reason to question them. But now there was reason to question them.

The sheltered, reclusive, reticent singer talked to no one about such delicate, life-changing issues. Consequently, Michael put himself under enormous strain, concealing the utter frustration of being denied the right to explore his own life.

The pressure and strain that can contribute to anorexic behaviour were there. Michael painted a picture to interviewers of a homelife that was as rosy as the well-tended gardens surrounding the Jacksons' Encino estate. His approach to work was tireless, he was forever reaching for that last reserve of creativity, strength. He was stubborn, full of pride. As always, his reaction to inner fears was to work harder. Work harder on anything.

Inside the anorexic, doctors say, there's an underlying torment, an unsettling sense of ineffectiveness, a constant fear of failure, disappointment, a terror of not having one's accomplishments acknowledged. Indeed, Michael could've asked himself,

'Why, with all my hard work, is my family crumbling? Why is there never enough money? Why isn't anything I do ever enough?'

Something had to give. Michael's back was up against the wall. He had to make a break. He couldn't go on burying his individuality within the group. But how would he summon the courage? He couldn't ask his father, his co-manager, for permission; he would simply say no. His brothers would also say no. His mother didn't get involved in these issues. No, something had to push him.

And then it happened. In between the release of the *Triumph* album and the related tour, the Grammy nominations for 1979 were announced. *Off the Wall* had been among the year's top albums, if not the top all by itself. Many critics felt that way and the worldwide sales figures backed them. Yet the LP received only one nomination. A single nomination. For Best R&B Vocal Performance. A black award. It smacked of tokenism. Of mistrust. Of a lack of respect. Here's your sole acknowledgement, Michael. We'll give you the award for having the best voice in black music. Not all music, but black music.

For Michael, like anyone who's compelled to push out the envelope of pain and endurance, this was a crushing blow. He watched the award programme on TV and then fell apart. 'I felt ignored by my peers,' he says with great restraint in his book. But it was much worse than that. To a reporter, he offered a more accurate picture of his distress. 'It bothered me,' he said. 'I cried a lot. My family thought I was going crazy because I was weeping so much about it.'

Not such an unexpected reaction from a young man who drew satisfaction from numbers – sales figures, awards. It didn't matter that his mother told him he was still loved. It didn't matter that Liza Minnelli, Diana Ross and Katherine Hepburn called and expressed their sympathy. Nor did it matter that his brothers told him he was robbed. His achievement wasn't being acknowledged.

Michael resolved to turn the tables. As a matter of self-preservation, he needed to go back to the beginning. He needed to establish his credibility once and for all. He needed to prove his uniqueness to the ignorant voters who nominated him for only one award. He had to show everyone how wrong they were. He said to himself, 'Wait until next time – they won't be able to ignore my next album.'

9

Ocean Way Recording Studios, Los Angeles. Spring 1982.

The night before, Michael burst into LaToya's room full of excitement. He was clutching a tape player. 'Listen to this!' he exclaimed.

LaToya reluctantly put down her book and looked askance at her younger brother, who stood anxiously in the dim shadows of her reading lamp.

'What?'

'Listen to this, Toya.'

Michael set the tape player on her bed, pressed the 'play' button, turned the volume up and waited. A moment later, a demo version of the song he had just finished in the backyard studio blasted out of the speakers. An insistent beat and red hot vocals made it impossible not to dance. Michael bopped in place, LaToya bounced on her bed.

'It's great,' she said when the song finished.

Michael was smiling. 'I think it's going to be a big hit,' he said. 'But do you think I should change the name from "Billie Jean?"'

'Why?'

'People might think it's about the tennis player.'

'That's even better,' said LaToya.

A person whose decision-making process relies more heavily on emotion than logic, Michael immediately believed this new song was the big, spectacular one Jones had been pushing him to write before wrapping *Thriller*. He had risen to the challenge. No one pays more attention to inner feelings than Michael, and the message he sensed this time was perfectly clear: 'Billie Jean' was a sure fire hit. He rarely ever felt so sure about something, but from the moment the infectious melody came to him, which happened to be while driving down Ventura Boulevard in his Rolls, he was convinced. LaToya's reaction confirmed it.

Never mind that it was late at night and most of his neighbours were getting ready for sleep. Michael lit up, kissed his sister and spun around the way he might do on stage, a crisp, quick turn. Tucking the recorder under his arm, he walked briskly down the hall to his room and disappeared inside. A few moments later, he was playing the song again, this time for himself. As the music pulsed out from under his closed bedroom door, he danced himself into a considerable, satisfying sweat.

'I could tell Michael was really happy with his work,' recalls LaToya. 'He was dancing and singing. He can be very secretive, but around us, he has a hard time hiding his feelings.'

The following afternoon a white, stretch limousine with smoked glass windows pulled in behind Ocean Way Recording Studios. Michael, his high hopes spilling overboard, got out clutching demos of his two latest compositions. In addition to the one he played his sister, there was another new song entitled 'Beat It'. Shedding the self-absorbed reticence he wore while away from the studio, he darted inside the low-rise building ready to work, with a surplus of energy, a powder keg awaiting the flame.

His producer was already there, waiting for him at the control board. Michael's presence filled the room with electricity. Following what had become a practised routine during *Off the Wall* and now this album, he and Jones embraced like two friends who'd been apart for years, even though they'd been together nearly every day for months. Jones greeted his upstart pupil as 'Smelly'. 'He's got an uncanny ability to smell out a good business deal,' he explains. Michael, like everyone else, called the producer by a singular consonant: 'Q'.

The only thing singular about Quincy is the manner in which he displays his sophistication and elegance. Jones' musical education began with trumpet lessons in his Seattle grade school. At age fourteen, he teamed up with another local prodigy, Ray Charles, for some after-hours gigs in soul clubs. The following year the burgeoning jazzman was all set to embark on a world tour with Lionel Hampton's big band when Hampton's wife insisted he stay behind and attend school.

It was but a temporary delay. Two years later Jones, now an ambitious seventeen-year-old, won a scholarship to Boston's respected Berklee School of Music, where he excelled in a full load of classes and earned extra money playing strip clubs at night. The ensuing years fill several pages of contemporary music history. By 1982, Jones had scored over thirty-five films, composed more than a dozen television show themes, recorded numerous albums of his own, and won an Academy Award for his score for 'In the Heat of the Night'. He'd also been nominated for fifty-five Grammy Awards and won eleven.

If Michael failed to become a well-rounded individual for lack of the proper guidance at home, he received the necessary tutelage to further develop his musicianship from the statesmanlike producer. 'In the beginning Quincy led Michael a lot and taught him a great deal,' says guitarist David Williams, a fixture of their recording team. 'Q adds his production trademark to all the music. If Michael did it by himself, it would sound totally different. Q is magic and Michael knows that.'

More like a mutual admiration club, their friendship is easy to define. Both possess a love of all styles of music, adventurous intellects and the ability to laugh and joke. Age differences aside, the two superstars enjoy a rapport that quickly blossomed well beyond their professional teacher-student relationship. 'We have a big brother-little brother thing,' says Jones. 'He listens to everything I say.'

Outside the workplace, their conversations are starting points for Michael's insatiable curiosity, which often attempts to understand the mundane events of everyday life, events that are to him foreign. 'He's asked me about everything – except marriage,' intones the producer, who divorced his second wife, actress Peggy Lipton, in 1987. 'But he sometimes questions me about relationships – what they're about and all that – because I've had lots of them and he's never really had one.'

Despite their close friendship, Jones admits that Michael's pathological modesty can be a formidable obstacle. 'He can sing in front of 90,000 people, but in front of three it's very difficult for him,' he explains. 'We've sat in my studio when he was going to sing me a new song and I've had to close my eyes and turn my back.'

Not this time, though.

Jones had been pushing Michael hard lately. Only a few weeks earlier, the album was thought by everyone involved to have been completed. Michael had composed 'Wanna Be Startin' Somethin'', a holdover from the previous LP, and a slew of other originals. Rod Temperton contributed three songs: 'Baby Be Mine', 'The Lady in My Life', and 'Thriller'. Toto's Steve Porcaro and John Bettis wrote the lush, beautiful ballad, 'Human Nature'. Soul crooner James Ingram and Jones penned 'P.Y.T. (Pretty Young Thing)'. And if these names weren't enough, Paul McCartney shared a co-writing credit with Jackson on 'The Girl is Mine'.

It certainly looked nice on paper. Yet when the producer played the record, he didn't get the sense that this was a finished project. It didn't move him. Even though the record company was clamouring for another Michael Jackson product, Q told them it wasn't ready. 'We had everything in the can for *Thriller*, and we were about to leave the studio,' says Jones. 'I played the tapes a few more times, and I didn't get that feeling. I told Michael that he had to write some stronger material. Everyone thought I was crazy.'

Except for Michael, the pernickety perfectionist, who never believed a project, be it a song or an entire album, was finished to its ultimate level.

Jones' pronouncement was exactly what Michael wanted to hear before any mistakes were made. To claim success, Michael was convinced that this album needed to surpass *Off the Wall*, which had produced four top ten singles and sold more than seven million copies. It was a tough act to follow. But it was also a matter of necessity. From day one, the hyper-motivated superstar had brought an obsessive vision to the making of this album. The LP was his personal mission, the Mount Everest he had to climb. No distance was too far for him to travel in order to make the absolute perfect album. In a statement reflecting the superhuman expectations he sets for himself, Michael says, 'Just doing as well as you did last time is not good enough.'

That should've been clear to everyone, but it wasn't. One day Michael was playing a pinball game during a break. Songwriter Rod Temperton and Jones were in the studio with him, and one of them off-handedly asked, 'If this album doesn't do as well as *Off the Wall*, will you be disappointed?'

Michael was suddenly confused. Good God, didn't they understand? He was crushed that they even needed to make such an inquiry. Couldn't they see?

'I told them *Thriller* had to do better than *Off the Wall*,' Michael recalls. 'I admitted that I wanted this album to be the biggest-selling album of all time.'

They laughed. Michael didn't.

It wasn't the first time during the project that Michael was distressed that the people working with him didn't seem to understand his ultimate goal, and it wasn't the last time either.

94

His riveting intensity in the workplace was obvious to everyone. His colleagues couldn't help but notice his blind obsession with work, his marathon runner's determination to achieve his absolute best, even when every last ounce of his energy was expended, but they couldn't match it. 'It's just impossible to work as hard as that guy,' says Williams. 'When he has an idea, he goes with it all the way.'

Michael's work habits are shaped by a monkish zealousness. His sleep is often interrupted by the sudden arrival of melody, inspiration that's uncontrollable, whether his eyes are open or closed. Yet he often stays awake around the clock, fighting the urge to sleep, in order to complete his work. 'I'm a perfectionist,' he says. 'I'll work until I drop.'

This time around his effort paid off.

When the two new songs Michael had brought in, 'Billie Jean' and 'Beat It', finished playing, he looked at the producer for a reaction. Jones was smiling.

'He did it,' recalls Jones. 'With the pressure on, Michael came through with two great songs.'

As Michael himself would say, it was magic.

And magic, according to the singer, is the very best.

It was the first of several controversial decisions the increasingly enigmatic singer made concerning his appearance. To no one's surprise, he left this and the other decisions unexplained. Sure, they were private. But their drastic nature incited volumes of rash gossip and speculation that eventually besmirched Michael's wholesome public image.

On their own, they demanded as much, if not more, attention than his music, and to his dismay, they did. Throughout the world, people who wouldn't ever in their lifetime own a Michael Jackson album followed every detail. Some would describe it as strange, ghoulish, revolting; others would simply poke fun. A minority offered a defence for the silent pop idol, pointing to the long list of Hollywood celebrities, including Marilyn Monroe, who had also had their noses fixed.

Michael never once considered the myriad ramifications caused by his decision to have Los Angeles plastic surgeon Steven Hoefflin apply his trade to his nose. No, just a snip, whittle and tuck on either side of his fleshy proboscis and, he believed, all would be okay. Gone from his nose would be the bulbous width that he found unflattering when he studied his image. Better it should be replaced by a straighter, more mature downward slope and a healthier, happier, more contented self-image.

It's not often that entertainers go to extremes like changing their physical appearance when their images are already firmly established. Never mind a proven superstar. A readily identifiable face is as good as gold. But then, most entertainers don't have to deal with the emotional baggage that weighed on Michael. Between his dogged efforts on his new album, his strife-ridden family, and coping with his strange personal life, Michael was setting himself up for a hell of a ride as the sacrifices he made for unprecedented mass acceptance played themselves out to a shocked public.

Cynics have described the first of Michael's Pygmalion-like operations as 'a stroke of genius', a calculated attempt to refashion his image before the release of his forthcoming album. If only Michael was *that* calculating. To argue that he was fiendishly reinventing himself for the sole purpose of selling the public a face they couldn't help but remember is to overestimate his guile, desperation and bravery. Of course, he did gamely embrace the notion of a revamped, more mature image to accompany the polyrock sounds he was serving up on record. After all, among his primary aims was distancing himself from the public's perception of Michael Jackson as the squeaky clean cherub who sang frothy pop alongside his brothers.

Michael Jackson, solo artist, desperately wanted to eclipse whatever he'd done in the past, and, for that matter, whatever everyone else had done. *Off the Wall* was impressive, no question about it, but it wasn't ever mentioned among the all-time bests, which is how Michael wanted to show himself. If he was going to have a superstar's solo career, he knew he had to make a drastic move. 'Michael grew up marketed from the time he was a kid,' observes Bobby Colomby. 'He knew the value of image and publicity as well as anyone in the business.' Still, Michael's methods centred around work. Lots of hard work.

Dire as his pining was for success, he was no pop cultural sculptor given to redesigning his face as one might repackage a tired old product in the hope of kindling a fad like Elvis' Royal Crown Pomade or the Beatles' mop top haircuts. His reasoning, which owed itself to a lifetime's-worth of complexes, was much simpler. 'He simply didn't like the way his nose looked,' says his mother.

To a degree, that's the honest truth. Michael didn't like his nose. He hated it, in fact. The nose he saw in his reflection served as a painful point of reference for a childhood of sacrifice as well as a troubled adolescence. It was the exclamation point for all the discontent and anger he concealed within the tight boundaries of his flesh. Then Michael realised that his body was the one area over which he could exercise absolute control, and the decision to restyle his nose became a deliberate, though dire attempt to take charge of his out-of-control life.

In the three years it took to make *Thriller*, the Jackson family was ravaged by the slings and arrows of showbusiness fortune. When he surveyed the wreckage, Michael saw a family whose lives had been marked by the seductive temptations of greed and fame. Despite all the wonderful rewards the Jacksons had accrued over the years, they were an unhappy lot. The reality proved unsettling to Michael, especially on the home front.

Katherine had spent the past two years in a trial separation, during which time Joe brooded, worked on his business affairs and grew increasingly distant from his family. She was now ready to call it quits. When she examined her personal situation, the pious matriarch concluded that she could no longer ignore the unrelenting heartache caused by her husband's adulterous behaviour. Nor could she tolerate the way he used hundreds of thousands of dollars of money earned for him by their children to support his illegitimate child and her mother. When she examined the realities of Joe's double life, the indignation and pain were too much to bear.

When interviewed by the press, the Jackson offspring – at least those who spoke publicly – provided a rosy picture of family life. Descriptions never varied. They were a close, happy and undivided family. Yet quite the opposite was true. In 1982 their soft-spoken mother, torn, unhappy and depressed, secured the services of an attorney and quietly filed for divorce from her husband of more than three decades. Although frightened, she received unanimous support from her children, especially Michael, the son who wielded the most clout within the family. Joe, meanwhile, continued to deny any trouble existed whatsoever. 'It was just the kind of minor problems everyone who's been married for a long time goes through sooner or later,' he says.

However, Joe's problems definitely were not minor. His clandestine social life and free-wheeling business schemes landed him in the position he most feared – being financially insecure. Never mind that he was exiled from the family nest. When he moved out of the Jacksons' rambling home and resettled

97

in a nearby townhouse, one of the few solid investments he made (actually, the group's longtime attorney, Richard Arons, was responsible) with money earned in the early days of the Jackson Five, he was having severe financial difficulties. 'At that time,' says a woman who kept company with the family, 'they were furious with him. They didn't want him around. He'd embarrassed the family and lost all his money.'

Joe's empire was weakened by lousy investments. A series of disastrous real estate deals, soured movie investments and failed recording projects, all under the auspices of Joe Jackson Productions, placed the befuddled patriarch in the midst of financial ruin. 'He fashioned himself a Berry Gordy-type wheeler-dealer,' says a former employee. 'But he was not very sophisticated when it came to business.'

Businesswise, Joe's children suspected he often favoured his personal interests more than theirs. 'I wanted to be an actress,' muses LaToya. 'And my father always encouraged me. But somehow all the scripts that came into his office went to his secretaries.'

In this dense haze of family strife, one fact was certain: Joe needed money. Large sums of cash. 'I was trying to launch singing careers for Janet and LaToya,' he explains, ignoring the cost of his extracurricular activities. 'That cost money – lots of money.' But how to get it with a bad track record that preceded him? When he pitched new projects, his usual backers retreated. Also, the co-management deal he had with his sons allowed him only limited funds. Finally, with his options exhausted, Joe got an idea that he hoped would breathe new life into his pocketbook.

He set up a meeting with his second youngest son and put a business proposition to him: Would he like to buy his old man's half-interest in the family's home?

How drastically the tables had turned from when Michael was a little boy fearful of his father's wrath. He was, at this juncture, the wealthiest of the musical Jacksons, having pocketed upwards of $15 million in royalties from *Off the Wall*. He was also the child most disturbed by the dissolution of his parents' marriage, since he had always assumed responsibility for the family's well-being, and he was anxious to end the bickering that plagued his only refuge from the outside world.

When his father spelled out his proposal, Michael jumped at the deal. He was no dummy. Not only would the transaction give him additional control over the schisms dividing his family, it would give him leverage in any future disagreement with his father, and give him title to a valuable piece of real estate. A calculating businessman who feared poverty and had given his personal finances scrupulous attention from the time he turned twenty-one and inherited the several million dollars held for him in trust, Michael paid his dad an estimated $500,000 for his share of the family residence.

The property's new co-owner wasted no time in laying out his latest plans. With his mother's consent, he made immediate preparations for a massive razing and remodelling of the estate. 'Foremost on his mind, Michael wanted to build a castle for his mother,' says a former intimate of the Jacksons. 'He wanted to prove to her that he could take care of her, that she didn't have to rely on Joe for financial support. A home was his way of protecting her.'

Michael, ever the dutiful son, readily agreed with the analysis. Not only was the purchase a reaction to the jealous sparring that had divided his family, it was also a testament of faith to his beloved mother. He wanted to provide whatever material goods would heal her emotional wounds. 'I've always wanted to do this for my mother,' he said. 'She loves homes and everything, and I do things by feeling and force.'

As for himself, he made it clear that he wasn't about to pack his belongings and escape Katherine's maternal pampering. 'If I moved out now, I'd die of loneliness.' The emotional ties were too strong to ignore. In addition, Michael was set on creating a monumental residence, a dream home that fulfilled all his childlike fantasies. 'I don't feel it's time for me to move away yet,' he explained during the construction. 'There are so many things I want to do just staying here.'

Not the stuff one ordinarily hears from a passionate young man driven by relentless ambition. It's also not the kind of talk that usually flows from the mouths of rock and roll stars. But then Michael, just short of turning twenty-five years old, was no run-of-the-mill pop music hero when he offered these comments.

As far as the music world, notoriously indulgent of bizarre behaviour, was concerned, he was something of a musical savant, a pleasant, not-too-worldly but multi-talented loner who knew little more than the business that had consumed him from earliest childhood. The public had even less of a clue to whom Michael actually was, which was okay with him.

When it came to his public image, all he desired was unrefutable evidence that his accomplishments carried the weight of consequence.

The subject of his personal life was one he guarded with obsessive care and secrecy, sweeping aside all inquiries about his puzzling character with a frail whisper. 'I'm shy,' he retorted ever so timidly. Even that was tantamount to a full-blown interview. As far as Michael was concerned, his offstage conduct was an extremely delicate matter, 'just like a haemophiliac,' he said, 'who can't afford to be scratched in any way.' The contrast between his fame and his private life, he felt, was his concern only.

Yet Michael's family members and associates indicate that his thoughts and behaviour were increasingly influenced by the traits that doctors use to define an eating disorder. Michael gave the impression of great stamina and sense of purpose. He was stubborn, unyeilding in his determination to achieve perfection. 'He's the hardest worker I've been around,' guitarist Williams says. 'He doesn't know when to quit.' Outside the studio, though, Michael's inexhaustible stamina yeilded to an underlying fear of not being rspected. 'It's hard to say if he feels good about what he's done,' says Marlon. 'Michael is rarely satisfied.'

His perspective was skewed. Michael not only set high goals for himself, which is not unusual in itself, but he also convinced himself that more was expected from him than anyone else. And if he did not fulfil these expectations, he believed, his world would crumble like a house of cards. 'He has always had a special sense of purpose,' muses his mother. 'He just became more private with it as he got older.' Past successes meant little to him. He set new standards for himself, inventing new scales on which to measure his accomplishments, such as when he told Quincy Jones that *Thriller* could not simply be a hit but had to be the biggest album in history.

Personal aims completely occupied Michael. His parents had long ago realized they exercised little influence over his development and thus Michael was allowed to shape himself. Not surprisingly, without parental guidance, his behaviour and his thinking grew more and more idiosyncratic. People who came into contact with Michael repeatedly described him as a man-child, impressed by his childlike innocence. It was a personality purposely cultivated by Michael, who sought never to leave the comforting world of childhood. And like a child,

Michael had a narrow, simple-minded view of the world that placed himself at the very centre.

This childlike egocentricity, medical experts say, is often the core of the self-image of one who suffers from an eating disorder. They do not want to leave childhood, and many times they ascribe concepts of magical effectiveness to themselves in an effort to underscore their uniqueness and set them apart from others. From early childhood on, Michael believed himself to be graced with powers greater than himself. It was his way of explaining his talent, his life and creativity. 'I must endure for the power I was sent forth,' he wrote in a letter to a journalist, 'for the world, for the children.'

Michael embraced the notion of magic. Magic became his favourite word. It was a catchall to describe anything entertaining, enchanting, anything beyond the grasp of his vocabulary. Walt Disney was 'magic.' It was magic, Michael claimed, the way he would open his eyes from sleep with a new song playing in his head. 'I wake up from dreams and and go, "Wow, put this down on paper," ' he said. 'The whole thing is strange.' His talent was owed to God or some like-minded supernatural power that happened to select him as its medium. 'The thing that touches me is very special,' he said. 'It's a message I have to tell. I start crying and the pain is wonderful. It's amazing. It's like God.'

The notions Michael entertained often seemed like something that would be dreamed up by a child and not an adult. For instance, he believed in the power of wishes. 'I really do,' he told an interviewer. And Michael once let on that he actually believed man possessed the ability to fly. 'We can fly, you know,' he intoned. 'We just don't know how to think the right thoughts and levitate ourselves off the ground.'

The power of the mind was everything to Michael, and one of the minds he most admired belonged to his pal, director Steven Spielberg. Quincy Jones had introduced Jackson and Spielberg during production of the hit film *E.T. The Extra-Terrestrail*, and the two young entertainment heavyweights became close friends. 'I even gave Steven a present,' Michael revealed. 'A book on Walt Disney, as he's the only person who's inspired me in my music as much as Disney.'

During the film of *E.T.*, Michael took time off from his own recording project to visit the movie's set. He wanted to meet the strange, loveable alien creature, and when he did, on a dark, empty sound stage, it was love at first sight. 'He grabbed me, he put his arms around me,' Michael beamed. 'He was so real that I was talking to him. I kissed him before I left.'

Michael's enchantment with the fantasy creature was so great that he took time off from recording *Thriller* to work with Spielberg on *E.T. Songbook*, a children's album adapted from the movie. Spielberg was not at all surprised that Michael so closely identified with E.T. 'I've never seen anybody like Michael,' he said. 'He is an emotional star child.' If E.T. was real, the director said, he would defiantely visit Michael. Michael watched the movie repeatedly in his home theatre. 'The first time I saw *E.T.* I melted through the whole thing,' he said. 'The second time I cried like crazy.'

Michael found that narrating the songbook provided him with an almost lifelike intimacy with the character he adored. 'I felt like I was there with them, like behind a tree or something, watching everything that happened,' he said. When he read the part where E.T. is dying, Michael broke down and cried in the darkened studio. What made the scene so poignant is that E.T. appeared to be so much like Michael himself. 'I love E.T. because it reminds me of me,' Michael admitted. 'Someone from another world coming down and you becoming friends with them and this person is, like, 800 years old and he's filling you with all kinds of wisdom and he can teach you how to fly.'

The kinship was understandable. Michael regularly felt like an alien among his fellow humans, and his music, he believed, was no less inspiring that E.T.'s brand of healing magic. Both, he reasoned, espoused a message of love, and both of them were more readily accepted by children than by their adult counterparts. In his videos Michael nearly always cast himself in a magical atmosphere. When he steps on a stone, it glows. When he flips a coin into a beggar's cup, the bum is transformed in a white tuxedo. In real life he believes Michael can heal, too. It is the reason he visited the children at a Stockton, California elementary school where a crazed gunman opened fire with an automatic weapon during recess and shot dozens of students. 'He felt he could make a difference,' one of Michael's spokesmen says. 'He represents good and little kids seem to know it.'

The flip-side to Michael's belief in his magical effectiveness is the pain he endures for being Michael Jackson. Privately, he suffers. He's come to believe that it's his obligation, his burden. 'The pain is wonderful,' he said of the special powers that course through his creative soul, and it is this wonderful pain that supplies him with the tangible evidence of his special role in life. Michael's whole existence has been bound by sacrifice. He gave up his childhood. He toiled for his family. He expended tremendous amounts of extra effort on his career to distance himself from his rivals. He was obsessed about his diet, losing the baby fat he hated and changing his appearance. In everything, he exercised an enormous willpower that allowed him to succeed. The pain, no matter how great, was worth it, he believed.

Pain was the justification of all Michael's aspirations and fears. If he felt no pain, there was no gain. Consequently, he fashioned his daily routines around the unforgiving partnership of sweat and solitude. He ate little, setting up strict rules on what he could and could not eat. He laboured arduously. His private rituals could be punishing. Every Sunday he fasted all day, ingesting nothing but fruit juices, no matter how his stomach moaned and growled. And he danced until he dropped, thoroughly exhausted, laughing and crying in a pool of perspiration, feeling that 'wonderful pain'.

The suffering was as self-fulfilling as Michael's refusal to relinquish his childhood. He did not have the amusements and friends of a normal twenty-five year old. Instead he played with his backyard menagerie of exotic pets, which included Louis the llama, Muscles the boa constrictor, and a lamb named Mr Tibbs. Michael identified so strongly with children that, in down moods, he often pedalled his bicycle to a nearby schoolyard and stared longingly at the little ones. 'When I come back to the studio, I'm ready to move mountains,' he admitted. 'Kids do that to me. It's like magic.' He also spent hours each week watching the Bugs Bunny, Disney and MGM animated classics in his extensive collection of cartoons. 'It's real escapism,' he confessed. 'It's like everything's all right. It's like the world is happening now in a faraway city. Everything's fine.'

However, these examples pale in comparison to the plans Michael made during the renovation of his new house, which was fashioned as an amusement-packed diorama for the grown-up demigod, a bubble-like playground where he could end-lessly amuse himself without ever having to cross into the scary outside world. It was like Elvis' Graceland, but for kids. His sisters fussed endlessly over their rooms. Michael didn't care about his. 'I wanted room to dance and have my books,' he said.

But when it came to the space he had reserved for recreation, he inspected every minuscule detail of the design. He wanted a screening room with the latest equipment, a room stocked with videogames, an exercise gym and all the accoutrements that would give the mansion the look and feel of a royal palace. He even consulted with Disney technicians about installing a room full of animated pirates that would scream and shoot at each other with guns and cannons, just like his favourite Disneyland ride, Pirates of the Caribbean.

Even though this elaborate, hugely expensive creation never got beyond the drawing board, despite widespread rumours that an entire electrifying ride was constructed beneath the six-bedroom residence, Michael continued to exercise a Hearstian appetite for consumption, filling his castle-like home with an array of whimsical distractions. His intent was obvious. While attempting to win the public's adoration with his music, he was erecting an impenetrable fortress in which he could hide from them. 'I'm putting all this stuff in,' he explained, 'so I will never have to leave and go out *there*.'

10

Westlake Studios, Los Angeles. November 1982.

As afternoons go, this one looked just like any other work day, one more air conditioned, windowless, thoroughly professional stint in the acoustically perfect recording studio to add to the hundreds just like it that had already passed. As usual, Michael and Jones arrived at the Hollywood recording studio in their separate limousines and cloistered themselves behind closed doors.

However, this was no ordinary work day.

What had begun in the sixteen-track recording studio behind the Jackson's Encino home three years earlier was finally thought to be finished. In between, Michael and Jones had selected cuts from more than three hundred songs. They'd spent an estimated $750,000 on the recording process, during which Michael had come into his own as a musician, taking charge like never before, often motioning with his arms or singing to musicians so they'd understand exactly what he wanted them to play.

After all this, the project appeared completed. Michael and Q sat down to preview the nine song mixes before copies of the album were pressed. The air was filled with expectancy. A CBS executive was waiting to uncork the champagne.

Oddly enough, neither Michael nor his usually upbeat producer felt in synch with the partytime atmosphere. Both were exhausted. With the record company levelling heavy pressure on them to get the long-overdue album out of the studio and into the stores, they had been following a gruelling schedule of sixteen-hour days and hard deadlines.

Outwardly, at least, Michael and Jones were a picture of laid-back L.A. casualness, who could have been lolling away a few empty hours rather than unveiling the project that had consumed nearly every waking hour of the past three years.

However, inside their baggy silks and denims, they were nervous. 'When we finally arrived, it was a big, nerveracking moment,' says Jones. 'We'd been working so hard we didn't know what to expect.'

The first single, 'The Girl Is Mine', which had been released in October, was already nearing the top of the charts. Before starting work on the album, Michael had phoned Paul McCartney in London and arranged a visit so they could collaborate on new songs. 'It was Christmas day,' says Paul, 'and I didn't believe it was him. I didn't think it was Michael. Eventually I said, "Is that really you?" He was laughing on the phone, he said, "You don't believe me, do you?"'

Michael wanted to pay back Paul for giving him 'Girlfriend', which he used on *Off the Wall*. 'I said, "Well, you know, great,"' says Paul. '"Let me think about it." And I thought about it and thought, "Well, why not?"' At McCartney's picturesque Scottish estate, in the midst of rolling green hills and spacious pastures, they watched cartoons and old Fred Astaire movies and talked business. The Fab One told the younger superstar about his vast publishing investments, including the rights to Buddy Holly's songs, and let him sift through a hefty book that held all the song titles he owned.

Michael was inspired by McCartney's publishing interests. He had learned valuable lessons from his father's business errors. He also paid close attention to stories of how other artists were cheated out of royalties or lost their fortunes, and he vowed that wouldn't happen to him. There doesn't seem to be a time when Michael wasn't a hard-nosed businessman with a keen awareness of his value as a musician and merchadising staple on the market. 'He's a tough negotiator,' Dileo says from first-hand experience. 'I'd hate going up against him.'

The idea of owning songs – his own and those by other artists – excited Michael, and the year after McCartney clued him into the business Michael acquired a major publishing catalogue, including all of Sly and the Family Stone's hits. Three years later he defeated McCartney in a multimillion dollar bidding war for ownership of the prestigious and profitable ATV publishing catalogue, which contained virtually the entire Lennon-McCartney oeuvre. The victory forced Michael to ante up $47.5 million, but it also cost him his close friendship with the former Beatle.

That was unfortunate. But where business is concerned, Michael exercises the same tyrannical control he does over his body. He makes all his own decisions, from where his money will be invested to how the sequins on his jacket are to be sewn. He's constantly in touch with his attorney, John Branca, and his accountant, Marshall Gelfand. 'He's briefed weekly on what's going on with his investments,' says Branca. 'For a star of his stature he's incredibly well-informed of his financial situation.'

When it comes to doing business Michael is a worrier. He frets over the smallest of details, as if even the tiniest slip up could cost him a notch or two in chart positions. He claims he can be a harsh, exacting interviewer when it comes to employees. For a time, he ran through a string of secretaries, firing one when he discovered that she had hung a black and white photograph of the Beatles given him by lensman Harry Benson in her own apartment and then claimed that it was lost. 'He didn't like doing that,' says his mother, 'but she lied to him.'

The Jackson-McCartney partnership proved fruitful, which isn't surprising, considering between them they had recorded thirty-seven number one singles. Despite its unadventurous refrain, 'that doggone girl is mine', which left reviewers yawning at Michael's first new music since 1979, 'The Girl Is Mine', spent three weeks at number two in January 1983. Two more middle-of-the-road Jackson-McCartney collaborations cropped up soon after. 'Say, Say, Say', which went to number one in December 1983 (competing directly with *Thriller*'s sixth single, 'P.Y.T.') and 'The Man', both appeared on Paul's *Pipes of Peace* LP.

George Martin, McCartney's producer, was surprised by the strong impression Jackson made in their sessions. 'He actually does radiate an aura when he comes into the studio, there's no question about it,' said Martin, whose inventive work with the Beatles is well-documented. He was also taken by Michael's mastery of music, something he didn't expect. 'He's not a musician in the sense that Paul is; he's not a great keyboard player or guitar player,' Martin said. 'But he does know what he wants in music and he has very firm ideas.'

Those ideas didn't jive with what he heard when he and Quincy finished listening to the master pressing of *Thriller*. The whole album finished playing without anyone saying a single word. Expectations plummeted. Never mind that the champagne was primed to pop. The mood in the studio was as sombre as a funeral. 'I felt devastated,' says Michael, who got up and left the room with tears in his eyes. 'All this pent-up emotion came out.' He passed the word: the album wasn't coming out. Not yet.

Jones faced up to the problem, which stemmed from the overbearingly rushed schedule under which they'd been operating. 'We'd been going day and night,' he says, 'and we were tired and not paying proper attention. We were conveniently ignoring the principles of physics – that you can put only eighteen or nineteen minutes of sound on each side, and then no more. But we had twenty-five and twenty-six minutes on each side because we were too tired to think. And the result was puny sound. It was all squashed. It didn't sound good at all.'

Exercising his calming influence over Michael, Jones' solution was simple: ride out the depression and then face the music again. 'After we cried,' he says, 'we went to bed for two days and then came back to the studio with renewed insight and direction.' Upon their return, they worked at a slower, more careful pace, mixing two songs a week. 'We were nervous,' says Jones. 'The one song was out and we hadn't even finished the album yet.'

The remixes showed a difference that was obvious even to the record company executives who'd been applying all the pressure to release the album. This time when they listened to the finished mix, Michael was excited. He loved it. The album was finally completed. There was no celebration, just the quiet acknowledgement of a job well done among friends, comrades who'd slogged it out together for more than one thousand days and nights. 'We hugged,' says Jones. 'This time we were all very cool.'

Only one question remained: Would *Thriller* be able to satisfy Michael's expectations by becoming the bestselling album in history?

Thriller was released on 1 December 1982, an inauspicious winter day that left plenty of time for Christmas shoppers to purchase the latest offering from Michael Jackson. Those who enjoyed reading the small print of liner notes learned that Michael's new album was 'lovingly dedicated to Katherine Jackson' and that special thanks were extended to such disparate personalities as Steven Spielberg, Vincent Price, Eddie Van Halen and Valerie Bertinelli, Janet, Joseph and LaToya Jackson (there was no mention of any Jackson brothers) and a slew of musicians, managers and friends.

Little more than a month after the LP's release, 'Billie Jean', the second single, hit the stores, entering the charts at number forty-seven. Six weeks later it went to number one. The album collected a four-star review from *Rolling Stone*, which noted that Jackson had 'cooked up a zesty LP . . . a gorgeous, snappy step in the right direction . . . that marks another watershed in the creative development of this prodigiously talented performer.'

Indeed, *Thriller* was a turning point for Michael. There was no rehashing of *Off the Wall*'s hackneyed funk. It was replaced by an array of uptempo tunes that spanned virtually every genre of pop music. And the boyish vocals that cooked up only a moderate flame when compared to Prince's four-alarm screeches on *1999* were replaced by the fiery yelps of a seething adult who, beneath the agreeable veneer of infectious melodies rich with toe-tapping hooks, seemed more than a little pissed off about something.

But then the LP marked Michael's musical coming of age, and when examined lyrically, there surfaced the bleak, dark, frightened soul of a tormented young man. It was as close and as unfiltered a look at the reclusive superstar as most people had ever got, and Michael's state of mind was startling. Most people never noticed the rampant doubt, confusion and fear of songs like 'Billie Jean' and 'Beat It', which didn't fit their image of cute little Afro-crowned Michael. Or perhaps they didn't want to cast cloudy aspersions on his character. All the more shocking it made Michael later on.

But it was right there, the singer's own inner storm laid out in front of the glad-to-hear-ya swirl of wonderful pop music. Though 'Billie Jean', an irresistible tableau of pulsating funk, is the story of a man who denies fathering the child of a relentlessly pursuing female, 'a composite of the people we've been plagued by over the years', says Michael, it also contains a clear expression of his obsession with privacy when he sings, 'And be careful what you do cause the lie becomes the truth.' On the rapid-fire 'Wanna Be Startin' Something', whose raw verses trace a scattered, confusing portrait of a pained character, he grouses, 'Still they hate you, you're a vegetable,' and then later retorts, 'No one can hurt you now/Because you know what's true.'

The two most popular songs from the album delineate Michael's harrowing world in the starkest terms. *Thriller*, the LP's spooky title track, illustrates the fright-filled world in which he resides. 'They're out to get you, there's demons closing in on every side,' he sings as if on the run. 'They will possess you unless you change the number on your dial.' Then, 'Beat It', a standout, macho barn-burner that quickly crossed over onto rock radio, unfurled his rampant paranoia. 'They're out to get you, better leave while you can . . . you wanna stay alive, better do what you can.'

Equally revealing were the comic-like sketches gracing the inside record sleeve. Drawn by Michael, an excellent renderer, the first shows him seated beside a girl while watching a monster-filled television screen out of which are reaching the hairy, clawed arms of a frightening monster. Other apparitions, including a werewolf, ghost and skull, float in the background. There is a look of bewilderment on his face. The scene is a textbook depiction of paranoia and panic.

The other picture portrays Michael, looking quite forceful and strong, engaged in a tug-of-war with Paul McCartney, each one of them pulling on the arm of a buxom young lady. Titled 'The Girl Is Mine', it's an obvious illustration of the song they wrote together.

In addition, directly beneath his signature, exploding like Fourth of July fireworks from under the M on the first drawing and the N on the last, Michael adds a large, radiant starburst, a reminder, lest anyone not notice, of his magical sparkle.

Commercially, it was nearly impossible to miss the sparkle of Michael's magic. 'Billie Jean' hit number one on 5 March, six weeks after its release. But even before that milestone, Michael's record company pulled a manoeuvre that cut against the grain of regular procedure. They released the album's third single, 'Beat It'. Usually, a record company will wait until one single has run its course, rising and then faltering, before issuing the next one. But Epic's sharp v.p. of promotion, Frank Dileo, convinced everyone that even though 'Billie Jean' was still ascending, it was time to release 'Beat It', too.

By mid April, 'Beat It', which climbed to number five at the same time 'Billie Jean' was concluding the last of its seven weeks at one, was the most talked about song on radio, thanks to the scorching guitar virtuosity of hard rock demigod Eddie Van Halen. Ironically, Van Halen nearly missed the opportunity when his telephone malfunctioned the first two times Jones called. When he answered the third try, he was so annoyed that he shouted a string of expletives into the receiver, until he heard, 'This is Quincy, Quincy Jones,' on the other end. But Van Halen's masterful solo aside, the real magic was being worked behind the scenes by Dileo. He had visited the studio when Michael and Jones were still mixing *Thriller*, and he'd loved 'Billie Jean' and 'Beat It'. 'They were obvious hits,' he recalls. 'Of course, the one song I loved more than he did was "P.Y.T." I always liked that.'

Opposites in personality, the gregarious, fun-loving Dileo, then thirty-six years old and the father of two children, and Michael, the super-shy superstar, struck up a friendship based on mutual respect for each other's expertise. 'He kept calling me and I kept calling him,' says Dileo. 'We had this ongoing relationship where I'd take him here and there to promote the album.'

Meanwhile, back in January, Michael had ventured to London for the filming of his 'Billie Jean' video. His longtime fascination with motion pictures had prepared him for the revolutionary influence of MTV, which gave the music video common currency when it was introduced in 1981. Michael, who loved the opportunity of presenting his music visually, hired Steve Baron to direct his initial foray, which was given a budget of $250,000 by the record company. At first, they argued over the concept, since the director didn't envision any dancing in the video, but obviously, Michael won out.

On the set Michael conducted himself as if he were moving inside an isolated bubble, breathing his own rarified air in a world only he inhabited. When his makeup was applied, he hardly took notice of anyone around him. One morning, his oldest brother, Jackie, was hanging around the set, sipping orange juice and confirming rumours that the Jacksons would be touring throughout Great Britain later in the year, virtually ignoring the fact that Michael was the only brother with an album out, and he was making plans for his own tour.

But Michael didn't raise an eyebrow to his sibling's comments, choosing instead to focus all his energy on the video, which portrays him on the run from a detective who follows him down streets, past shops and into a bedroom where he climbs in next to a woman. Yet, whenever the detective catches up with him, Michael's image goes poof, and disappears, as if he's demonstrating once and for all that his private life is out of bounds to everyone.

Not surprisingly, Michael is also shown to possess a Midas-like magic. Every grimy object he touches lights up. When he skips away at the end, for instance, the stones underneath his feet turn an incandescent white. MTV started showing the

'Billie Jean' video only after the song became a chart topper, though it was widely rumoured and subsequently denied that Walter Yetnikoff, the powerful chief executive of CBS, had threatened to pull all other CBS videos off the network until Michael's was aired, which it was by mid-February.

For his next video, Michael eschewed record company financing and plunked down $150,000 of his own money to produce a cinematic translation of 'Beat It'. When Michael wrote the tune, he says, he envisioned the tough, warring urban gangs of Los Angeles whose murderous violence is chronicled almost daily in local newspapers. The song's translation, he thought, should be literal, and the director he hired, Bob Giraldi, agreed. Consequently, he filmed on location on the dangerous streets of East Los Angeles and hired real life gang members.

Borrowing from *West Side Story*, one of Michael's favourite musicals, the rival gang members meet like two angry armies in the middle of the street and act out the rituals of what appears to be the start of a deadly clash. Or so it seems, until Michael pulls on his red leather jacket, leaps into the thick of this violent cauldron and secures peace. Giraldi, who had already won hundreds of awards for his work in commercials, was impressed by Michael's tireless effort during production, especially at the way he involved himself in details that ranged from the overall concept down to the wardrobe. 'He's an absolute perfectionist,' says the director.

'Beat It' began airing in March. Several weeks earlier, on 21 February, *Thriller* hit number one on the LP charts. 'Michael was very happy,' says Jones with typical understatement.

Michael's album was still comfortably atop the charts at the end of February when his management team, Freddie DeMann and Ron Weisner, informed him that Motown was putting together a television special celebrating their twenty-fifth anniversary and had inquired about the possibilities of a Jackson Five reunion. The brothers hadn't performed together since the night in 1985 in Las Vegas when Motown chief Berry Gordy telephoned Jermaine backstage and demanded that he not go on with the rest of his family.

Michael said no. He didn't like television, a carryover from the uninspired days of the Jackson's variety show. But since the Jackson Five had played such a crucial role in Motown's success, and likewise the record company had fostered the Jacksons' rise to fame and fortune, his managers rephrased their request, over and over, asking him to ponder the situation. They spelled out the benefits of prime time exposure on network television as well as pointing out that the gossip would dog him when it was leaked that he alone had prevented a reunion of the Jacksons on a show that included Diana Ross, Stevie Wonder, Marvin Gaye, Smokey Robinson and the Four Tops.

'We all wanted to do the show, except for Michael,' says Marlon. 'We were very excited to be a part of it. But he just had to be persuaded that it would be good.'

That job fell to Gordy himself, an old master of friendly persuasion, who paid his former protégé a visit in person. Michael, who was in the middle of editing the 'Beat It' video, eventually succumbed to the influential pleas of his former mentor. However, though he agreed, Michael, now a huge star on his own, could demand his own terms, and he did. He wanted to sing 'Billie Jean', the only non-Motown song that would be performed onstage that evening. That was fine with Gordy.

Then, according to Michael's account in *Moonwalk*, he called his brothers together and rehearsed them into shape, choreographed their routines and then took them onstage, like a has-been boxer returning heroically to the ring after a lengthy absence. Ironically, his version of the pre-show preparations, which grants a passing mention to contributions made by Marlon and Jermaine, puts him in a position of domineering authority similar to that once occupied by his overbearing father. 'But Michael wasn't doing all the work, which is how he makes it seem,' says Marlon.

As expected, Marlon's version differs from his younger brother's. It goes like this: 'Actually, what happened is we sat down, all the brothers, and said these are the three numbers we're going to do, and then we just did them. We were at Jackie's house then, and we rehearsed there a little. Then we spent some time rehearsing at my mother's house. Michael and I mainly choreographed, which was really simple, though everyone made suggestions, and that was it. Getting the entire routine down took about three or four hours, then we watched the videotapes, improved on certain areas and that was it. We were all ready.'

Except for Michael. Granted, the television show was a glitzy celebration of Motown's array of music and performers, featuring, among other greats, the Jackson Five and their bubblegum classics, but for Michael, the star-studded, two-hour special boiled down to the few minutes he'd have the

113

stage all to himself, performing 'Billie Jean'. At dress rehearsal the day before taping, with his brothers offstage, he still didn't know what he was going to do with the number. His excuse: 'I was so busy rehearsing the group.'

Truth be told, Michael had never performed the number before. Consequently, the night prior to the taping, he stood by himself in the kitchen of his home, listened to the song and let the music inspire the movements, following whatever came naturally. His office had purchased a spy's hat for the routine, and holding it in his hands, he posed and stepped, juked and slid, twirled and high-stepped and simply had fun doing what he loves most, until the choreography simply fell into place.

He knew only one thing: that during the extended break he was going to do a fragment of a street dance whose style was called 'body-popping'.

The next evening the brothers, now grown men rather than children, came out of their dressing room and huddled in the wings just like the old days, paying little attention to the swarm of stagehands rushing around them and the commotion beyond the curtain. 'We said a little prayer, put our hands together and said, "Let's do it,"' recalls Marlon. Then, like a basketball team moving in perfect synch, they sprinted onstage to thunderous applause as the announcer attempted to be heard over the rising din, 'Now, the original Jackson Five.'

Dressed in black, Michael spun whippetlike centre stage, his teeth clenched, his hips pumping. 'Come on everybody,' he shouted, 'clap your hands.' The crowd stood on its feet. They swayed to and fro when the group slid into 'I'll Be There' and Michael draped his arm around estranged brother Jermaine. 'It was a very emotional time for all of us,' claims Marlon. Nonetheless, after three songs, the brothers marched dutifully off the stage, leaving the youngest of the five, Michael, all by himself.

'You're beautiful,' he said to his brothers, who were already hidden from sight. 'I'd like to say those were the good old days.' As he spoke, Michael was a mix of emotion and self-assured showmanship, catching his breath, saying the words the audience wanted to hear, and manoeuvring himself into position for his solo number. 'Those were magic moments with all my brothers, including Jermaine. But what I really like . . .' – here, the opening blasts of 'Billie Jean' started – '. . . are the newer songs.'

With that, Michael launched himself into what one critic

called 'his greatest dance soliloquy', a 'struggle so prolonged, intense and obsessive that it suggests a man trying to purge himself of an evil spirit.' The audience was on its feet, screaming at this once-in-a-lifetime performance. Then, during the extended break, Michael took the crowd, and himself, a step higher when he 'Moonwalked' across the stage, a fanciful glide backwards while walking forward at the same time that caused people to look at their neighbour and ask, 'Did you see that?' The effect was dazzling.

It is little known that Michael did not invent what suddenly became his terpsichorean trademark. Jeffrey Daniel, a former member of the pop group Shalamar, arranged for Michael to learn the move in 1980. Daniel, who used to dance on *Soul Train* with R&B singing star Jody Watley, caught Michael's eye often enough that he taped several performances from the television, and later travelled to Disneyland where Shalamar were in concert. 'Michael stood in the wings, wearing funny glasses, a fake nose and moustache,' says Daniel.

'Then he got in touch and asked me to teach him the move,' says the dancer, who, because he was touring, instead sent an assistant named Casper to Jackson's Encino mansion, where he showed Michael how to do the Moonwalk. 'Only it was called the Backslide then,' says Daniel with an ironic chuckle.

Finding inspiration in the raw, untutored body-popping of urban street dancers, Daniel had picked up the now-celebrated move a year earlier from an obscure Long Beach-based dance group called Electric Boogaloo and used it in Shalamar's stage act. 'Originally, it was one part of a four-step move,' he says. 'But I separated it, then put the distance in it. I wanted the illusion of going forward on a backward escalator.'

Unfortunately, says Daniel, Michael, uncharacteristically, chose not to acknowledge the tutelage he received, not even with a thank you, and Daniel, who's since helped choreograph Jackson videos, wouldn't have minded the nod. 'He could've done a favour for me and Casper by acknowledging us,' says Daniel. 'That would've been more important than the money we got for working with him.'

Nevertheless, Michael finished his Motown performance to a standing ovation that catapulted his rising star into an even higher stratosphere. Offstage, his brothers lavished hug after hug on him. He knew that he'd pulled off a good show. True to form, though, Michael distanced himself from the adulation by concentrating only on how he had not been able to stay on his

115

toes long enough after a particularly difficult spin. That one slip, detectable to no one but him, tainted the entire performance for Michael.

He was happy, sure, perhaps even elated, that much Michael admits. But overriding all other emotions, hugs and standing ovations was an overwhelming sense of disappointment. In his own mind, Michael failed to achieve perfection, and, as always when that happened, it ruined the whole achievement. 'That's his thing, if he wants to be upset,' says Marlon. 'No one else could tell, I'm sure of that.'

That's for certain. Not one of the forty-seven million people who tuned in to Motown's anniversary party that night could tell. Nor could legendary master danceman Fred Astaire, who telephoned Michael the following day. 'You're a hell of a mover,' he said. 'Man, you really put them on their asses last night.' Astaire then mentioned that he had videotaped the show and issued another compliment. 'I watched the special last night, and I watched it again this morning. You're a hell of a mover.' Michael was truly touched.

From triumph to trouble. That's the rocky road Michael travelled immediately after his stunning performance on television. It wasn't by choice. And it wasn't discernible to anyone outside his inner circle of family and business associates. But on 12 March, about one month before taping the Motown special, the co-management contract Michael had with his father and DeMann-Weisner expired without fanfare. Michael allowed the situation to slide.

By choice, he waited before making a move, setting up a situation where DeMann and Weisner, his father Joseph, and others who wanted to guide his career, acted out their struggle for power in front of him. 'Michael's style has become one where he prefers people to come to him,' says Jermaine. 'He would rather watch people and see how they work than make a decision.'

As managers courted his favour, the twenty-five-year-old multimillionaire made a good move. He alligned himself with fast-track attorney John Branca, a cool, long-haired sharpie who'd earned a reputation as the most powerful legal eagle in the music business by representing a roster of true heavyweights, and a smart accountant named Marshall Gelfand. It appeared that Michael was locking his family out. 'Michael is secretive about his finances,' says Marlon. 'He is very private, and we [his family] are very often the last to know anything he does.'

After *Off the Wall* earned so much success, Michael decided to be furtive. His solo accomplishments only increased his desire to distance himself from his brothers, which worried those around him. In 1980, Joe sent a letter to DeMann and Weisner, expressing his concern that the managers were devoting too much time to Michael and not enough to the rest of the brothers. A copy went to the record company. Within his concern, Joe was also attempting to protect his own position, however slight Michael made that.

By the time the contract expired in March 1983, these silent worries had been simmering unresolved on the back burner for three years. Then, in June, the situation blew up in everyone's face. Joe Jackson, who no longer had a contract with Michael, or his sons, announced that DeMann and Weisner were finished. 'As far as I'm concerned it's over,' he said. 'They don't have a contract and my boys are not re-signing with them.'

Then he added insult to injury. 'There are a lot of leeches trying to break up the group,' he continued, referring to the upcoming Jacksons album slated for production after *Thriller* and Michael's lack of interest in rejoining his brothers. 'A lot of people are whispering in Michael's ear. But we know who they are. They're only in it for the money. I was there before it started and I'll be there after it ends.'

Joe painted himself as the architect of DeMann's and Weisner's involvement, which dated back to 1978, and, in coarse street parlance, indicted they were hired only, 'Because there was a time when I felt I needed white help in dealing with the corporate structure at CBS and thought they'd be able to help. But they never gave me the respect you expect from a business partner.'

Weisner wasted no time in responding to the elder Jackson's charges. 'That's Joe's personal point of view,' he said. 'There's no great love between us, and it's no big secret. I haven't talked to the man in six months. But we have no problem with Michael or the Jacksons. The problem seems to be with their father more than anybody.' Weisner claimed that Joe took no interest in dealing with Epic. 'He doesn't talk to anybody up there. He doesn't have any relationship, and from what I gather, he doesn't want to.'

DeMann countered Joe's seemingly racist comments with a

117

pointed barb of his own, reflecting the rampant behind-the-scenes dissension plaguing the once-united group. 'Joe made the deal with us, but since then we've worked directly with the group – with Michael and the Jacksons,' he said. 'He hasn't been involved in any of the major issues for the past five years. We don't have a good relationship with him, but I don't think he enjoys a good relationship with anyone whose skin is not black.'

Michael, meanwhile, was aghast at this public outburst, embarrassed by the racist intimations and sickened and humiliated by his father's outrageous sentiments. 'I don't know what would make him say something like that,' he said. All the hateful sentiments Michael harboured towards his father, which had lain dormant while he laboured on *Thriller*, suddenly resurfaced. 'To hear him talk like that turns my stomach. I don't know where he gets that from.'

Michael immediately issued a strong-willed statement distancing himself from his father and asserting his own independence in matters of career. 'I happen to be colourblind,' he wrote. 'I don't hire colour; I hire competence. The individual can be of any race or creed as long as I get the best. I am president of my organization and I have the final word on every decision. Racism is not my motto. One day I strongly expect every colour to love as one family.'

Meanwhile, as the imbroglio raged, Michael's attorney fielded upwards of fifteen inquiries from managers hoping to meet the singer whose album was securely situated atop the charts, having already spawned three gold singles. The calls were declined. 'He just wants to concentrate on the album and think about other opportunities,' said one of Jackson's associates. 'Michael knows exactly what he wants. He's calling the shots.' Yes, but even Michael admitted he was inundated by the task. 'There are so many things I've got to make decisions on,' he said. 'There's so much going on.'

There was, and not all of it was pleasant. First, the dirty work. On 22 June, DeMann and Weisner received a letter by messenger from Michael and his attorney, Branca, informing them that they were no longer to function as Michael Jackson's representatives. With that final volley, it appeared Joe had finally won the heated struggle for his son. Weisner, who had spoken to Michael earlier that day, was shocked. 'Everything seemed fine,' he said. But Michael had made his decision, if not to hire new management, to at least get rid of the old team. 'There was a lot of pressure on Michael,' said Branca, referring to Joe's background lobbying.

However, Michael didn't rush out and hire new management just because he fired the old team. Instead, he returned his obsessive attention to business, seeking consultation and companionship from a man in whom he was placing more and more trust: Frank Dileo. The good-humoured, crafty promotions executive was delivering the kind of results that Michael liked as single followed single up the charts. 'Wanna Be Startin' Somethin'', released in May, went top five; 'Human Nature', out in August, climbed into the top ten; 'P.Y.T.', issued in October, also flew up the flagpole. 'The kid was hot, and we were working our butts off for him,' says Dileo.

Oh, was Michael hot. His temperature? Well, he was hot enough for the press to call the public's mounting fascination with him Michaelmania. Hot enough for people to copy the white socks he wore dancing to 'Beat It'. Hot enough to have sold more than eight million albums. Hot enough for people to finally notice the single white glove he'd been wearing on his hand since 1979. A fad was born. Suddenly, in fact, superstar was an inadequate way to describe Michael. Now, he was the Great Gloved One, ascending even further into the stratosphere of stardom, thanks partially to some twelve-hundred rhinestones of Austrian crystal each individually sewn on to cotton fabric, and then slipped over his fingers, turning Michael's hand into a magic wand. 'It makes me feel never offstage,' he says.

In late October Dileo flew out to Los Angeles to talk Michael into making one more video. 'I told him we'd like to have him do something with "Thriller", which was going to be the next single,' says Dileo. Michael hemmed and hawed, not really enthusiastic about the additional work, what with all the distractions in his family. 'But you're right,' he told Dileo. 'That's the only song that can be done.' The promo man, who has a knack for simplifying the most complicated matters with a shrug, gave him a dose of encouragement. 'Look,' he said, 'all you have to do is get the director from *Psycho II*, make a real scary dance in it, and everything will be fine.'

Michael agreed. However, when that particular director wasn't available, the Gloved One hired John Landis, one of Hollywood's much-heralded young turks, who had made *An American Werewolf in London*, a movie Michael had enjoyed though it suffered at the box office. The video followed pretty much the same story as Landis' movie: boy turns into werewolf and ruins outside relationships. It was also a thinly disguised version of Michael's own life.

Since the record company's budget for this video wasn't nearly enough to cover the extravagant costs of what Michael planned, the singer dipped into his own deep coffers and financed the fourteen-minute horror flick himself. However, when the costs soared, Michael's attorney came up with a brilliant idea: sell the rights for a documentary video on the making of the 'Thriller' video, which they did, and eventually *The Making of 'Thriller'* became a bestselling videocassette on its own. Well before this happened, though, Dileo got word of the budget overruns, grew alarmed at what Michael might be up to left alone on the West Coast, and flew out.

Dileo checked into a bungalow at the Beverly Hills Hotel, where Michael met him the following afternoon. They exchanged information; Michael talking about the film, the record executive updating Jackson's sales figures. 'Then, out of the clear blue,' says Dileo, 'he said, "Did you ever think about managing me?"' The normally loquacious Dileo was taken aback. 'No,' he sputtered. 'My goal is not to be a manager but to be president of CBS records.'

'But do you think you'd ever want to manage me?' Michael persisted.

They made an odd pair. While Michael grew up in the protective confines of a large family, Dileo was forced to fend for himself at sixteen when his father died suddenly on the operating table without any medical insurance. Never mind his big-headed dreams of entering politics and maybe, one day, becoming mayor of his hometown, Pittsburgh. Instead, he landed a job busing tables and working the kitchen in a restaurant. 'An Italian joint,' he laughs.

One night, when a guy came in the kitchen and asked if anyone wanted to get in the record business, Dileo jumped at the offer. He took a job at Columbia records. In a short time, he went from selling albums to promotions. 'That's where the pizzazz was,' he says. 'It was showbusiness, expense accounts, hang out with artists, stay out all night. It was like a job made for me.' At twenty-one, he became national director of promotions for RCA. 'I was so young American Express wouldn't give me a card,' he laughs. 'Now I have four.'

Dileo ricocheted through the industry, learning all facets

of the business, rising in responsibility as he changed jobs. However, in 1977, at the height of the disco craze, he grew disillusioned with the record industry. 'The business became infested with people who looked great but knew nothing,' he snarls. 'I didn't work all my life to hang out with assholes.' So he quit. Just like that. He took two years off, went back to Pittsburgh, got married, and had the first of two children.

'Then the worst disaster of my life occurred,' he intones. While attending the funeral of his wife's grandmother, Dileo's house burned down. Underinsured, he and his family lost everything – clothes, cash, belongings – and found themselves closer to broke than they'd ever dreamed. 'I told my wife we'd never be in this position again,' he says. Within days, he sold his Cadillac for $2,000, bought two blue suits, three white shirts and a one-way plane ticket to New York. He lucked into an opening at Epic, worked longer and harder than anyone else, going so far as to have limo drivers wait in the driveway while he snagged three hours sleep at his Connecticut home, and ended up a vice president.

Dileo, whose nickname since childhood has been Tookie (Uncle Tookie to most Jackson intimates), relished the payoffs of hard work. He spoiled himself in luxuries. Shortly before Michael popped the big question, he set himself a new challenge. After all, he'd ushered four singles from *Thriller* into the top five as well as launched a dozen new acts. 'Hey,' he thought, 'why not get an audience with the Pope?' Four months of string-pulling later, he was face-to-face with John Paul II at the Vatican.

Michael was merely exercising his acute shrewdness when he asked Dileo to manage him. The cigar-smoking, steak-eating, chocolate-loving, wine-drinking, late night-partying, incessantly-talking, squat Italian family man was just the complimentary companion the skinny, reclusive vegetarian needed. The more Michael drifted away from reality, the more he needed Dileo for ballast. They were opposites made for each other. Over lunch, Michael smiled when Dileo said, 'I'm very honoured and flattered you'd ask me to manage you. But I think we might be caught up in all the excitement and success we're having.'

Dileo himself was having a difficult time containing himself. 'Rather than do something spontaneous, let's think about it a few days. I'll think about it. You rethink it. Call me back on Friday. And if you don't want to, there's no hard feelings because I was never looking to be a manager any-way.'

'Okay,' said Michael, on his way out the door.

Alone in his hotel room, Dileo was, to put it mildly, excited. 'But I didn't know who to tell,' he laughs. He phoned his wife; she was excited, too. 'Then I said, "God, who do I tell after my wife?"' No one. Not a soul. 'Because then, I thought, "Maybe it's not true. Maybe Mike's just being a nice guy who wants me to work his records."' Then Friday rolled around, the day Michael was to call back. 'A little before midnight, I got this call and it was Mike. He said, "I thought about it, and I want you to do it." I said, "Okay."'

Eight months passed before their negotiations, which were as near as a superpower summit, were settled in March. Dileo couldn't believe how tough a businessman Michael was. 'He demanded I work with him exclusively the first part of the contract,' says Dileo. 'He knew the tour [the Victory tour] and a movie were coming up. He had the contract written so the guaranteed part was enough to interest me, and the incentive part was enough to keep me motivated.'

11

Encino, California. September 1983.

Cloaked in secrecy, the meeting took place in the high-ceilinged living room of the large Tudor mansion. It was unlike most big-time Hollywood deal sessions, where hot air and bluster feed off greed and self-promotion. This was a family matter. There were no agents, managers or promoters present. No accountant or attorneys to pacify. That route had been tried and tested to no avail.

Unlike the many other family meetings dotting the calendar over the previous few months, there were no brothers around this time to consult with. That hand had also been played, with similarly poor results. In what amounted to an emotional, last-ditch plea to their most famous son, Joe and Katherine Jackson demanded, and got, a face-to-face confrontation with Michael.

They felt the time had come for their most famous son to discover the honest facts of financial life.

His brothers were hurting for money.

His father was hurting for money.

The whole family was hurting for money.

Michael, on the other hand, was worth tens of millions of dollars, and the through-the-roof success of *Thriller* was taking his stock higher than anyone imagined. In two months, purchases of the LP would pass the ten million mark, making it the bestselling release in CBS history. With Christmas still ahead, there was no sign of a slow down. In addition, the album's sensational title cut and accompanying fourteen-minute video, laden with special effects were still in the ammo bin.

The family's salvation, according to Joe, was a Jacksons world tour. A tour that would be bigger than any ever launched before. A tour that would capitalize on Michael's phenomenal popularity by circling the globe and playing to every paying customer in the world. 'It was time,' says Joe. 'The timing for

123

that kind of extravaganza was perfect. Millions of dollars were waiting for us.'

There was just one problem: Michael wanted no part of the action.

This wasn't the first time the issue had been raised. As far back as April Joe began meeting with prospective promoters, testing the market value of a tour. His initial go-round included half a dozen people. 'But the best offers coming in were for $200,000,' says Joe. 'That was too little. I just couldn't let it happen for that amount.'

That's when Joe phoned up flamboyant boxing promoter and ex-convict Don King, who flew out to L.A. for a meeting with the brothers. They weren't impressed. A second meeting was arranged and this time King fared better. 'There's no one better at selling "black" than King,' says a friend of Michael's. 'That's exactly what Joe wanted to hear, too.' More important, Papa Joe's eyes lit up over the sum of money King offered: $3 million. Each brother was guaranteed $500,000.

'Don King was also the only one to offer my parents money, too,' says Marlon.

Still, up until September, Michael continued as the Jacksons' lone holdout. Then his parents, who were roughly six months into a reconciliation, confronted him. 'They'd asked him before many times,' says a close adviser of Michael's. 'Finally, though, his mother and father got him alone and simply pleaded with Michael. His mother broke down and cried. She told him that the brothers were broke, or close to it, and they all needed the money from this tour. Basically, they applied the guilt so thick he couldn't resist them.'

Michael caved in to his parents' wishes, a not-so-subtle reversion to a long-established pattern of burying his pride and independence for the family's benefit. Almost immediately, a contract was signed with King. But it was obvious the Jacksons' main drawing card was no fan of the wild-haired, fast-talking promoter. 'Don King was not Michael's first choice to promote the tour,' admitted his attorney, John Branca, whose on-the-record comments were an obvious clue to the rancorous backstage politics. Branca also then alluded to the pressure put on his client, saying, 'This tour is important to Michael because it's important to Michael's family. I'm not sure the tour was Michael's first choice. He might've preferred to do other things. But he found it important to tour at his brothers' request and his family's request.'

124

Michael put his plans temporarily aside, but his father's manipulative reappearance in his life and career was an unpleasant intrusion. Without Michael's consent, Joe and King made a multimillion-dollar deal for the Jacksons to film a commercial for Pepsi, a product the health food devotee neither drank nor liked. But the soft drink company was sponsoring the Jacksons' tour, giving Michael little leverage. Joe also concocted a deal with a Hollywood producer for a movie based on 'Beat It', which would also star Michael. But the superstar didn't know about his father's manoeuvrings and eventually came to disown anything to do with the project.

As a result, Michael, magnanimously playing the role of the beneficent, good son, once again erected a barrier between himself and Joe, which left the single-minded patriarch confused. 'I don't know what he had against making money,' shrugs his father. 'You can always need money. You never get to a point, I don't care how much money you have, where you don't need more. And at that time everybody in the family, except Michael, needed it.'

Family dynamics being what they were, Michael wasn't too aware of his brothers' situation. 'After *Thriller* came out, we saw him less and less,' says Marlon.

The last thing Michael needed was a tour with his less-talented brothers The start of December was marked by the double release of 'Thriller', the single, and *Thriller*, the video. The result was unanticipated. Millions more people went out and purchased the album, and 'Thriller' became the LP's fifth top five and seventh top ten single, setting new industry standards.

However, the flipside of the upsurge surrounding him was the Jehovah's Witnesses' troubling reaction to it all. Michael's earnest belief in God and the Bible was clearly stated. 'I believe in the Bible and I try to follow the Bible,' he explained. Still, he found himself far from the saint he needed to be in order to survive the oncoming apocalypse that Witnesses believed only Witnesses would survive. 'I know I'm an imperfect person . . . I'm not making myself out to be an angel.'

Nor was he all that bad, either. However, Michael's public comment was an obvious attempt at sending a message to the Witness elders, who were soundly criticizing him for attracting attention to himself. Whether he meant to or not didn't matter. His success resonated like a virus throughout the Encino Kingdom Hall he attended three times a week. Michael was no longer another worshipper. He was no longer a kindred soul who could innocuously perform the humble field ministry of the Lord. His fame drew inordinate attention. Among the angry church preachings directed towards him was a particular warning against the sin of pride.

Raised on the stern constraints of the Witness, including prohibitions on premarital sex, homosexuality and too much interaction with the secular world, Michael fought a constant battle against the influences of the world in which he laboured. Despite his phantomlike existence, his work regularly brought him into contact with all kinds of people, shady characters, drugs and glamorous ladies, situations that make one worldly but that he chose instead to close his eyes to. 'Michael has always fought to protect his innocence,' says Jones.

Perhaps this is one way to explain some of his reclusive behaviour. But it was a battle, and Michael rebelled the only way he knew how. In his music. The ruminations slipped out subconsciously, unintentionally and they gave a hint of the fervid undercurrents of thought swirling beneath the surface of his consciousness. Lyrically, *Thriller* touched many of the Witnesses' taboo subjects, including out-of-wedlock sex, vampires, gangs, unwed mothers, fame.

The *Thriller* video, with its symbolic allusions to sex and horror (which the Witnesses interpreted as satanic), proved controversial enough to bring the clash between church elders and Michael to a head. There were meetings conducted at which Michael was present. There were discussions about the state of his soul. By the end of December, the Jehovah's Witnesses' headquarters in New York released a statement condemning the work. On the West Coast, there were more meetings with Michael. 'Shortly after one of those meetings,' reported *Spin* magazine, the Gloved One 'issued his own statement repudiating' the widely popular video, 'promising never to present such images and ideas again. The public embarrassment left him shaken.'

A little after six p.m. The cavernous Shrine Auditorium was cold, the crisp January air tinged with the faint burning smell of high-powered lights, the residual spent explosives and the silent pinings of an overworked crew waiting to go home. Thousands of people were sitting in stands, simulating a live concert audience, and an army of technicians milled about the floor. The director was between takes. The brothers, oblivious

126

to the buzz from out front, talked backstage. 'I don't remember what, just talk,' says Marlon.

A moment later, it was time for another take. The action was winding down, finally. This particular scene, the razzle-dazzle opening sequence – Michael's flashy descent down a staircase to the accompaniment of 'Billie Jean' – was one of the last remaining scenes scheduled during the four jam-packed days the Jacksons spent filming a top-secret Pepsi commercial. The multimillion dollar ad was scheduled to debut on the Grammy Award telecast in February. Video whiz Bob Giraldi was the director.

The first sign of something gone drastically wrong was the large explosion that rattled that stage like an angry thunderclap. Amid a swirl of acrid white smoke there followed immediately a sudden incandescent burst of flame. That, too, was followed by a shrill scream, and then the sight of Michael grabbing the back of his head, pained and surprised. There was panic. Confusion. Some people on the set thought the superstar had been shot. He hadn't been. But the truth was only slightly less traumatic: his head was on fire.

He was dancing down a flight of steps. 'Billie Jean' thrumped in the background. Pyrotechnical airbursts discharged all around him. 'During rehearsal,' recalls Marlon, 'I saw what he was supposed to do and said to myself, "Those flashpots – airbursts – seem pretty low." But being a high-budget commercial, with lots of professional people working it, I didn't even raise the question.'

The first to reach the panic-stricken superstar was Miko Brando, Marlon's brawny son and Michael's close friend and security aide. 'I tore out, hugged him, tackled him and ran my hands through his hair,' said Brando, who scorched his own fingers performing the valiant effort. The fire was extinguished in seconds as commotion immediately gave way to chaos. 'Everything just stopped,' says Marlon. 'My brother Tito was right there with Michael.' So was a nimble-minded fan who wrapped a handful of ice in a borrowed T-shirt, making a compress that was applied to the injury. Paramedics arrived moments later, placed Michael on a stretcher, and then sped him to the emergency room at Cedars-Sinai Medical Center.

This wasn't the first serious tragedy to hit the Jacksons. In 1980, Randy, the youngest brother, who enjoys the L.A. night life, wrapped his sports car around a telephone pole in a nearly-fatal high-speed crash. Katherine Jackson received a

127

telephone call from the hospital at two in the morning. 'We all went out to St Joseph's Hospital in Burbank,' says Marlon. 'It was a rainy night. When we got there I remember lifting up the covers and seeing both his legs split open, with blood everywhere. It was as if you had taken a knife and opened up your legs. But he didn't feel anything because they had him doped up. He was just sitting there, talking.' Though doctors considered the possibility of amputating both his legs, Randy eventually regained full use of his legs after a painful, two-year period of recovery. 'That was more of a shock than Michael's accident.'

On the way to the hospital, Michael clung to the only security he knew. Fairly alert but shaken, he told the ambulance attendants to keep his jewel-encrusted glove on. He was determined to lose neither his consciousness nor his trademark. Doctors worked quickly. His vital signs were stable. The palm-sized wound on top of his head, diagnosed as a second-degree burn, was initially treated with antiseptic cream. At first, Michael refused a pain-killer, since he avoided narcotics, but he later accepted an analgesic. 'It was quite a shock for Michael, and when I got there he was in a daze,' said his personal physician and plastic surgeon, Dr Steven Hoefflin, who rushed to the hospital. 'After I examined him and told him he would be fine, he felt a lot better.'

About two hours after the accident Michael, accompanied by his parents, his brother Randy, two bodyguards and his doctor, was transferred to the Burn Center of the Brotman Medical Center in Culver City. He settled into a private room, but was suffering the disorienting effects of mild shock. Recalls nurse Kathy McGrath, 'He was still pretty shaken up and cold, so we put about five blankets on him.'

Several hours later Michael felt possessed of renewed strength and clarity and appeared to be on the road to his old self again. He asked his nurse for a videotape player. Since it was already late at night, staffers broke into a padlocked cabinet to get the machine and found a cache of videotapes for their famous patient to watch. He chose *Close Encounters of the Third Kind*, a film by his pal, director Steven Spielberg. When the movie ended around one a.m., Michael swallowed a sleeping pill and put an end to a long, nerveracking day.

Upon awakening the following morning, Michael, feeling stronger and more composed, sipped a lightweight breakfast of fruit juice. He was overjoyed when presented with an

128

assortment of the hundreds of messages that had flooded the hospital, including get-well calls from Diana Ross and Liza Minnelli, and by the time of his doctor's afternoon check-up, Michael was sitting in bed, bopping to *American Bandstand*.

This wasn't the superstar's first time in the Brotman Burn Center. The previous month Michael had visited a 23-year-old mechanic who had incurred third-degree burns over ninety-five percent of his body. By coincidence, the young mechanic was in the adjoining room when Michael checked-in, having recently undergone his fourteenth operation. He had also been in regular contact with another patient treated by Hoefflin, Bessie Henderson, a 41-year-old seamstress who was grappling with depression. 'When Michael started calling,' reported her doctor, 'she turned around and now she is doing a lot better.'

Convinced long ago that his life had been touched by a unique, God-given power, Michael didn't have to be persuaded to visit the other patients on the floor. With the back of his head covered by a gauzy, netlike cap, Michael slipped into black trousers and white socks, leaving his hospital jersey on. Walking down the drab, antiseptic-scented corridors, you couldn't help but notice that his right hand was sheathed in his sequined glove. The effect was obvious. Though a patient himself, he wanted to make it clear that he was not like the others. After all, he was Michael Jackson.

He shone while making rounds, smiling, posing for pictures, and exchanging small talk, looking remarkably comfortable in his role as soother of the less fortunate. As if anointed with magic, the superstar reached out and touched each bedridden patient with his glove, bringing immense joy to each person he met, similar to the display of magic he affects in his music videos when everything he touches is suddenly recharged with a luminous glow of life.

Only one out of the six patients he visited couldn't believe Michael was actually beside his bed, prompting the understanding superstar to make a return visit to prove he wasn't just a figment of someone else's imagination. Another patient then did exactly what hundreds of reporters wished they could do: he asked Michael why he wore the single white glove. 'This way,' he answered, 'I am never offstage.'

Michael's unexpected brush with catastrophe, his first close encounter with mortality, became a cornerstone of his consciousness. He sensed that his life was moving at a pace too

129

rapid for him to control, and it appeared that the top speed had not yet been reached. His frightening accident was a warning signal. The result was a series of shockwaves whose reverberations were felt for years. Almost at once, definite patterns in his behaviour began to emerge where before Michael's forays were tentative steps in unexplored territory.

Domination of every unexpected possibility was the new objective. A tightly-knit organization, whose first lieutenants were manager Dileo and attorney Branca, formed around the superstar, and it would soon become apparent that the once-obedient child had been transformed into a bold decision maker. As awareness of his worth increased along with his bank account, the shroud of secrecy surrounding his movements became increasingly harder to penetrate. More than before, he exerted his power and influence in matters concerning him. Most of all, his mania for absolute control reached new heights.

None of this was outwardly apparent the following week at the American Museum of Natural History in New York, where Michael's record label threw a star-studded megabash celebrating the record-breaking success of *Thriller*. By this time, the freakish accident, in perfect synch with the smash album's ghoulish themes, seemed like one more incredible, gasp-inducing frolic dreamed up to enhance the superstar's mystique. Invitations, the hottest ducat in Manhattan, were delivered on single white gloves. And that evening, as the limos idled in single-file procession, hundreds of zealous fans clustered outside the monumental building in the snowy cold, hoping to catch a glimpse of the Gloved One.

Amid the frantic swirl of gay activity Michael generously ventured outside twice, standing on the granite balustrade encircled by a covey of police and bodyguards, a spindly twig in a thick forest of flesh, obliging his freezing admirers with friendly waves. Inside, surrounded by dinosaurs and beasts that looked downright terrifying, the doe-eyed guest of honour kept dutifully to his own small circle of intimates. He graciously observed the gala proceedings with less than his customary aloofness, smiling what appeared to be a genuine smile. Dancers caught his eye and the festive revelry didn't pass unnoticed. But he was unapproachable in his sequinned outfit and dark, impenetrable shades.

The evening's highlight, at least for Michael, came packaged in the form of a lavish coronation when Norris McWhirter, the stately, grey-haired creator of the *Guinness Book of World*

130

Records, who had one month earlier been forced to holler, 'Stop the presses!' on their latest paperback edition, crowned Michael with honour after honour, including the most top ten singles from one album. Of course, the most significant accolade bestowed upon Michael was the one he cherished most: McWhirter's recognition of *Thriller* as the bestselling album in music history.

Michael's thin-lipped grin was hard pressed to contain the enthusiasm and delight bubbling inside him. He had mentioned this moment to Quincy Jones at least two years earlier and been derided for setting such an outrageous goal. He had dreamed about having the biggest selling LP in 1980 after *Off the Wall* failed to win as many awards as he felt it deserved. And now, here it was, materialized. This, Michael felt, would show everyone. Here was irrefutable evidence of his talent. 'He was very happy,' says Dileo. 'He had proved his point.'

Perhaps. But there were a few exclamation marks to add. Several days later, Michael cleaned up at the American Music Awards, raking in a record seven trophies. 'A gratifying number,' is the way he describes that honour. In February, just a few weeks after his sweep, Michael triumphed yet again, this time at the prestigious Grammy Awards ceremony, where he collected a record eight trophies.

Seen by tens of millions on national television, Michael, dressed in a showy, sequinned jacket with epaulettes and a sash, and his lone white glove, barely uttered more than a whispery thank you each time he took to the podium. He hid behind his sunglasses, playing his shyness to the hilt. Perhaps that was just Michael's concession to the Witness elders who might have been monitoring the broadcast. Or perhaps it was a rather crafty publicity ploy designed to enhance the image of someone who knew he had nothing further to say after thanking the Almighty. Ironically, the television audience was utterly captivated by his strangely humble and evasive behaviour.

Privately, though, Michael was trembling with a hard-to-contain sense of joy. Eight Grammys. Though he posed as the picture of icy coolness in his front row seat, framed on one side by Quincy Jones and on the other by date Brooke Shields, Michael relished the goose flesh-raising curves of one stunning victory after another as he might a Disneyland rollercoaster, relishing every second he received a Grammy on TV in front of millions of witnesses. Rather than openly delight in the moment, though, he embraced the intoxicating feeling of recompense for the Academy's earlier slight to *Off the Wall* like a selfish child, locking the giddiness inside himself.

'I spoke to him later that evening,' says Marlon, 'and he was really very happy. He'd gotten everything he wanted. I don't know why he didn't say more on television. He felt he's too shy, I guess. But he didn't say a whole lot to his family, either.'

The rumour mills churned out speculation over Michael's relationship with his Grammy date, Brooke Shields, the former child model who'd grown up in the glare of spotlights and television cameras and matured into a tall, intelligent young woman who later graduated from Princeton University. Michael's latest love interest was the word; Tatum O'Neal's replacement. The truth, however, is that Brooke was nothing more than a friend, and far from choosing her as his date, Michael had indulged her forthright request to attend the glitzy event on his arm, which was certain to earn her a nice bit of publicity.

'Brooke was just a friend of Michael's, not a real girlfriend,' says LaToya knowingly. 'She wanted Michael to be the one chasing her, but that's not the way it was.'

Not at all. 'A little before the Grammys, Brooke was over visiting Michael at the house,' she explains. On her way out, Brooke brazenly asked her friend to take her to the awards. 'Michael didn't really want to, but he didn't know what to say,' says LaToya. 'Me and Janet were both there, sitting in another room, and he kept coming back, asking us what to say. "Tell her no, if you don't want to," I told Michael. But he couldn't. Michael was scared he'd hurt her feelings. And Brooke just kept asking. Finally, Michael just laughed it off and said, "Well, okay."'

Michael was pissed off. The scene was a jam-packed press conference at Tavern on the Green, the ornate Central Park restaurant in New York, where Don King, the boxing impresario, publicly announced that he was promoting the Jacksons' upcoming tour, which the hypemaster promised would be the biggest and richest rock and roll show in history. With each syllable the P.T. Barnum-like orator issued, the smell of money lingered in the air like bad breath.

Before rows of jostling reporters, the ever-smiling King flooded the room with a tidal wave of self-congratulating hyperbole, finishing his monologue with a fifteen-minute promotional film on – what else – himself. The Jackson brothers sat directly behind him, their eyes, mirrored by dark sunglasses, fixed unflinchingly straight ahead. Though silent, their sullen, grim-faced dispositions revealed their opinion of the promoter's grandiose manner of handling this question and answer session.

Michael was never in favour of hiring King and his displeasure with the circus-like event rose to new heights when the motor-mouthed promoter gave in to reporters' repeated calls for comments from Michael and handed the microphone to the reticent superstar. 'I don't really have anything to say,' Michael mumbled coolly, while inside he was fuming.

At this same time, King was the recipient of a letter written by the Jacksons' star attraction, which bristled with anger. Couched in measured, businesslike formality, it delineated specific guidelines for the way King was to conduct himself. A) He wasn't to make any comments concerning Michael Jackson without prior permission; B) Michael's own representatives, and not King, would collect whatever share of money was due him from the tour; C) He could not initiate any business deals concerning Michael; and D) the free-wheeling King 'was not to hire any personnel, any local promoters, book any halls or, for that matter, do *anything* without Michael Jackson's personal approval.'

The whole tour gnawed at Michael like a bothersome sore. What could be more disastrous to a control freak than losing control?

The distance Michael put between himself and his brothers was more than just a play for power. More than the simple brooding of an unhappy sibling. Michael appeared to be the picture of confidence, but inwardly he was floundering, feeling out of control and panic-stricken. No matter how detailed his plans, he couldn't get a firm grasp on his life, which seemed to be on autopilot. Too much had happened lately: *Thriller*'s out-of-this-world success; being manipulated into participating in the tour with his brothers; Don King wresting control of the action; then the accident; the Grammys; the rush of money streaming into his bank account. Not to mention that he was grappling with his age-old fear of losing his hard-won achievements to yesterday's news, of having to master every situation, terrified that any single mistake might let the air out of his high-flying balloon.

To quash the roiling stress and worry dominating his thoughts, Michael desperately needed to assert himself and regain control – plainly, forcefully and without any outside interference he couldn't forecast. It was a tall order. Yet in early spring 1984 Michael did exactly that, and he did it in the only way he felt completely certain of attaining results. He arranged for Dr Steven Hoefflin, his plastic surgeon, to use his skill with the scalpel a second time on his nose.

When the bandages were removed a week later, Michael looked in the mirror and the man he saw wasn't the same person he had seen a few days earlier. No, this recast version of Michael Jackson now had a smaller nose than before. A nose with pinched sides, smaller nostrils and a slight upturn. A pug nose. He looked in the mirror and saw features that were darn near fashion-model perfect. Beautiful, in fact. He looked again at his reflection. He smiled and, at least for the most, felt better about himself.

12

North Hollywood. May 1984.

Wearing faded blue jeans and a red sequinned jacket, Michael strolled into the large rehearsal studio, a lone, meek figure standing tall and regal and surprisingly relaxed. Without the usual entourage or any formal announcement, his entry was startling for its subdued informality. After all, Michael was the world's biggest, most reclusive star. Yet here he was. In person. Suddenly, an electricity crackled throughout the dark-walled room.

As Michael strode into the cold hall for his first full day of rehearsals, white socks visible above his polished black shoes, which clicked slightly on the hard, uncarpeted floor, he smiled an easy grin and shook the hands of familiar individuals, ignoring the stares that even seasoned technicians had difficulty concealing. Then in one sharp, athletic movement, he jumped up on the three-foot-high stage and greeted the members of the Jacksons' tour band.

Rehearsals, minus main attraction Michael, had started several weeks earlier in the same studio when Tito addressed the assembled musicians, whose casual jamming had naturally drifted into the all-too-familiar get-up-and-dance chords of 'Billie Jean'. 'We start at seven,' he intoned. 'That means seven. You're not expected to come in carrying your instruments at seven and be ready to play fifteen minutes later.'

Later, Nelson Hays, the Jacksons' road manager, laid down the rules of conduct. 'I've been under contract with the Jacksons since 1981,' he said. 'They don't like drugs. Do anything like that on this tour and you probably won't be with us by the time the tour is over.'

Naturally, everyone wanted to know where the star was. But Michael's absence was shrouded in secrecy. Only a handful of people knew that he was back in the hospital, undergoing minor surgery at Brotman Medical Center to replace scar tissue on top of his head, which would promote hair growth. The operation, on 18 April, wasn't necessary. But Michael wanted to repair the small bald spots that remained after his accident. He'd been wearing a tiny hair piece and was self-conscious about it.

Checking in the night before, after sneaking in a back entrance, he ate a vegetarian dinner and then visited acquaintances in the burn unit where he'd been treated two and a half months earlier. The following morning he was wheeled into the operating room. The procedure, minor, relatively painless but sophisticated, lasted eighty minutes, and Dr Steven Hoefflin predicted a three-week period of recovery for his patient.

Interestingly, Dr Hoefflin noticed that Michael had grown increasingly fascinated with medicine between hospital visits. He said Michael had read several medical books. He was curious about everything, insatiably so, inquiring about how certain operations were performed, asking questions about strange and rare diseases and investigating the different floors in the hospital. He spent hours in the burn ward, playing checkers with one patient, chatting with another, and later, Hoefflin arranged for Michael to visit the maternity floor at Santa Monica Hospital.

Meanwhile, because Michael's top-secret surgery slipped by the media, attention went to the rehearsals. That was real news, anyway. It was a positive sign. For months stories of heated backstage bickering among the brothers and their lawyers, agents and assorted hangers-on had circulated. Many predicted the tour would never get off the ground. But with the brothers' latest album, *Victory*, completed and scheduled for a June release, it appeared that this much-ballyhooed extravaganza might actually take off.

But taking the tour on the road wasn't as simple as showing up for rehearsals on time. Aside from several niggling, multimillion dollar problems, one glitch overrode everything else. 'Michael didn't want to do the tour,' says Marlon. 'He wasn't happy about it. Not from the word go. Even after rehearsals started, Michael was still making demands and arguing about various details, threatening not to participate at all unless he got his way. Before the Victory Tour, which was a great tour, got underway, it was already the most painful tour we'd ever done.'

Just naming the darn thing pitted family members against

each other. Michael, underscoring his unspoken but obvious intention to cut musical ties to his siblings, wanted to call the tour 'the Final Curtain'. 'But none of the other brothers liked that,' says Marlon. 'Our parents didn't like that either. Michael was making it sound like a funeral, like someone had died. But we weren't dying.' The brothers felt that calling it the Victory Tour, the same as their forthcoming LP, better reflected the sentiment behind the tour. 'It was a victory just naming the tour that,' laughs Marlon. 'That was the only time I recall Michael losing an argument.'

Michael remembers it quite differently. 'When it came down to the actual tour,' he claims, 'I was out-voted on a number of issues.' In the short run it didn't matter, since Michael's long-term objective was to get this thing over with as quickly as possible. 'It was the wrong thing for him to do,' says an insider. 'Make that the worst thing for him to do.'

However, for the brothers, the Victory Tour was a gold mine that would rejuvenate their struggling careers as well as their pocketbooks, and give them a chance to share in the spotlight Michael had recently had for himself. 'Michael's had very big success, and sometimes the success of the Jacksons has been undermined,' said Tito with diplomatic restraint. 'I think the tour is a chance for us to show our success, too. It's not going to be the Michael Jackson show. It's going to be a Jacksons show.'

Onstage, maybe that would be true. Behind the scenes, though, Michael was not shy about flexing his considerable muscle to sway opinion to his side. 'On lighting, on design, on choreography, he always got his way,' says Marlon.

Everyone knew that without Michael, there was no tour, and he fought against the whole thing from the start. His fame was astronomical. A writer for *Rolling Stone* figured that if sales of some of the year's biggest albums in the U.S. were added up, all the copies of David Bowie's *Let's Dance*, the Police's *Synchronicity*, the Rolling Stones' *Undercover*, Culture Club's *Colour by Numbers*, Quiet Riot's *Metal Health*, and Duran Duran's *Seven and the Ragged Tiger*, and then that figure was doubled, that was roughly how many albums Michael had sold in America alone. Twenty-five million copies. More than one million copies of *Thriller* sold in the five days following his sweep at the American Music Awards. Another 700,000 sold in Los Angeles alone the week after his accident.

Michael didn't need the $500,000 that each brother was initially guaranteed for the tour. Individual success had Michael enjoying the highest royalty rate in the music business. He received roughly $2.10 for every album sold in the U.S. Multiply that by sales and the gross on *Thriller's* U.S. sales alone works out to be nearly $32 million. Add in another $15 million for worldwide sales. And this still doesn't include his millions in publishing residuals from the four songs he wrote on *Thriller*!

In other words, Michael could afford to play hard ball and his brothers couldn't. 'We were all proud of what Michael was doing,' says his father, the instigator of the Victory Tour. 'But Michael's money didn't matter to anybody but Michael, and he was always very secretive about that. More important, the brothers needed the money to enhance their situation. Like any other group, they needed to tour.' At stake was a tantalizing figure that had ballooned to $100 million, and everyone wanted a slice of that juicy pie.

However, in the several months following Don King's announcement, the reality of such a complicated, expensive, over-burdened tour ever coming off seemed more and more like a figment of the boxing czar's florid imagination. Forget, at least for the moment, that Michael first told his family that he flat out didn't want to do the tour. A nightmarish guilt trip took care of that. And don't pay any notice to his disenchantment with King, who had no experience promoting a musical event. He let the promise of much-needed millions for his mom and dad temporarily mollify his fears. Maybe they would quit asking him for loans.

No, the real problems had more to do with the number of people who wanted in on the action. Promoters came and went as quickly as they could ante up the $10 million good faith money, a fraction of the $40 million that potential promoters had to guarantee the Jacksons. There were all sorts of rumours about who was promoting the tour, with names ranging from entertainment mogul Jerry Weintraub to Elvis Presley's old manager, Colonel Tom Parker. Veteran New England promoter Frank Russo eventually emerged as the man, announcing that he had won the coveted honour. 'All the brothers were hugging me,' he said. 'They started popping champagne. I couldn't believe it was really happening.'

It wasn't. Three weeks later he was booted out. Far from celebrating, Russo was talking multimillion dollar lawsuits against the Jacksons and King. Why the sudden change of heart? 'That's when Michael and his people began making various demands and trying to take control.' says Marlon.

138

In the midst of this fracas, pressure from Michael got King demoted. King blamed Michael's lawyer and manager for the move. 'They fed him all kinds of lines about how I was going to build something from my relationship with him and he wouldn't be part of it,' said King. 'And he swallowed it.' What it boiled down to, argued King, was issues of race. 'I see that Michael has nobody black around him – nobody.'

King's comments were ignored as power was solidified around him. Michael and his camp were rightly concerned about a lack of experience on the money/promotional end of the tour, and hiring Azoff, former manager of the Eagles and Steely Dan, was their way of instituting some safeguards. But Joe Jackson, his control being whittled away, aligned himself in a defensive move with the brothers who were having their own difficulties. The brothers also had trouble accepting Michael's defiant stance. 'If they weren't already there,' says a source, 'battle lines were definitely drawn. The brothers were on one side and Michael was on the other.' Adds Marlon, 'It was a bad situation all around.'

The situation was made worse by countless advisers, attorneys, agents, acountants and assorted other showbiz hangers-on who were brought into the picture by the Jackson brothers. Everyone wanted a pinch of the profits. 'They want to be stars themselves,' lamented Jackie. 'They want people to think they're doing a lot. Everybody wants to play a very, very important part and feel important. Don King's that way. Irving Azoff's the same way. Sometimes I can't believe it. It's like power games they're playing. I know it. We all know it. They must know we know it.'

When Joe Jackson surveyed the distressing situation, it was with the mounting exasperation of a man who'd accidentally created a monster he could neither control nor understand. 'The way we planned it, this was going to be the greatest tour that had ever been done in the world, but the problems were so overwhelming from the start I didn't know what to do,' he sighs. 'The real problem was with outsiders. They came between the brothers. Eventually, the brothers were battling each other.'

This quickly became the worried patriarch's primary concern. 'People were always talking about how it was going to be a Michael Jackson show,' Joe says. 'But we were more worried about just talking to Michael, simple as that. He was never around. He had his manager and his lawyer and his accountant do everything, and who knows what they were saying in his ear. Like the rest, they were probably telling him to keep away from his family.'

Publicly, the brothers, as was their habit, denied all reports of ill will and hurt feelings between them. 'We are family first,' said Tito. Which is how it appeared on Michael's first appearance at rehearsal. Everyone showed up but Marlon, who was busy producing Janet's solo LP. Despite the backstage bickering, the brothers all embraced each other before diving into that day's lesson: a run-through of 'Wanna Be Startin' Somethin' ', from the Gloved One's *Off the Wall* album. Jermaine strapped on his bass, Randy stood behind his rack of keyboards, and Jackie stood alongside the lead mike. But it was the other Mike who took charge. 'That's not it,' interrupted Michael, finding a trouble spot in the arrangement. 'It's got to be big, really big, right there.'

The band hit the song again. And again. And again. Michael worked on adjusting the band's arrangement of his song. Tito picked out a guitar harmony that wasn't quite right. Jackie asked for more sock on a particular drum part. Three hours later, along towards one a.m., the song was not just glitchless, not just ready to thunder through the vast reaches of huge stadiums across the land, but perfect enough to satisfy even Michael – for the night, at least. As the music's high-voltage hum faded, the brothers were pumped with the exhilaration of piloting such power, adrenalin racing through their bodies, big smiles on their faces and jealousies temporarily forgotten. 'We still have that unity,' oldest brother Jackie chimed during a break. 'We don't look at each other as competition.'

The once-precious boys had grown into determined men, many with children of their own, and if there wasn't competition between them, there was change, especially in Michael. The band noticed the obvious. 'I sensed something was different about him,' recalls guitarist David Williams, a mainstay in the group's touring band. 'He walked in and he looked different. Then someone told me it was his nose. He'd had it fixed again.' The brothers, meanwhile, were dealing with intangibles band members couldn't fathom. 'He had changed,' says Marlon. 'After *Thriller*, Michael was a different person. At least where we were concerned. For instance, we used to talk all the time about how we were going to work on this or that project. All of a sudden, he didn't want to talk about anything.'

Indeed, the Jacksons' proclaimed unity existed only on the

140

surface. Take their process of decision making. Everything from lighting to costumes to programmes were determined by group consensus, with the majority vote deciding the outcome. Still, when the Jacksons sat down to select T-shirt designs, Michael was the lone no show. In the early stages of rehearsals the superstar was away in New York, posing for photographs with Shirley MacLaine while his brothers were engaged in important tour negotiations. When the Jacksons appeared on television to promote their closeness and deny dissention in the ranks and rumours that this tour would be their last together, there was one significant absentee, and no one needed a programme to recognize that it was Michael.

Millionaire developer Chuck Sulllivan, former owner of the New England Patriots and chairman of the Stadium Management Corporation, who captured the hot seat of promoter, got a hint of the undercurrents during his negotiations with the Jacksons. From his objective perch, there were too many personalities, too many special interests. 'People who are closely associated with Michael – Branca, Dileo – just want to get the thing over with,' he observed. 'And people who are associated with the other brothers look at it as the most significant opportunity they will have. They want to maximize the return on that. All these guys are interesting characters.'

Michael was crushed by what he read. What he heard was equally distressing. In the weeks counting down to the long-awaited launch of the fifty-five city Victory Tour, the onslaught of negative publicity raining on every aspect of the front page event had penetrated the distant, isolated, environs where Michael conducted his life. The Jacksons were being criticized for record ticket prices, $35 a seat, not including service charges, which had their fans up in arms.

But what caused Michael fits of anger was the gossip concerning him personally. There seemed no end to the ghoulish tales that caused him so much pain. His exotic lifestyle and bewildering ways were on the lips of practically everyone who took a breath of air in 1985. People speculated on his sexuality. Was he gay? Did he even have sex? They gossiped about his plastic surgeries. His androgynous appearance prompted comparisons to lookalike Diana Ross. To the public, the enigmatic superstar was frightening, curious, odd and wonderful all at the same time.

Damaging backlash like this is exactly what Michael and

141

his coterie of associates had feared might result from the participation of Joe Jackson and Don King and the rest. 'It was a joke how everyone was out to snag their share of the dough,' says one man who was involved with the tour for a brief time. Michael, who played hard ball as well as anyone in music when it came to business, always maintained distance between his money and the image of innocence he projected to the public. 'It made him sick to see what was going on,' says Dileo.

By the time all two hundred and forty people associated with the Victory Tour, the most massive undertaking in rock history, arrived in Kansas City for the 6 July opening, the camps were openly divided. Michael and his group were on one side, and the brothers and their various minions were on the other. The two rival factions met only when the brothers climbed onstage. 'It was already very obvious that Michael was going to keep to himself on the tour,' says Marlon.

Not that apparent, though, was the stress and woe Michael was suffering by the persistence of the rumours concerning him. They gnawed at him, and his refusal to set the record straight by granting interviews only backed him deeper into a corner, convincing him for good that no matter what he did he'd be misunderstood. 'He was miserable,' says LaToya. 'He tried to hide it. Michael has a good idea of who he is as a person. But I can't recall him ever being that upset.'

With the pomp of visiting royalty, Michael arrived in Kansas City three days prior to the first curtain. His first night there he went to the movies, sneaking out of the Alameda Plaza Hotel to see *Ghostbusters*. The next day, 4 July, Dileo sifted through hundreds of messages, including those left by the city's mayor, the NAACP, politician Jesse Jackson and Las Vegas entertainer Wayne Newton, all of whom wanted private meetings with Michael. As for himself, Michael watched fireworks and took phone calls from friends.

It wasn't a good night. Michael was more than just upset. He was irate. He could no longer tolerate the soiling of his good name. With Dileo, he stayed up long into the wee hours of the morning, debating what was to be the most bold and controversial decision of the entire tour. In two nights he'd be onstage with his brothers, yet Michael felt it necessary to further separate himself from them, from the tour's promoters and to somehow address the rumours that were dogging him unmercifully, and to do all this publicly.

The next day, roughly twenty-four hours before the concert, a menacing security force led Michael through a corridor of screaming fans in the hotel to a press conference. Motor-driven cameras whirred; reporters jockeyed for position. The sticky air was thick with tension. Michael couldn't hide his anger, even from behind the sunglasses that attempted to conceal his overwhelming emotion as his stocky manager read an extraordinary message from the Silent One off a prepared text.

First, Michael wanted it known that he was donating his proceeds from the tour, at that time thought to be in the neighbourhood of $6 million, splitting it between his three favourite organizations: the United Negro College Fund, Camp Good Times for terminally ill children and the T. J. Martell Foundation for leukaemia and cancer research. Then, Michael addressed the queries of the gossip mongers, using a strong tone that made it clear he felt the best defence was a good offence.

The voice was Dileo's, but the words were Michael's: 'For some time now, I have been searching my conscience as to whether or not I should publicly react to the many falsehoods that have been spread about me. I have decided to make this statement based on the injustice of these allegations and the far-reaching trauma those who feel close to me are suffering.

'I feel very fortunate to have been blessed with recognition for my efforts. This recognition also brings with it a responsibility to one's admirers throughout the world. Performers should always serve as role models who set an example for young people. It saddens me that many may actually believe the present flurry of false accusations.

'To this end, and I do mean END –

'No! I've never taken hormones to maintain my high voice.

'No! I've never had my cheekbones altered in any way.

'No! I've never had cosmetic surgery on my eyes.

'Yes! One day in the future I plan to get married and have a family. Any statements to the contrary are simply untrue.

'Henceforth, as new fantasies are printed, I have advised my attorneys of my willingness to institute legal action and subsequently prosecute all guilty to the fullest extent of the law.

'As noted earlier, I love children. We all know that kids are very impressionable and therefore susceptible to such stories. I'm certain that some have already been hurt by this terrible slander. In addition to their admiration, I would like to continue to keep their respect.'

The entire spectacle lasted less than five minutes.

It was nearly ten o'clock the following moonlit evening, almost two hours late, when a thick puff of white smoke signalled to the 45,000 fans inside Arrowhead Stadium the start of the Jacksons' Victory Tour. First, a handful of menacing Kreeton monsters appeared onstage, their arrival heralded by flashing strobes and billowing smoke, only to be slayed moments later by Randy Jackson, resplendent in his sparkling stage armour, who drew a *Star Wars* type laser sword, restoring peace as an offstage voice intoned, 'Arise, all the world, and behold the kingdom.' The message: 'We were out to prove something to all the people,' says Marlon.

The opening salvo belonged to Michael, the man everyone wanted to see, whose song, 'Wanna Be Startin' Somethin'', provided a fitting start to the glitzy show. Of course, whatever magic occurred onstage belonged to him. Inspired by a two-week vacation at Florida's Disney World, his ideas turned the Jacksons' concert into a special effects extravaganza, replete with pulsing lasers that shot the length of the stadium, explosions, fire, thunder and trap doors. Musically, too, this 'tight, well-drilled production', as one reviewer described it, belonged to the Gloved One. The ninety-minute production featured most of the hits from *Thriller* and *Off the Wall* as well as a rousing medley of old Jackson Five tunes. 'We'd like to do the old songs the old fashioned way,' hollered Michael.

Noticeably absent from the seventeen-song performance, much to the consternation of Michael's brothers, was any material from the newly released *Victory* album. 'No one wanted that but Michael,' says Marlon. Earlier, while he was recording *Thriller*, Michael explained his reluctance to perform any new tunes in concert. 'I think that people should come to a show knowing all these songs in their heads,' he said. 'They shouldn't come to the show and feel you're forcing these songs on them.' But the other Jacksons were in sharp disagreement. 'Fine,' says Marlon. 'That's his opinion. But we were supposed to be doing everything by majority vote. This was the first time we ever toured and didn't do any songs from our new album. Everyone except Michael wanted to work some of the numbers in. That issue was brought up every day. But Michael refused to even rehearse them. How could we do them then?'

Though the five-month tour lacked any spontaneity onstage, there was a smattering of fun away from work, more the result of boredom than brotherhood, that recalled the Jacksons' early days of tomfoolery on the road. Michael remembered the night in Kansas City when Dileo fell in the hotel swimming pool and they hopped a wall onto an unprotected street to flee surprised fans. 'People saw Michael all alone on this street and did amazing double-takes,' laughs Dileo. In Jacksonville, Florida, Michael called his manager into his hotel room, where he tripped over his pet python, Muscles. 'I hate snakes,' he laughs. 'I wanted to destroy him.'

In Washington D.C. Michael pulled $100-bills out of Dileo's pockets and threw them over the balcony. In another city Michael, Randy and Marlon stood on their balcony and flung water balloons on unsuspecting bathers down by the pool. In Houston the same naughty trio filled empty hours by throwing buckets of ice cold water out of their windows and giggled as wind sent the cool wash smack into the car windows of waiting taxi drivers. 'The hotel manager called security to stop us,' laughs Marlon. 'But security was there helping us.'

The offstage event of the tour took place in Philadelphia, when Michael met the only other superstar of his calibre, Bruce Springsteen. The summit was a contrast of styles and personalities, witnessed by a crowd that packed the reception area in Michael's vast hotel suite. Springsteen sauntered in first, the consummate blue-collar rocker, wearing boots, faded jeans, and a wrinkled short-sleeve shirt whose rolled-up sleeves showed his straining biceps. His face carried several days of stubble. Then Michael entered, clean, scrubbed and freshly showered after a concert, wearing a pink button-down shirt over a white T-shirt and a pair of dusty rose pants that bunched up over his blue slippers with his initials stitched in gold.

'I hear you play long concerts,' Michael said. 'How long do you go?'

'Oh, about three hours,' replied Springsteen.

'How do you do it? Do you take a break?'

'Yeah, about a half hour. It works out pretty good, I guess.'

Springsteen, relaxed, held a drink in his hand, smiled, casually sucked on an ice cube. Unable to stand still, Michael fidgeted. He was nervous, uncomfortable. His eyes darted about the room. They spoke briefly about writing songs. Neither thought the road was conducive to composing. When a reggae song came over the stereo, Michael started moving his feet, then stopped himself. Although both worked similar magic onstage, mesmerizing millions with their music, they didn't

145

seem to have a thing in common. Or maybe they did, but couldn't find the common ground.

'Do you talk to people during your concerts?' asked Michael. 'I read that you do.'

'Yeah, I tell stories,' said Springsteen. 'People like to hear your voice do something besides singing. They go wild when you just . . . talk.'

'Oh, I could never do that. It feels like people are learning something about you they shouldn't know.'

Springsteen nodded and said he knew what Michael meant. There were more questions, more polite answers. Just small talk really, talk that masked the embarrassment of two men whose meeting was an event that could never amount to anything more significant than the fleeting images captured by photographers, who enjoyed the few moments more than the participants. Their worlds were just too different.

'I read you go right to sleep after you perform,' said Michael. 'You can't really do that, can you?'

'No, I feel good after a concert, because I feel like I've worked hard,' replied Springsteen. 'I stay up till about four. What do you do?'

'I watch TV or read. I can't go to sleep.'

'Don't you ever go out?' asked Springsteen.

'I can't.' Michael shook his head. 'Too many people would bother me.'

Back home LaToya complained about the haunting quiet that blanketed the Encino mansion like a dense fog. 'With all the guys on the road, it was so lonely,' she says. 'There were just a lot of workers, and I spent time with my mother and Janet.' During one of her regular phone talks with Michael, he bemoaned all the round-the-clock security surrounding him on the road, describing his life as too claustrophobic. 'He told me, "Oh, if only I could breathe, for once." ' she recalls.

Michael's level of frustration reached breaking point on a brief visit home, a much-needed respite from the Victory Tour. LaToya saw him run out of the house, exclaiming, 'That's it! I don't want any security. I'm going for a ride.' Then he jumped into her black Mercedes 450 SL and sped out of the driveway. Immediately, there was trouble. 'Girls,' giggles LaToya. 'Michael was followed by two cars of girls. Then the car ran out of gas and they blocked him in the middle of the street. He didn't know what to do. Since the car was out of

146

gas, he just left it right there in the middle of the street and ran over to Quincy's house.'

Several months later, in September, LaToya was the only one minding the family home when she received some shocking news. Her baby sister, Janet, had got married to singer James DeBarge of the group DeBarge. They'd eloped. 'Was it ever a surprise,' says LaToya, who took it upon herself to call the rest of the Jacksons on the road. 'They were terribly angry.' Deluged by calls from her family, Janet changed her story. 'She told us she wasn't married because she felt we'd all be against it, which we were,' says LaToya. 'I know that Jermaine would've killed her if he'd gotten his hands on her.'

Why the unanimous disapproval? 'James DeBarge had some habits that the Jackson family doesn't approve of,' says Joe. 'He was not the sort we want in this family.' Under heavy pressure to reverse the painful situation, Janet, then a semi-regular on the television show *Fame*, sought an annulment. A year later, her feelings on the arrangement still weren't clear, but her ex was obviously heartbroken. 'I can pretend that I don't think about her and that I don't love her, that it's over, but deep down inside I'm fooling myself,' said DeBarge. 'She wasn't just my wife, she was my sister, my mother, everything.'

The camaraderie the family mustered in confronting Janet was merely a temporary product of their life on the road. After all, Michael travelled in his own private jet, while the brothers usually made their way from city to city by commercial jet. Several times Pia Zadora's husband, multimillionaire businessman Meshulam Riklas, lent them his personal jet. When the brothers nearly got stranded in New York after shooting the Torture video the night before a show in a different city, Michael generously sent his plane to pick them up. 'We also started out riding to shows in the same van,' says Marlon. 'But eventually, Michael branched off into his own van.'

Demands coming from Michael's camp constantly rankled with the brothers. 'At some point during the tour, we got word from Michael's people that if we didn't fire the publicist, Howard Bloom, then Michael wasn't going onstage,' says Marlon. At first, they ignored the threat. 'Then Frank Dileo came to us before one show and said, "I told you that if you didn't fire Bloom then Michael wasn't going to perform,"' he recalls. 'The motive wasn't clear. But we sent Howard to New York and his assistant continued the tour.

'Another instance that got all the brothers upset was Michael's refusal to let us film the tour,' continues Marlon. 'There was someone who wanted to pay us several million dollars to film it, and then release the video on the market after the tour. But Michael didn't want to do it. His argument was that if anybody filmed the tour, it should be for personal use only. Not for sale or anything like that. We agreed.

'Then, about the third date, I was onstage, and I bumped into this cameraman. I looked into the audience and there's a crane out there with another cameraman. Then I saw another cameraman in the wings. Right there I realized they were shooting for Michael. Which I didn't mind. At least somebody was capturing this on video. Later on, we confronted Michael about this. He said it was just for personal use and that he would make copies and give us all one.

It seemed the Jacksons made rules only to break them at every opportunity. For instance, early on they decided nobody was to ride with them in their van. Then Michael showed up before one show with his actor pal Emmanuel Lewis. Another day Marlon brought tough guy star Mr. T. 'No one minded,' says Jermaine. In New York the Jacksons, who had to take a helicopter to the Giants' stadium, agreed in a pre-show meeting that no one could tag along. However, when the brothers got in, Michael was already inside with his friend, Julian Lennon. 'None of us minded,' says Marlon. 'But if we were going to go to the trouble to make rules, we should've lived by them. That was a problem all along.'

From Michael's point of view, his demands were like the flailing arms of a drowning man – vain efforts to save a losing situation. By the time of the tour's finale in Los Angeles, he was more than ready to say goodbye to everyone concerned. At the end of the Dodger Stadium show, in fact, he left no doubt of his intentions to leave the rest of his family behind. 'It's been a long twenty years,' he said from the stage. 'This is our final farewell tour as a family.' And then, in a puff of pastel smoke, Michael was gone.

The entire five months had been one enormous let-down. Instead of a victory, it was, for Michael, a long, arduous torture. 'I was disappointed with the tour from the beginning,' he said. Although more than two million people watched him perform in the various cities, Michael's expectations had not been met – not with the staging, the lighting, or his choreography – and his thoughts, in retrospect, were typically extreme. 'I wanted it to be so much more than it was,' he wrote in *Moonwalk*. 'It killed me to have to accept these things and settle for the way I did.'

The Victory Tour inflated the bank accounts of each brother by roughly $7 million. But, according to Joe, that figure would've been a lot higher had Michael not jumped ship when his brothers wanted to take the tour on to Europe. 'That's ridiculous, wishful thinking,' says Dileo. 'Michael never agreed to that.' Argues Joe, 'Don King and I planned to take it around the world. Michael knew that. But after the L.A. show, his people said he wasn't going to perform any more. That that was the final show. No one else thought it was going to be the last one, which is too bad for everyone.'

When all was done, it was obvious that not all had been said. King, the original man in the middle, was still irate over his diminished role on the tour, which was reported to have made him a cool $5 million. 'There's no way Michael Jackson should be as big as he is and treat his family the way he does,' King said. 'He feels that his father did him wrong? His father may have done some wrong, but he also had to do a whole lot right.'

King's solution: 'What Michael's got to understand is that Michael's a nigger. It doesn't matter how great he can sing and dance; I don't care that he can prance; he's one of the megastars in the world, but he's still going to be a nigger megastar. He must understand that. Not only must he understand that, he's got to accept it and demonstrate that he wants to be a nigger! Why? To show that a nigger can do it!'

Michael and Dileo talked the day after the tour ended. Their conversation, reflecting their overall feelings for what they'd just endured, went something like this:

Dileo: 'It's over.'
Michael: 'Right, it's over.'
Dileo: 'You know, the Friday, Saturday and Sunday nights of every week that we were out there were the most exciting nights of our lives.'
Michael: 'Right.'
Dileo: 'But the days were terrible.'
Michael: 'Right.'

Michael rested for several days. Then Dileo phoned over to his house, expecting to hear about the superstar's vacation plans. Someone else answered Michael's line. 'Where's Mike?' Dileo asked.

'Oh, he's out in the studio,' came the reply, 'working on some demos for the next album.'

13

Encino, California. January 1985.

Michael's version of the historic song places its origins inside the closet. According to him, he and Janet would periodically search out rooms with good acoustics and he would summon from the depths of his soul a solitary note. A single, soaring note – a sound meant to disturb the flesh, trigger the mind, wrinkle emotions. Then he'd ask what image that sound conjured up in her mind.

One particular time, recalls Michael, he asked what she thought of when she heard him sing and his soft-spoken sister replied, 'Dying children in Africa.'

Michael was thrilled. That's exactly what he was attempting to express. He also remembers that from this extraordinary meshing of heart and mind was born the extraordinary song, 'We Are the World', the landmark recording that became the emotional anthem for USA for Africa, the charity devoted to providing relief to famine-plagued Ethiopia.

Unfortunately, there was much more to the monumental undertaking than he lets on. In fact, Michael wasn't even the first performer called. Nor was he the second or third entertainer asked by Ken Kragen, a high-powered manager with a fund-raising background, to participate. He was the fourth superstar to receive a phone call, right after Kenny Rogers, Lionel Richie and Stevie Wonder. Wonder proved unreachable by phone, but was corralled in a Beverly Hills jewellery store by Brenda Richie, who helped him select gifts in exchange for his participation in the project.

Several days later it was Richie who telephoned Michael and asked if he would perform on the recording. 'Yes, sure,' he replied. 'I'd love to. But only if I can write the song with you and Stevie.'

'No problem,' said Richie.

From the start, Michael was convinced that he was the perfect man for the job. After all, the flip-side of his talent for song, he believed, was his gift for healing. But Michael truly believes in his talent, that it's God's special endowment to him. It's the core of what he considers his mission in life. If the millions of dollars he donated prior to the Victory Tour wasn't proof enough, by the time of USA for Africa, he already had a long history of helping the sick and afflicted, especially children.

Take David Smithee, dying of cystic fibrosis at age fourteen, who had only one wish: to meet the Gloved One. Before the Victory Tour, Michael invited the boy to his home, where they ate lunch together and played in the backyard with the superstar's menagerie of animals. When it was time to say goodbye, Michael gave his new friend the red leather jacket from his 'Beat It' video and the black-sequinned glove he had worn to the American Music Awards. 'He said the glove had special magic, that I should never let anyone else wear it,' David later told his mother.

Seven weeks later, David died. Michael didn't forget him. In July, when the Jacksons' *Victory* LP was released, the boy's mother learned that the album dedications went to Katherine Jackson, the late Marvin Gaye – and David.

Michael, who genuinely loves children, has replayed that scene dozens of times, giving his special touch and wellspring of love to his frailest of fans. Late one night during the Victory Tour, in the small hours of the night when the superstar and his manager usually went through their business, kidded around, and entertained VIP guests, a nine-year-old boy suffering a brain tumour and spinal cancer was hastily wheeled into Michael's suite on a stretcher.

The boy weakly reached up his spindly arm, extending his gloved hand to touch his hero. Dileo, who broke down in tears, turned away, though he realized once again the depth of tenderness and compassion in Michael, his 'inner godliness', as Quincy Jones says. Taking the boy's hand, Michael turned to his tough manager and said, 'Don't feel sad, don't cry. This is why I'm here.'

'Helping kids, that's not the stuff he likes publicized,' intones Dileo. 'It's part of his private life. He is very genuine in his feelings for them. It kills me. But Michael has a very deep understanding of the beauty of life. He's not afraid to look into the worst suffering and find the smallest part that's positive and beautiful.'

Michael was more than ready to commit to a project of some kind when Richie telephoned him about USA for Africa. 'Most every Sunday Michael, my mother and me watched the various programmes on television that showed film of the famine conditions in Africa,' says LaToya. 'We would always talk about doing something to help, but we didn't know how to do something that large.'

Fortunately, others did. The progenitor of the project was singer Harry Belafonte who, impressed by the British famine effort and stunned by news accounts of the Ethiopian tragedy, had first conceived of the American initiative in mid-December. Several days before Christmas, he phoned Kragen with the idea. 'He figured, after all, the national song charts are dominated by black artists,' says Kragen. 'If Jews were starving in Israel, American Jews would have raised millions.' Kragen went to work right away.

Meanwhile, the gold-plated trio of megastar composers turned into the not-too-shabby duo of Michael and Richie when Stevie Wonder left town to spend Christmas with family in New Jersey. For nearly a week, Lionel visited the Jacksons' Encino home, arriving for dinner, 'which we eat at six sharp,' says LaToya. 'Afterward they'd go up to Michael's room and work.' Both men like working at night, finding inspiration in the stillness of the dark and quiet.

Creatively, Michael and Richie ignited sparks in each other, though first they had to accustom themselves to working with another person. 'See, we both like to write in private,' explains Richie, 'and now we know why. 'Cause we talk to ourselves. Lines just come zinging out, and we were doing them out loud, in front of another person. That means you have to allow yourself to sound stupid and have somebody who you respect hear you sound stupid.

'There were times I'd draw out a line and Michael would fall down laughing. I'd say, "Sounds kinda dumb, eh?" He'd nod. But you have to give that ego up. It's all in the nature of discovering that your style happens to be somebody else's style, or close to it. The pleasure about writing with someone who also writes lyrics is that as fast as I come up with one line, he's coming back with the other. I didn't have to tell Michael where I was trying to go. He knew exactly.'

The first couple of days of Michael's and Richie's collaboration were spent exploring their feelings and thoughts on the subject. 'I'd go into the room while they were writing,' says LaToya, 'and it would be very quiet. Which is odd. Since Michael's usually cheery when he works. I said, "You're supposed to be working," and they told me they were. It was very emotional for them. Some nights they'd just talk until two or three in the morning.'

'The trick to this,' continues Richie, 'was that we spent about two or three days talking about the concept, about what we were trying to do – we wanted an anthem, a theme; we wanted something that appeals to all ages and cultures. We didn't have a song yet, we didn't have lyrics, we just had this concept.

'On the final day, at last, we started coming up with the lyrics and the melody. There were certain lines that would be corny to record if one of us were singing alone. We would never use a line, "Let's stand together as one". But when you have forty-five of the top music people in the world as your chorus, you can get away with "Let's stand, let's fight" and so on. You can use all the great lines.'

The tune was still just a few related ideas and melodic splinters when Richie left the house that night. The pressure was rapidly building. Only four days remained until Quincy Jones, taking time out from producing the movie, *The Color Purple*, was scheduled to lay down the initial tracks. 'I'd been barging inside the room, saying hi and fooling around with them,' remembers LaToya. 'I'd say, "How are you guys doing?" and Michael would go, "Nothing accomplished." They were laying on the floor, just laughing out loud over something.'

And the song? 'Well, Lionel had a line or two,' she recalls. 'Then after he left, Michael went out to the studio and wrote the entire song. The next day he told Lionel and Quincy that it was finished. But he's never felt it's necessary to say that.'

In the days between Christmas and New Year, Kragen set about lining up an all-star chorus to sing the song. 'Basically, I started at the top of the record charts and began making phone calls,' he says. Steve Perry, lead singer and creative heart of Journey, came home to a message on his telephone answering machine. 'I was real excited,' he says. Then Bruce Springsteen, on tour, was called. 'Do they really want me?' asked the Boss modestly. Assured that he was wanted, Springsteen also signed on. 'That was something of a turning point,' concedes Kragen. 'It gave the project a great deal more stature in the eyes of others.'

Kragen's final lineup read like a *Who's Who* of gold record collectors. Among them: Tina Turner, Bette Midler, Willie Nelson,

Billy Joel, Huey Lewis and Waylon Jennings. Michael asked LaToya the week before. Jeffrey Osborne was approached by Richie just hours before the taping, while both were rehearsing for the American Music Awards. 'Keep it silent,' cautioned Lionel.

Michael and Richie completed the lyrics 21 January, the night before the top-secret recording session that included forty-five of the most luminous names in pop music. Around nine p.m., a seemingly endless motorcade of sleek polished limousines nosed up La Brea Avenue, pulling into the gated compound of A&M Records, at Charlie Chaplin's old film studio. A sign outside Studio A, tacked up by Jones, bore a single admonition: 'Please check your egos at the door.'

Some, like Cyndi Lauper and Richie were coming straight from the American Music Awards. Springsteen, who flew in the night before from Syracuse, New York, where he'd concluded his American tour, parked his rented car across the street and strolled in without entourage. June Pointer, of the Pointer Sisters, followed him in. Guests of the musicians, including Dyan Cannon, Ali MacGraw, Jane Fonda, Dick Clark, Penny Marshall and Donna Dixon, were situated in the building's large Charlie Chaplin soundstage, which creaked under a $15,000 spread of roast beef, tortellini, imported cheese and other goodies.

Television monitors allowed them to watch the proceedings inside Studio A, where early birds like Ruth Pointer, James Ingram and Smokey Robinson encountered Michael laying down 'over dubs' that gave them a tantalizing taste of the song they would soon learn. 'But during the first hour,' says Osborne, 'it was impossible to get anything done. Everyone was congratulating each other, meeting people they hadn't met before.' Michael happily posed for pictures for Ruth Pointer. 'I have two kids, and they would've killed me if I hadn't,' she laughs. The room was supercharged with excitement. Says Kenny Loggins, 'I've never before felt that strong a sense of community.'

Around ten p.m. the sheet music was passed out, and several people stepped forth to address the group. Kragen talked of plans for the funds they hoped to raise. Referring to the decade-long 'Bangladesh situation, I assured the artists that if it came down to seeing that the money got to the right places, I would go over with the supplies personally.' Then Bob Geldof, the eloquent, outspoken leader of the Boomtown Rats and organizer of the British Band Aid singalong, offered a moving speech about his own travels in Ethiopia, telling of a 'good day' in one village he had visited when only five people had died. 'Geldof's opening speech was pretty intense,' noted Loggins. 'You could hear the truth in his voice.'

Then it was Michael's turn to come forward and speak to the assembly of stars. Thus far, Jackson had kept mostly to himself, either working or chatting with Diana Ross and Jones in the engineers' booth. 'Michael was quiet beyond his well-known shyness, and I think that was his own way of showing how emotional the evening was for him,' says Belafonte. In this rare public moment, Michael maintained his composure and quietly introduced the song he and Richie had written, 'A love song to inspire concern about a faraway place close to home,' he whispered.

Taping then began, with Jones on a stool directing his million-dollar chorus and Richie on a chair next to him. Michael might as well have vaporized. Standing off to the side, dispassionate behind his sunglasses, he separated himself from his peers, who willingly clad themselves in USA for Africa sweat shirts. Michael remained in his sequinned jacket. There was no question the group's unity moved him – 'I know he was choked up,' says LaToya – but Michael somehow managed to remain aloof, filming himself with the chorus by using a special effects lens filter and later splicing it in.

By three a.m. the choral section of the song was completed, and only the solo sections remained. 'Everybody was drained, but also hanging on to the thread of magic in the night,' says Ingram. During a short break, Diana Ross started collecting autographs on her sheet music, and everyone quickly followed her lead. Then Jones positioned the twenty-one soloists in a semicircle around him. Starting with Richie, they sang their parts, and the singing moved round and round the semicircle until it was completed.

By dawn most of the performers had finished, and the emotional recording session was chugging to a weary close. Michael hung in there till the end, conferring occasionally with Jones but keeping pretty much to himself. 'It was odd the way Michael removed himself from the group, considering how loose everyone was,' says a musician on the project. 'He was very gracious. But I think he was too frightened of not doing his part absolutely perfect. I guess he felt he had a lot to live up to.' Dylan and Springsteen, obviously drained by the marathon, remained until around seven-thirty. With little more to do, a very tired Diana Ross sat on the floor, tears filling her eyes, and said, 'I just don't want this to end.'

But there was nothing more for anyone except the technicians to work on. Osborne, after trading a few last-minute ad lib vocal licks with Wonder, Richie and others, finally walked out the studio door with Michael sometime before eight. 'Michael was as exhausted as anyone,' says Osborne. 'He didn't say much, maybe something about being very happy, but I could tell that he was delighted.'

From May 1985 to September 1986.

That's how long it took from the start of production to the world premiere of *Captain Eo*, the marvellous 3-D movie attraction Michael made for Disneyland. The folks at Disney had asked Michael to dream up an amusement ride for them, and he developed the story of a space voyager whose singing and dancing saves a forbidden planet from destruction. Michael described it as 'a great celebration of good over evil'.

The seventeen-minute, $30-million sci-fi short, which combines *Star Wars* cinematography and MTV choreography, came loaded with Academy Award-calibre credits: George Lucas was executive producer and Francis Ford Coppola directed. But the theme – Michael as saviour – belonged solely to the star. 'The story is about a young guy who goes on a mission to this miserable planet run by an evil queen,' writes Jackson in *Moonwalk*. 'He is entrusted with the responsibility of bringing the inhabitants light and beauty.'

When he dreamed up this parable, it's probable that Michael was dealing with himself more than anyone realized. The 'miserable' planet he had in mind was Earth, and he no doubt saw himself as the 'young guy who goes on a mission'. Little more than two years later, Michael would tender a heartfelt plea for understanding in a letter to *People* magazine that revealed virtually identical sentiments. 'I must seek truth in all things,' he penned. 'I must endure for the power I was sent forth, for the world, for the children.'

In making the video Michael brought many idiosyncracies to the set. There was no shooting Michael on Mondays. That was policy. 'The first dance rehearsal,' says one who worked on the picture, 'was an interesting introduction to Michael's ways. Per his request, all the curtains in the rehearsal room had to be closed. All the lights had to be turned off.'

Michael arrived every day promptly on time. 'He always

seemed friendly,' says another individual involved with the project. 'But he kept to himself, staying in his compound, when he wasn't working.' Michael was never alone, though. His entourage was always hovering close by. 'He had several body guards, a cook, a makeup person, his security chief and lots more people watching out for him during the three months it took to shoot,' the source says. 'His cook would bring him carob brownies every day and make big vegetarian meals. But it wasn't like he ever ate a regular sandwich.'

Always 'heavily made up', Michael hid his eyes behind mirrored sunglasses, even in the pitch black of the cavernous sound stages, taking them off only when the cameras were ready to roll. And on several occasions the timid superstar hid lots more than his eyes. 'Jeffrey Hornaday, the choreographer, would go through a routine for Coppola, and Michael was supposed to be watching,' recalls another source. 'But he'd be gone. Michael would just disappear. The crew would spend half an hour looking for him, and he would be hiding in a crevice or a crack somewhere, having literally slipped into the woodwork, where he'd watch everyone looking for him. I guess it was a game to him.'

Michael spent most of his free time entertaining a ten-year-old blond boy named Jonathan. 'He'd been burned in the past,' says a woman from the film, 'and they were very close.' Adds another worker, 'Jonathan was the only person allowed nearby Michael at all times. He carried a towel to wipe sweat off Michael's face, and they seemed to nuzzle and hug a lot. There was nothing sexual going on. But it was definitely a close friendship.'

Other friends, like Barbra Streisand, Sophia Loren and Toni Basil, dropped by, but outside of Jonathan, Michael's most constant play companion was his close friend Elizabeth Taylor. 'She was there more often than not during filming,' says a source. They spent breaks together in his trailer, alone. 'And God knows what they did,' he continues. 'But apparently, he and Liz had some wild food fights. Weekly damage reports to the trailer ran up to $3,000.'

While working on the 3-D gem, the crew often donned ear plugs. Not that the two new songs Michael composed – 'We Are Here To Change the World' and 'Another Part of Me' – weren't up to his usual standard. That wasn't the case at all. It was because Michael stipulated that the music, which he composed around his dance, be played at the highest possible volume. 'You could hear it six to seven stages away,' says the source. 'Michael always said that he wanted to "feel" the music.' There was no questioning his methods, no matter how bizarre they seemed. Michael knew what he was doing. 'His dance scenes were positively exciting,' says the source. 'He was a completely different guy. He came alive dancing and singing. It was magic, electric.'

After filming was completed, Coppola was forced to reloop the star's voice several times to get him to sound more masculine. Otherwise, Michael finished *Captain Eo* and dropped out of sight for the rest of 1985 and 1986. Oh, there were random spottings. He showed up in London to visit his wax statue at Madame Tussaud's, and he was photographed at a Springsteen concert with Liz Taylor, her black hair teased and spiked and the rest of her pressed into a black leather jacket. He was also seen by commuters peddling his bicycle along Ventura Boulevard in the early morning traffic, wearing nothing odder than faded Levis, a windbreaker and Sergeant Pepper sunglasses.

Michael was scheduled to attend the heavily-touted world premiere screening of *Captain Eo* at Disneyland in September. It played simultaneously at Disney World in Florida, too. But the Gloved One was nowhere in sight among the cavalcade of stars who arrived at the Magic Kingdom that sunny afternoon, including Lucas, Coppola and co-star Angelica Houston, who brought her boyfriend, actor Jack Nicholson. Jane Fonda brought her son Troy. Actor John Ritter had daughter, Carly, and Alana Hamilton, Rod Stewart's ex-wife, came with their children, Sean and Kimberly. Other attendees included Debra Winger, Molly Ringwald and Sissy Spacek.

And Michael? Only the week before, a photograph of him supposedly sleeping in a hyperbaric oxygen chamber, a complicated piece of high-tech equipment used to treat burn patients, appeared in the *National Enquirer*, touching off a spate of new stories concerning his health. His non-appearance touched off a vitriolic confrontation between Michael and Disney executives, chairman Michael Eisner and president Jeffrey Katzenberg. 'They really had it out with him for not coming,' says an insider connected to the movie.

By the time of the post-screening party, a rumour was circulating that Michael was actually in attendance, and much of everyone's time was spent guessing whom he might be. 'Michael was there,' says Dileo. 'He was just in disguise.' But in the land of make believe, which one was he? A few incorrect reports had him dressed as one of the film's sci-fi supporting characters. Not true. 'Michael Jackson is here,' declared Eisner, 'but he's disguised either as an old lady, an usher or an animatronic character.' Only that wasn't correct, either. 'He came dressed up as a nurse, pushing a wheelchair,' claims another source.

It really didn't matter. Whatever disguise Michael wore, he had already convinced everyone he was Goofy.

14

Encino, California. August 1987.

On the one hand, it was a fine day. Frank Dileo settled back into a comfortable overstuffed chair in the roomy cabana behind his ranch-style home in Encino. The walls on either side of him were decorated with black and white photos of he and Michael acting chummy with celebrity buddies like Marlon Brando, Jane Fonda and Elizabeth Taylor. Outside, the warm morning sunshine nourished overflowing gardens and chirping birds filled the air with loud song. 'For a guy from back East, this is paradise,' he mused.

On the other hand, Dileo was squaring off against the toughest challenge of his professional life: convincing the world that Michael Jackson, at the ripe old age of twenty-nine years, was still as popular as he ever was. In a few weeks *Bad*, Michael's eagerly awaited follow-up to *Thriller*, whose history-making sales now topped thirty-eight million, was going to hit the stores, and Michael wanted not just to shatter that record, but to triple his sales.

There was just one problem: in the two years since the Victory Tour creaked to its agonizing halt, the public's opinion of Michael had changed from admiration into fascination of the bizarre figure he'd somehow become. For good reason, too. During that period Michael was reputed to have proposed marriage to Elizabeth Taylor, built a shrine to her in his home, offered $1 million for the Elephant Man's bones, taken female hormones to keep his voice high and facial hair wispy, had his eyes, lips and nose surgically altered, his skin chemically bleached, and taken to sleeping in a hyperbaric oxygen chamber in the hope of living to be 150 years old.

Dileo confronted the bizarre list of questions with a straight face and the utmost seriousness. A man with a good sense of humour, he didn't show it. That would've been inappropriate.

161

It was Dileo's job to sell Michael, to present the singer as something more sympathetic than a flighty aberration of a human being, and he refused to cave in during what must have been one of the strangest interrogations ever concerning a pop idol. Instead, the manager casually bit the tip off the day's first nine-inch Dunhill Monte Cruz. 'Mike's a hard person to describe,' he said. 'He's part Howard Hughes, part E.T.' A few days later, Quincy Jones added his opinion. 'He's one of the most normal people I've ever met,' he said.

Right. Either Jones hangs out with some odd ducks, or he didn't catch the intimation of Dileo's clever comments, which pegged Michael as some kind of lovable weirdo. The real Michael, of course, remained elusive. Not a word was going to pass from his own tightly pursed lips, that was for sure. 'Michael knows the public thinks he's weird and strange and all that,' scolded LaToya. 'But he knows who he is and is sure of where he stands. He says he's always misquoted or misunderstood. So why give an interview?'

There was truth in her words. Michael couldn't voice it himself, but the crux of his self-imposed silence was his absolute certainty of being misunderstood. Forget the misquotes, that's nothing more than a symptom of his real fear. Actually, Michael didn't know how to begin to explain the roiling mess of emotions he kept locked inside himself. This was the core of his dissatisfaction with himself.

By this time, though, Michael's life was governed by a set of stringent rules that he set for himself. No doctors would talk for attribution, but off-the-record comments indicate that Michael's odd behaviour was the result of an eating disorder. His habits were distinct: he ate like a bird, danced himself into a dither, worked himself into a Type A frenzy, and lived a self-imposed isolation in a fantasy world he created. He thought himself unique, yet he yearned for signs that would assure him of his significance.

Friends and family members noted with concern the diligence and suffering required for Michael to maintain this existence. Close associates like Dileo and Jones were quick to deny anything wrong with Michael, but literature on anorexia offers a description that seems strikingly familiar. 'The longer the illness lasts, the more anorexics become convinced they are special and different,' writes Dr Hilda Bruch in *The Golden Cage* a classic primer on the disease, and 'that being thin makes them feel worthwhile, significant and extraordinary.'

Left untreated 'they feel they are no longer able to communicate with ordinary people who won't understand them. . . . In isolation, their thinking and goals become bizarre and they construct weird ideas about what happens to food . . . their own bodies become an arena for their only exercise of control.'

'During the height of the illness, anorexics are so preoccupied with how they appear in the eyes of others, constantly absorbed in proving their superiority or camouflaging their inferiority, that their style of communication is rather stilted, often prententious and always dead serious, completely lacking in humour.'

Whether or not Michael suffered from anorexia can't be substantiated, but there's little question that this textbook summary provides a fairly accurate sketch of the enigmatic superstar, or at least the way he was perceived through his actions. More than a year before Dileo sat down to defend Michael's increasingly strange behaviour, he admitted that on occasion he too was baffled by Jackson's thoughts. 'Sometimes Michael has the most bizarre ideas,' Dileo said, around the time of Michael's preoccupation with the hyperbaric oxygen chamber, 'and he'll just refuse to listen to anyone.'

Michael spent most of 1985 sequested inside his 48-track home studio, recording demo after demo, including a cover of 'Come Together', a favourite Beatles song that he would later include in his *Moonwalker* movie. He worked at a frantic pace. It was as if *Thriller*'s imposing success haunted him, drove him to work at a heightened pitch, even frightened him. 'After the Victory Tour, Michael basically disappeared into his work,' Marlon says. 'We rarely saw him and really didn't know what he was doing.'

In relative secrecy, Michael laboured with feverish intensity like a man trying to exorcise private demons. The satisfaction of *Thriller*'s record-breaking success was short-lived. Michael felt his next LP had to do even better, had to shatter even *Thriller*'s previous records. His expectations, unrealistic, soared off ordinary scales of human endeavor. 'He was already number one in the world,' says Marlon. 'All the records were his. But I guess he felt like he had to prove himself all over again.'

It appeared that way. When Michael and his producer began putting tracks to tape at the Westlake recording studio in the first week of August 1986, it was obvious to everyone that the demands Michael imposed upon himself were excessive, the pressure immense. 'There was so much stress,' said regular

163

guitarist David Williams, 'and so much tension' that 'I was doing the exact same part at least five different times on each song. They were trying to match the other one, the *Thriller* album, at least.'

But this is getting ahead of the story. Prior to this, Michael's yearning for outward signs of success was combined with his mania for control when he completed two stupendous business transactions that caused his net worth to leap into the hundreds of millions. First, during the third week of August 1985, Michael outfoxed and outbid his rival for ATV, the jewel in the music publishing crown because it included nearly every song Paul McCartney and John Lennon wrote between 1964 and 1970, including classics such as 'Let It Be', 'Hey Jude' and 'Yesterday'. The cost: $47.5 million. His rival was none other than his pal, Paul McCartney.

Make that ex-pal. With Michael's purchase, which completed eight months of transcontinental negotiations that had all the trappings of a high-powered corporate takeover, there was a definite cooling of relations between the once-chummy superstars. 'Yeah, that's true,' says Dileo. Four years earlier McCartney and Yoko Ono, John Lennon's widow, attempted unsuccessfully to buy ATV for $40 million. At the time of the deal, royalties from just eighty of the two hundred Beatles' songs listed in the publisher's catalogue were generating some $3.2 million annually for ATV. Ownership made Michael one of the fifteen largest music publishers. But it also prevented McCartney from acquiring the rights to his own work.

'From Michael's point of view,' explains Dileo, 'he didn't see why McCartney would be upset. Michael wanted ATV all his life, and when it became available, he bought it. Paul also knew it was for sale. You don't think he knew about it before Michael? He had an equal, if not better, chance. It's like seeing a sweater in a store window and walking by every day wondering if you should buy it or not. Eventually, someone else is going to come in and get it and you're going to be angry at yourself. Same thing happened.'

Pushing the value of his publishing concerns past an estimated worth of $100 million didn't come close to satiating the hungry superstar. More money, $15 million, came his way seven months later, in March 1986, when Dileo, attorney Branca and Pepsi president Roger Enrico inked a second endorsement deal between Michael and the soda pop company. The deal called for Michael to make two commercials and for Pepsi to sponsor his world tour. The figure was a record for commercial endorsements.

Yet the most astonishing detail of the agreement called for Michael to be paid the entire $15 million up front. In cash. Apparently, Michael had his reasons for requesting the enormous cheque. First, he needed the income for tax breaks available to him resulting from the ATV purchase. Second, Branca and Dileo were already plotting to renegotiate the deal for other participations that would tag another $10 million onto the price ticket. 'The third reason,' reported *Rolling Stone*, 'was completely irrational but perhaps the most important: the $15 million was about three times the previous record for such a deal, and getting the record-setting amount all at once would make Michael happy.'

The ego-flattering transaction surprised no one more than Michael's dad. Not because his son wasn't worth it. Far from it. Rather, the gruff man who thinks of little but money couldn't fathom Michael being concerned with the dollar side of stardom. 'For as long as I can remember, he wasn't ever really interested in money,' says Joe. 'That wasn't Michael. When he was little I'd give him his share of a night's earnings and the next day he'd buy ice cream or candy for all the kids in the neighbourhood and watch 'em eat it. But these days, money is about all he seems interested in.'

Not without reason. With his ample financial resources, Michael was able to calculate his success in real terms and finance undertakings like expensive video projects. More important, though, he could buffer himself from the outside world and indulge in whatever fantasy fed his childlike visions. Actress friend Jane Fonda suggested that the refuge Michael sought in animals, children and make-believe was his way of protecting his creativity. 'He's an extremely fragile person,' she said. 'I think that just getting on with life, making contact with people, is hard enough, much less to be worried about whither goest the world.'

Yet it was more than an artist's fragility that inspired Michael to confine himself within the gates of his mansion and to cloak his various movements in the murky shadows of secrecy. It's doubtful that Fonda or any of Michael's friends, celebrities such as Liz Taylor and Marlon Brando, who were favoured, in part, for their ability to keep probing outsiders at bay, ever glimpsed the darkness of the superstar's private life.

But it was clearly there. By the middle of 1986 many of

165

Michael's close associates were seriously concerned by his behaviour, since it was also becoming obvious to the public. The accident during the making of the Pepsi commercial triggered in Michael a fascination with medicine. He purchased volumes of medical books, all kinds, and read them endlessly. After mastering the workings of the body, he began studying every rare and gruesome disease he could find. He became obsessed with germs, convinced that he would somehow catch some horrifying disease. He even took to wearing a surgical mask in public.

Then apparently confident that he'd stumbled onto an important discovery, Michael went too far, prompting several people from his inner circle to scold him publicly, an unheard of occurrence, even in private. But the week of 16 August 1986, headlines blared the sensational story: 'Michael Jackson's Bizarre Plan to Live to 150.' 'Michael's Next Thrill: An Oxygen Chamber.' Too odd for most people to fathom, it was absolutely true: Michael planned to buy a hyperbaric oxygen chamber, a device used to treat burn victims. The coffinlike contraption encloses the patient in an atmosphere of one hundred percent oxygen, under increased barometric pressure up to several times the pressure at sea level, flooding body tissues with oxygen. It was the cornerstone of his personalized health regimen.

Sechrist Industries Inc., the manufacturer of the $65,000-machine, refused Michael's request to buy one of the chambers, which are sold only to hospitals. Undaunted, he looked elsewhere to satisfy his whim. An outraged Dileo issued a warning. 'I told Michael, "That damn machine is too dangerous. What happens if something goes wrong with the oxygen?"'

There was that likelihood. A photograph of Michael lying in a chamber, taken on a tour of the burn unit he funded at Brotman Medical Center, showed him wearing street clothes, which is especially dangerous. Patients using the device are always dressed in fire-retardant clothes. Otherwise there's a high risk of spontaneous combustion and certain death in the oxygen-rich environment from the slightest spark of static electricity. 'But Michael won't listen,' fumed Dileo.

Michael had taken several long naps in a chamber, declaring 'when I awoke I felt like a new person.' He couldn't be dissuaded from his scheme. Hoefflin warned that the hyperbaric chamber was to be used only under supervision. His manager protested that he was acting carelessly. 'But Michael ignored all the warnings,' said Dileo. 'He wants to put one in his bedroom, and have one of his staff trained to operate the machine.'

Of course, the hyperbaric oxygen chamber was only the most elaborate cog in Michael's overall health plan.

There was also Michael's self-prescribed approach to nourishment. Michael ate only fruits, nuts and steamed vegetables. He never touched meat, obviously, but he also abstained from chicken and fish. Despite his endorsement of Pepsi, he never touched the sugary liquid. Instead, he allowed only the purest fruit juices and natural bottled water to satiate his thirst. 'Michael also takes massive doses of vitamins,' added his manager. 'I've seen him take about fifty assorted vitamin and mineral pills in one day.'

Michael was only following his personal blueprint for the future. 'I want to live to see world peace, a world without hunger, a world where children and all mankind know no suffering,' he explained. 'And I want to help achieve that goal. I believe if I can stay healthy in mind and body, I can help make a difference in the world. The longer I live, the more I can do.'

Michael approached his health and appearance in the same way as all his other projects. He aimed for absolute perfection. Or as close as was humanly possible. Lookswise, it was as if he had spent days paging through every fashion and exercise magazine, taking note of each fitness or beauty trend, and then decided to embody every single one of them. He would, he concluded, become the model human being, inside and out, impervious to criticism. If he was reinventing Michael, it wasn't for reasons of commerce. It was for Michael himself.

The changes were harsh. Maintaining his diet for several years, Michael took on a harder-edged, sinewy appearance. The weight peeled off him. His skin pulled tighter. The extra padding on his hips and around his stomach disappeared. Gradually, with the loss of fat, the bones on his sculpted face protruded, giving him prominent features that seemed chiselled out of stone. Or lifted straight from a beauty manual.

To look at Michael was to see a beautiful face completely void of imperfection, a visage that displayed every feature society esteemed without a single humanizing blemish. The small, upturned nose. High cheekbones. Gaunt cheeks and big, square chin. Wide eyes accentuated with eye liner. Rough, scarred skin smoothed with thick makeup. The effect was frightening. It left the public wondering if Michael was a real person or something manufactured in a cold laboratory.

167

No matter how he made himself look, though, there was a lingering dissatisfaction in Michael. It was obvious even to casual friends. Singer-composer Paul Anka noticed it when Michael was his house guest. 'He spent hours sitting in the Jacuzzi, and every two minutes sent my wife out to buy the most bizarre food in the world,' said Anka. 'And instead of asking me about music, he only wanted to talk about plastic surgery.'

Michael was trying to sort things out. Shortly after beginning work on *Bad*, he made one of the biggest decisions of his life. He broke from the Jehovah's Witnesses. 'He did it himself,' says his mother, who was disappointed by his choice. 'Michael was very close to the church, but I guess he felt he had to leave. It really bothered me. I think it was too much pressure on him.' Surely, Michael didn't want a repeat of the harangues church elders delivered to him when *Thriller* shot his star to new heights.

Katherine wished her son had consulted her before severing his ties with the church. They had shared a religious bond his entire life. 'Michael felt he had to choose between the two, religion and music,' sighs Katherine. 'He could've continued, I think. I would've liked that very much.' One could only imagine the anguish Michael suffered from his decision, knowing that his deliberate break with the church drove a wedge between him and his mother, the woman he most desired to please, both on earth and in the hereafter. Katherine tried to understand. 'Just as I know Michael would never give up his music, I know he still believes in God. He has to.'

When CBS Records' chief executive officer Walter Yetnikoff heard that Michael had recorded two brand new songs for *Captain Eo*, the $30 million 3-D movie fantasy, he raged furiously. Why the hell wasn't he in the studio working on the album he owed CBS? Corporate profits had dropped after *Thriller*, and Michael's album was being counted on to ensure a profitable 1987. The gruff record executive threatened to sue his superstar, but then backed down and extracted a less-threatening compromise: no songs from *Captain Eo* would be released, and Michael would hightail it back to the studio.

Michael brought a distinctly wacky presence to the Westlake recording studios, where he and Jones began toiling in August. Some days three men followed him into studio D, carrying Crusher, his three-hundred-pound, twenty-foot python, who would slither across the engineers' console and wrap himself around knobs and speakers. 'Scared the daylights out of me once,' says guitarist Williams. Other times it was Bubbles, dressed in one of his many Osh-Kosh outfits, who would rollerskate across the slick floors. One day the chimp even rode around on the back of engineer Bruce Swedien's Great Dane. 'There's always something a little different going on when you work with Michael,' adds Williams.

Michael was difficult to predict. Sometimes he'd show up wearing jeans and a T-shirt, other times in a pricy designer suit, and still other times he'd arrive clad in what Jones calls 'this Captain Marvel stuff'. When Michael laid down vocals, he liked the lights to be turned off. 'So he could be alone with the music,' says a session musician. He also danced while he sang. 'If he's not moving, it ain't happening,' adds Williams. Friends dropped by constantly. Emmanuel Lewis. Elizabeth Taylor. Oprah Winfrey. Sean Lennon. 'I was happy to see all these beautiful faces come by and cheer us up,' explains Jones.

When he made *Thriller*, Michael's goal was to create an album that would shatter every sales record in the books. With *Bad*, his intention was even loftier. Namely, said Michael, 'That this album should be as close to perfect as humanly possible.' He had come up with more than sixty tunes by the time Jones began listening to the demos. Right away, the producer recognized that Michael's work had become more complex than earlier albums. 'His demos became real professional, with live string sections and lots of information he wanted to communicate,' says Jones. 'I liked it when it was rougher, more raw, which gave us all a little more room to participate. But it's nice to hear what's in his mind. We still have to determine if what he's put down still best represents the song.'

Ironically, Michael isn't a trained musician. His skill on instruments is extremely limited. Instead, he sings what he hears in his head, puts it on tape, and then hires musicians to record the parts. 'But he doesn't even have to do that,' says Williams. 'His voice is a great instrument. He hears and sings just as many notes and chords as a trained musician.'

Veteran musicians such as Steve Poccaro, Toto's highly-regarded keyboard ace, who played in sessions on *Bad*, discovered several years earlier that when they collaborated on songs, Michael didn't suffer from a lack of formal training. 'On this one tune we did, he sat down with a pencil and paper and just wrote lyrics until he was finished,' says Poccaro. 'I barely saw him lift his head. On another one, I just had a rhythm track

169

to it. He took it home and brought it back with incredible lyrics and melody that I never would've thought of in a million years. He's just an amazingly musical person.'

In the studio Michael and Jones are well aware of their separate roles. 'They really are a magical team,' says Poccaro. 'It's a lot of Michael, but Quincy is the glue.' Adds Toto's other keyboard whiz, David Paitch, 'When you get in the studio with Quincy and Michael, there's very little dialogue. A lot of what goes on is understood. Quincy does the speaking for Michael.'

Indeed, Jones is captain, protector, father, friend, coach and whatever else it takes to guide Michael through the treacherous shallows of the creative process. 'The first thing a producer has to provide to an artist is objectivity,' he explains. 'The main task, I think, is selecting the songs. That's fifty percent of the commitment right there. From then on, you deal with dressing and setting and colours, shades and textures, fast and slow, and all those decisions.'

With more than sixty tunes to choose from, Jones' initial decisions involved whittling the possibilities down to a manageable number. He, Michael and Dileo, together and separately, spent days listening to each song, noting their favourites and their discards, with the producer retaining the final verdict. 'I picked the first six or eight tunes that I liked, and we started to work away,' says Jones. 'Making an album is a process that's constantly metamorphosing. You're dealing with a blurry image that you're attempting to make clearer and clearer.

'It's total instinct. That's all you can hold on to. There's no way in the world you can prepare an album by trying to figure out what people like. You have to go with something that really touches you, that gets the goose bumps going. If that happens, then you have the basis of something to deal with. Otherwise, you're trying to guess what emotional reaction people are going to have, and I wouldn't know how to do that for fifty people, let alone thirty-eight million.'

However, the triumvirate of Michael, Jones and Dileo were all fishing around for some inventive touchstone that would enable *Bad* to stand on its own. An issue-oriented song, a duet, something. 'We didn't put the sequence together until we said, "This is it, no more playing around,"' recalls Jones. 'Before that, we had lots of things in mind.' In October, for example, Michael was scheduled to record an anti-crack song with rap superstars Run D.M.C.

Michael arrived looking casual in a red corduroy shirt, black pants, white sweat socks and black espadrilles. He had on shades and a brown fedora that covered his slicked-back hair, which had grown long. It was pulled back in a ponytail. Bubbles was tagging along right behind, dressed in overalls. Michael ignored the buffet of fried chicken, potato salad and assorted snacks that had been set out on a long table and waited for the rappers to show up.

Not long after, Run D.M.C. hit the studio with the subtlety of a sonic boom, streaming in wearing the latest in ghetto trendy. Their all-black outfits, white hightop Adidas tennies and thick, garish gold jewellery clashed with Michael's conservatism. 'Yo, what's up, Q?' they boomed. Quincy's introductions were awkward as Michael showed little interest in the rappers' loud, jive bravado. Run D.M.C.'s effort in front of the microphone fared not much better, and the song was shelved alongside scores of other unreleased Michael Jackson tunes. 'We felt strongly about the issue,' says Jones. 'But when it came time to put out the album, the song didn't seem to have the impact.'

Michael wanted this album to come out swinging; every cut had to be a knockout. From the start, everyone liked 'Bad'. Not yet the title track, it was Michael's interpretation of inner-city street life, inspired by the true story of Edmund Perry, a Harlem teenager who attended Phillips Exeter, an exclusive prep school, and was shot dead by a policeman who claimed Perry had tried to mug him. Jones loved the song's blistering swagger, the driving beat, and immediately suggested getting his friend, Martin Scorsese, to direct the video.

Michael wasn't familiar with the director's work, which includes *Taxi Driver*, *Raging Bull* and *Mean Streets*. The only Scorsese picture he'd seen was *New York, New York*. Michael had hoped to snag one of his pals, Spielberg or Lucas, to direct the short. But Dileo pushed for the gritty director. Aware that Michael needed to toughen his image, he knew that any more Peter Pan-type fantasy stuff would only perpetuate Jackson's wimpy image.

The filming of 'Bad', done mostly on location in New York City, kept Michael out of the studio for six weeks. According to one account, the shoot was 'a nightmare'. The pressure that pushed Michael towards neurotic stabs at perfection was transferred whole to the movie set. At his stubborn best, he insisted that Scorsese 'reshoot and reshoot'. Says one of the dancers, 'Michael was very nice, polite and all that. But he was also crazed. He'd want to do the same thing over and over, with no appreciable difference. He was like a guy who keeps slapping a wall with one coat of white paint after another, never convinced that it's really white.'

Scorsese kindly described Michael as 'a perfectionist'. However, because of that tendency the budget for the sixteen-minute movie, whose gangland dancers draw generously from *West Side Story*, soared two or three times over the estimated cost, totalling roughly $2 million. Michael footed the bill in its entirety.

Inside the Jackson camp, there was quiet hope that 'Bad' would cast a new, tougher light on Michael's troubled image. His manager had played a strong part in getting his star to de-emphasize the glitz and adopt a stronger, more macho personna, if that were possible. For his part, Michael came up with the leather and buckle-adorned garb he wore in the 'Bad' video, which he designed himself. 'He needed a new look,' says Dileo.

That much was obvious to everyone but the young man in question, whose initial, personally-selected cover portrait for the album generated instant alarm. When Yetnikoff, the CBS chief, saw it – a fey close-up of Michael's heavily made-up face hiding behind a veil of black floral lace – he blew his stack, reportedly telling Dileo, 'Look, this cover sucks.' The fragile, feminine-looking photo was discarded. In its place was substituted a shot of Michael in his 'Bad' neo-motorcycle outfit, which was actually a promotional picture taken during a fifteen-minute break in the video filming.

His handlers made little effort to shield Michael from the reams of adverse press he received in tabloids and gossip columns. He read most of it himself. 'We make sure Michael reads a lot of the stories,' says Jones. 'But he sees most of them himself.' But did any of it sink in? Did the Gloved One realize he had become the Unloved One in a reversal of worldwide adoration so sudden it caused whiplash?

Clues were plentiful. His 'Magic Beat' perfume failed. A short-lived line of Michael Jackson clothes and dolls proved a waste of $20 million. And then there were the multitude of stories and rumours. However, the message eluded Michael, who continued to feel isolated and persecuted. 'He sees himself as being misunderstood,' says an associate. 'He only knows that he's famous, that famous people are gossiped about, and that people go berserk when they see him. That's been his whole life. He doesn't understand that the fans are turned off because they can't find anything about him to identify with.'

By Christmas it was obvious the album's initial January release date was going to quietly pass without celebration. In fact, Jones was only beginning to sequence the LP. 'Even though we didn't have all the songs, I made a sequence and we never changed it,' says the producer. 'I laid out the songs on three-by-five cards, and on the songs we didn't have, like the duet with Stevie Wonder, I just wrote, "Duet with Stevie Wonder". It gave us a sense of where we were going.' At a Christmas party at Jones' house, songwriter Glen Ballard asked the host, half in jest, 'Need anything for Michael?'

'Yeah,' he replied, also joking, 'I need a hit.'

Later, he admitted he was still looking. 'We still needed some killer songs,' he says.

By New Year, Jones was a busy fellow. 'Dirty Diana' was the album's hard rocker, similar to 'Beat It', which boasted Eddie Van Halen's guitar wizardry. For six-string fireworks on 'Dirty Diana', Jones telephoned Billy Idol's flashy guitarist, Steve Stevens. 'Actually, I didn't believe it was Quincy,' he says. 'I picked up the phone and Quincy said, "I hear you're a bad motherfucker," and I said, "Well, in what context are you talking about?"'

The plan called for Stevens to lay down his tracks in the studio after the 'Bad' video finished shooting, since Jones was going to be in New York. 'But I said, "Well, I'd love to do it, but I want to make sure Michael's there when I play,"' says Stevens. 'At this point in my career, I've done things where the artist isn't there and it's not much fun.' Timing couldn't be arranged in New York, but Stevens was in Los Angeles for the Grammys in February and studio time was scheduled. 'I walked in and the first person I saw was Quincy,' he recalls. 'We sat around talking about films.

'Then Michael came in and said something to the effect of, "Oh, I like your suit." I'm known for wearing decent clothes and it made me think the guy was pretty cool. If I can play half decent, I thought, I've got it made. Michael was real literate musically; he knew what he wanted. There were some guitar guidelines, and Michael explained to me what kind of feeling he was looking for on the track. He wanted the neo-heavy metal sound, that white-boy metal over the bad-ass groove. So I ripped off a couple of different solos, and he liked the first one. It was my choice, too. He said it had more feeling. It seemed to me that Michael's a person who goes upon emotion rather than technique, which is how I've always worked with Billy. The funny thing is he kept telling me I was too thin, that I should eat something.'

In February Jones, still searching for new material, met his staff songwriters at his home. The meeting was at eleven o'clock. Siedah Garrett, one of Quest Records' contract writers and singers, showed up an hour late. 'I got lost,' she laughs. She took notes through the meeting. 'Basically, he said, "We need another smash for Michael's new album. I just want hits, that's all I want."'

The next day she met her collaborator, Glen Ballard, whom Michael mistakenly identifies in *Moonwalk* as George Ballard. He 'sat down and started playing a figure on the keyboard and Siedah opened up her notebook,' recalls Ballard. 'I started singing a verse idea melodically. I heard her singing something about a "man in the mirror", and I said, "That's great. I love that."'

Their demo was completed on a Friday. Garrett immediately telephoned Jones and told him, 'I know this is highly irregular, but I cannot wait until Monday for you to hear this song.' Though he was in a meeting, he said to come over. 'He calls me four hours later and says, "Uhh, I don't know."' Then he laughed and began raving about the song. 'But he cautioned me,' she says. 'He said, "I've been playing Michael songs for two years. We've been in the studio for eleven months. I don't know if he's going to take this song."'

Several days later Garrett found out that Michael loved 'Man in the Mirror'. It was just the type of message song that he loved, but was incapable of writing. His own lyrics about girls, sex, cars and monsters tended to be shallow, disjointed and gleaned through second-hand experience. The next week, when Michael decided to extend the tune's bridge, Garrett showed up at the studio to add her soulful twinings to the gospelly voices of the Winans and the Andrae Crouch Choir, who were adding backup vocals. When they met, Michael kissed her on the cheek. 'Externally, I'm very cool, you know,' she says. 'But my heart's going, "Omigod! I've just been kissed by Michael Jackson."'

She was the saving grace they needed to solve one of the LP's lingering problems: who to sing alongside Michael on the saccharine duet 'I Just Can't Stop Loving You'. From the start, the song had been pegged as the first single, a slow tease that repeated the same marketing pattern as *Thriller*. But it had been problematic from the word go. First, Jones had been forced to lend his help on the whispered confessional that introduced the song. Then Michael's top choice for a singing partner, Barbra Streisand, turned them down. 'She didn't like it,' said Dileo. Whitney Houston also said no. 'I didn't lose any sleep over it,' he says. That's when Jones phoned Garrett to ask if she'd received the tape he'd sent. 'Yeah, I got it,' she said.

'Do you think you can sing it?' he asked.

'Yeah, I can sing it,' she recalls saying. 'The next thing I know, Michael and I are standing face to face in front of a mike. I think we did three or four takes and they composited the best. That was it.'

Not quite. There were still more costly delays. In mid-February Michael took a two-month break to shoot an $8 million extended video for 'Smooth Criminal'. In March he began work on his ninety-minute movie, *Moonwalker*, a project that was encompassed by such tight secrecy that even the CBS brass didn't know at first that Michael had once again strayed from his overdue project. However, these interruptions were causing tremendous worry to those in Jackson's inner circle. A tour was already scheduled to roll through Japan in September. They needed the record out before that, no ifs, ands or buts. Dileo called an emergency meeting at Universal Studios, where Michael was working on the video, and announced that it had to be completed in final form by 30 June. 'This train has got to leave,' said Dileo.

'You need a dramatic deadline,' said Jones. 'I swear, it doesn't happen without that. We'd have been in the studio for another year.'

That they had to finally wrap up work on the album, select and polish the final product and then deliver it to the public hit Michael like a cold slap in the face. How could he be certain they'd done their best? He judged success by outward signs like sales and dollar figures; there was nothing to go on yet. What if people didn't like it? What if it didn't sell more than *Thriller*?

Dileo maintains that pressure was never an issue during the period of more than two years they spent recording *Bad*. 'Unfortunately, we never felt like we had to outdo ourselves,' he says. 'Michael, Quincy and I all have the same attitude – all we can do is make the best album possible and then present it.' But a musician with more than his share of top ten hits recalls discussing the album with Michael's attorney, who revealed, 'We really won't be happy unless it goes past *Thriller.'*

Michael himself would've preferred to labour in the studio another year or more rather than finish and risk public scrutiny of work that was inseparable from him as a person. 'He's afraid to finish the record,' an associate was quoted saying in a very detailed account of the recording in *Spin* magazine. 'The closer he gets to completing it, the more terrified he becomes of that confrontation with the public. Quincy Jones could only keep him protected from it for so long, then he leaves the studio and it's there. He's reminded that everyone is waiting for this record and he goes into a shell. He's frightened.'

Michael reacted to the uncertainty of his new album's reception the same way he did to the release of *Thriller*. He made an appointment with his plastic surgeon, exercising control over the only thing he could; his body. This time he had a cleft dimpled into the centre of his chin. Why? 'Because he wanted to,' says Dileo.

A series of seemingly preposterous stories made Dileo's August attempt at selling Michael all the more difficult. In October 1986, a report surfaced that Michael was so smitten by Elizabeth Taylor that he ordered special wallpaper with her picture on it. Also that he awoke every night at three a.m. just to eat some vegetables and then went back to sleep. Six months later a banner headline disclosed 'Michael Jackson Asked Liz To Wed – And She Said No.' Another item reported that Michael's preparations for his upcoming Japanese tour included packing enough Evian water for regular hot baths as well as inventing a plexiglass contraption that would separate him from the germs of his audience.

On 29 May came the topper. A two-paragraph press release sanctioned by Michael himself was sent out, informing the media that the superstar had 'submitted an official bid for the remains of the late John Merrick, known as the Elephant Man, from the London Hospital Medical College which has kept them since Merrick's death in 1890'. If people weren't convinced that Michael had gone over the edge, this did it. They couldn't in their wildest dreams imagine why Michael wanted this.

However, Michael had been utterly fascinated by Merrick and the odyssey of his life ever since watching the Academy Award-winning movie in his private theatre. 'He cried all through it,' says LaToya. 'He was really touched by the man's life.' Gradually, with repeated viewings, his fascination turned into an obsession. Michael read every bit of material on the Elephant Man and his disfiguring disease. He even made two personal visits to the London Hospital to view the man's remains. 'Jackson has a high degree of respect for the memory of Merrick,' said Dileo in the prepared statement, adding that he 'hopes to add them to his collection of rare and unusual memorabilia at his California compound'.

Strangely, it made sense to some people that Michael would want to own The Elephant Man's remains. Merrick, as portrayed in the dramatic film, was an absolutely pure soul, selfless and godly, embodying everything good and admirable, despite being ostracized, impoverished and gawked at by the public simply because his disfigured appearance was considered strange and frightening. It seems obvious that the Elephant Man's travails gave Michael something with which he could identify.

With these extraordinary events as the backdrop, Dileo cleared his throat and confronted the issues that had clouded the once-sympathetic image of Michael Jackson. Did he propose to Liz Taylor or didn't he? 'No, he didn't,' says Dileo. 'And no, there's no shrine to her in his house. Yes, they are very good friends. They dine together occasionally and visit.' Hormone shots? 'Ridiculous,' says Dileo. Eye surgery? 'He has never had his eyes done.' The nose? 'Yes, he did have his nose done, as every person in Hollywood has. Elvis did, Monroe did.' Cheekbones? 'No.' Did he have a cleft put in his chin? 'Yes.' Why? 'He wanted one.' Chemical or surgical skin lightening? 'Preposterous.' The hyperbaric oxygen chamber? 'He has a chamber. I don't know if he sleeps in it. I'm not for it. But Michael thinks it's something that's probably healthy for him. He's a bit of a health fanatic.'

Though the stories of Michael's eccentricities seem endless, there is only one word people use to describe him: 'nice'. 'I didn't see anything freaky,' said Helene Phillips, assistant choreographer on *Captain Eo*. 'No big ego. He was friendly and had a good time.' 'Always laughing and joking,' said Ola Ray, the female lead in the *Thriller* video. 'He seemed very happy.' 'Michael's a real sweetheart,' says guitarist David Williams. 'They don't come any nicer.'

All Dileo wanted was to smooth over the rough edges, bring Michael back into the public's favour, and get on with plugging his album and the tour. Michael is 'utterly devoted and very disciplined', he says. 'It sounds boring and stupid, like I'm hiding something, but I'm not. He realized that he's a good person. I think he hopes he's thought of as a good entertainer, since that's what he likes to do.'

Oh, and Dileo wanted to add one more thing. 'We see ourselves as a couple of regular guys.'

15

Tokyo, Japan. September 1987.

For reasons of security, the superstar avoided the front lobby of the Capitol Tokyo Hotel, slipping out of a side door for a photo session in front of a colourful Japanese shrine. Dressed casually in red trousers and a T-shirt, he had been taking the morning easy, goofing around in his hotel room, eating breakfast and watching television. His clandestine departure was a careful attempt to avoid the fans camped in front of the hotel. Still, a throng of nervous schoolgirls caught sight of his slim figure being whisked around the driveway. They shrieked with excitement and made a bee-line for him.

Instead of running, as was his instinct, he very calmly sat himself down on the cold sidewalk and, with an acquiescing silence, allowed the gaggle of young ladies in their prim school uniforms to click their cameras until they depleted their film. Out of this disbelieving cluster, one timid little girl mustered her courage and thrust out a pen and piece of paper. 'Excuse me, Mr Bubbles,' she said. 'May I please have an autograph?'

In the eyes of the Japanese, Michael's chimpanzee was a fully fledged superstar. 'If he could sing, he could sell out an arena all by himself,' said an incredulous Jackson associate. But the Bubbles' reception was nothing compared to the clamorous tizzy that greeted Michael's arrival. The moment Jackson stepped off the plane at Tokyo's Narita airport, he came face to face with a Nikon firing squad of six hundred photographers and more than one thousand fans who tried to cram into the airport. His was a welcome reminiscent of the Beatles' first trip to the United States. Crazed fans followed him everywhere; posters lined city walls; his face decorated shopping bags carried by commuters on the city's packed subways. In the heart of high-rent Tokyo, Nippon Television, attempting to recoup a portion of the $5 million they paid for exclusive TV

179

rights to Jackson's gig, opened a store that stocked only the fast-selling paraphernalia endorsed by Michael.

As he set up camp in his gigantic hotel suite, unpacking his three suitcases, two large trunks and the assorted video and stereo equipment he travelled with, Michael was a fairly happy fellow. *Bad*, out for just three weeks, had already zoomed to the top of the charts in at least eight countries. By Michael's third week in Japan, worldwide sales inched towards seven million. His first single, 'I Just Can't Stop Loving You', topped *Billboard*'s pop chart the week of 19 September. 'We have high hopes,' said Dileo from his three-room suite that was cluttered with video equipment, candies and flowers and disturbed by several constantly ringing telephones. 'Michael's taken aback by everything that's going on right now.'

Throughout his Japanese stay, Michael kept to a strict schedule. He stayed up until one a.m. and slept in his curtained room until noon. On show days he kept to himself, brooding, thinking, preserving his energy. He was served three vegetarian meals a day, though on Sundays he fasted, taking in nothing but orange juice. 'He really pops on those nights,' said one of his backup singers. 'His energy is really overwhelming.' As were his thrice-weekly performances. 'I have a hard time keeping my eyes off him,' said backup singer Sheryl Crow. 'He's so charismatic. When he's onstage, he keeps drawing you in.'

His auspicious return imbued Michael with a carefree spirit. In Osaka, he amused himself at a tea ceremony with the mayor by having Bubbles sit at the table and sip the warm potion with them. On off days he ventured out to shop for clocks, Japanese art books and a colourful Oriental screen. He also plundered two of Japan's biggest toy stores. Dileo wouldn't disclose what Michael purchased, but joked, 'His hotel room is a mess. I told him it's starting to look like his room at home.'

Rarely leaving the debris-strewn room, whose floors were littered with books and videotapes, Michael nonetheless kept a full schedule of fun and games. Gregory Peck, in town for the Tokyo Film Festival, dropped by to talk and invited Michael to a private afternoon screening. Katherine Jackson and LaToya visited and compared shopping tips; Michael preferred that his father, also in town, stay away. 'That's a touchy situation,' said LaToya from her suite at the Akasaka Prince Hotel.

When friends and family weren't around, Michael sought

amusement with Dileo. Late one night he burst into his manager's room and sprayed Silly String all over him. The next night they took Polaroid snapshots of each other making funny faces. He regularly chastized his overweight manager for eating too much as they watched television and discussed the news in local papers. Other evenings Michael chased after Bubbles down the hallway, playing tag and hitting him with pillows. 'We have a lot of fun late at night,' says Dileo. 'When it's quiet and the phone isn't ringing, we can goof off.'

If Michael often resembled a child, it was because he identified so closely with children. Quietly, he provided rafts of free tickets to handicapped youngsters, visited Japanese schools and hospitals and sent condolences and $20,000 to the grieving family of five-year-old Yoshiaki Ogiwara whose shocking kidnap and murder made front page headlines while Michael was there. At one concert he dedicated his entire Japanese tour to the boy, a gesture that brought tears to the eyes of the forty thousand adoring fans in the audience. 'People just don't have a realistic picture of who Michael is,' argued his makeup artist Karen Faye. 'He's innocent and inspiring without being preachy – and a lot of fun to be around.'

To tour intimates, Michael was obviously more confident than he had been on the Victory Tour. While the two hundred and forty crew members of the 1984 fiasco felt chaos around every corner, Michael alone presided over the ninety members of his solo show. He approved every photo and backstage pass, and he personally checked every detail of the show which lasted for one hundred minutes, contained sixteen songs, included lasers, explosions and a breathtaking magic trick that levitates him across the stage. The show cost $500,000 a week to run.

With fourteen shows before roughly 450,000 fans, the entertainer whom the Japanese press dubbed 'Typhoon Michael' raked in more than $15 million, and then departed for an October vacation and shopping spree in Hong Kong. His triumph should have provided a foundation of security. 'But Michael was worried about how people in the United States were receiving him,' says his mother, who was in Japan to support her son's first ever solo tour. 'The letter he wrote worried him. He wondered how people would take it.'

'A week or so later, I spoke to him,' says Bobby Colomby, who was recently made a CBS record executive. 'He was asking me why so many bad things were being said about him. He didn't understand. He said it really hurt him to read all that stuff. Basically, I tried to tell him that the problem was his. That he would never get the real story because everyone he hired was afraid to say no to him. He didn't have anyone around who could say, "Michael, you're full of shit."

'I explained to him, as I recall the conversation, that he'd never see Bruce Springsteen on the cover of the *National Enquirer* in a hyperbaric chamber. "Even if that picture came in, they wouldn't believe it," I said. "But you, Michael, spend so much time working on your mystique, on being reclusive and unusual that people will buy anything with your name on it." He said he understood, kind of.

'Then he told me that he wanted to see me, that I should just get on a plane and fly over to Hong Kong. I laughed. It was obvious that he wanted a friend, someone impartial to whom he could talk openly. But I couldn't just get on a plane like he couldn't just get on a plane and fly to Los Angeles. "But I'm there for you, Michael," I said. "I'm your friend. I always was and still am. All you have to do is call."

'There was silence. Then he said, "Bobby, I want you to come to my house and see it." I said, "I don't want to see it. Why don't you come to my house? Why don't you leave your entourage and come here? We'll sit and talk." He was quiet for a moment, and then he changed the subject.'

On a warm February afternoon Michael stood in front of a stage set up in a football stadium in Pennsicola, Florida. His untucked shirt flapped in the breeze as he watched his troupe of musicians, singers and dancers run through several of the new songs from *Bad* that were being added to the show. What he saw didn't make him happy.

'It's just not ready,' he told Dileo, who was sitting behind him. 'I'm gonna need more time to make it perfect.'

Dileo shook his head, remembering the ultimatum he'd been forced to deliver to get Michael out of the recording studio.

'We can't do it, Mike,' he said. 'We're in Kansas City in three weeks. New York in four. The train is leaving.'

'But I need at least another week,' he said. 'Another week or two and the show'll be perfect.'

'Impossible,' said Dileo.

Michael bit his lower lip. His brow furrowed, weighted by concern and worry. From Michael's vantage, the Japanese tour had been a warm-up. With little preparation, he had basically rehashed the Victory Tour minus his brothers while *Bad* caught fire in the stores. 'The Japanese leg was basically everyone go out and do whatever they do best,' said keyboardist Greg Phillinganes. Five sell-out shows in Australia followed the same pattern. Adds Dileo, 'We knew things were going to sell out and be fine, whatever we did. And we were rushing things, coming right out of the studio and not having much time to prepare like we wanted.'

The stakes were much higher now that the album was no longer brand new. The press-shy Jackson had his publicists working overtime, spewing out 'Hot Flash' releases that pressed the hype and, hopefully, increased the sales: 'Worldwide sales of Michael Jackson's *Bad* LP surge past eleven million; number one in twenty-three countries.' 'Michael Jackson voted top Male Vocal Artist in Scandinavian readers' poll.' 'Jackson received four nominations for American Grammy.' 'Ten-city ticket sales on Michael Jackson's European stadium tour have hit one million mark . . . promoters exert pressure to extend tour.' 'Prince and Princess of Wales will attend 16 July Michael Jackson Wembley Show.' 'Michael Jackson to make a substantial contribution from concert's proceeds to the U.K. Prince's Trust charity.' 'Michael Jackson to perform at this year's Grammys.'

For a guy who hated interviews, Michael sure liked seeing his name in print. He even permitted *Entertainment Tonight* to film some of his rehearsals and then provided some off-camera narration for the segment. Afterwards, he and Dileo shared dinner with that show's anchorwoman, Mary Hart. 'Michael liked her,' revealed an associate. 'When she left, he even called his publicist, Lee Solters, and asked if she was married.'

With the publicity machine rolling in high gear, Michael kept his eagle eye trained on the pop charts, monitoring the fate of each single *Bad* launched. The first had hit number one in September. The second, 'Bad', the title track that announced his tough new image, captured the first position on 24 October. The third release, 'The Way You Make Me Feel', a frothy number reminiscent of a Broadway dance tune, scored the Big One in late January. 'Michael was very happy, but restrained because it was still early,' says Dileo.

Nonetheless, each chart-topper fuelled the superstar's fervent hope that *Bad* would rewrite music history by surpassing *Thriller*. 'We had made a secret pact, a game plan,' says Dileo. 'I promised Mike that we'd get five number one singles off the album.'

Other factors weighed heavily on the superstar. His home life was miserable. He wasn't getting along with his father, who was in financial trouble, and his brothers were pressuring him to commit to another album, which he avoided without ever saying no. 'Michael's never said he's left the group,' says Marlon. Confrontation wasn't his style. But a successful tour would give Michael the courage to flee their prying, manipulation and influence. Without anyone's knowledge, he was searching for his own home.

In the meantime, home away from home was the stage, and as such, Michael's goal was clearly outlined: his performance not only had to live up to his superstar reputation, it had to be brilliant enough to erase all the year's-worth of rumours surrounding him as well as make it impossible for him to go back to his brothers. Which is why after hours and hours of rehearsal, he was still frustrated. The show wasn't flowing, not from his perspective, anyway. Calling a break, he took aside choreographer Vince Paterson, a lanky veteran dancer, and led the way down to a cold, barren room hidden deep within the dank bowels of the outdoor stadium.

When they finally reached the empty, dungeonlike room, Michael motioned for Paterson to take a seat, and then followed him inside. He closed the door, turned out the light and sat down beside his friend. It was so dark neither one could see the other. Which is exactly what Michael wanted. In the pitch black, time and place were suspended. Outside concerns were forgotten in the pervasive silence. Forgetting he was in the centrepiece of a multimillion-dollar venture, Michael transformed himself into a child who wanted to play a thrilling game of 'let's pretend'.

'Let's create a fantasy for ourselves,' said Michael.

'Okay,' replied Paterson. 'What?'

'Well, we have to do something incredible,' Michael whispered. 'We have to make something that's never been done before. It's got to be perfect. It's got to be absolute magic.'

'What do you have in mind?' wondered Paterson.

Michael got excited. He'd been pushed to the edge of tolerance by the unsatisfying grind of rehearsals and frustrated by immutable time constraints, but here in this dark chamber, he finally locked onto the inspiration that had been lacking.

'Let's say,' he said, 'that if we don't create the best show possible . . .' He stopped and giggled.

'What?' asked Paterson.

'Okay,' Michael started in again. 'Let's say that if we don't create the best show possible, the most perfect show . . . we'll get our heads chopped off.'

Facing a deadline, Michael needed to feel the desperation. He had to be forced into making a decision. He and Paterson talked into the night, and during the following day Paterson took notes during rehearsal. They went over them until a show to Michael's liking was carved out and practised. 'I really had to persuade him to add some new songs,' says Paterson. 'Michael wanted everyone in the audience to already know the songs. But I told him, "After selling twelve million albums, they're going to be familiar with the songs." '

Paterson simply 'wanted to convince the world that he [Michael]'s the most incredible Broadway performer, a guy who can out rock Whitesnake, and so on.' Dileo told him, 'Make this a show for Michael.' That was a challenge. 'He's so generous,' says Paterson. 'He'd hate taking away from other's solos.' Perfectionism was the rule. 'He always thinks there's room for improvement. Michael would rehearse a single phrase in a dance for one to two hours, until it became ingrained in his motor memory.' And despite the pressure, he was unfailingly positive in outlook. 'He never would say, "I don't like that." It'd be more like, "That's great, but I think we could do something cooler." Cooler is his word.'

What impressed Paterson most was Michael's willingness to receive criticism. It was almost as if he'd rehearsed in a cocoon all his life. 'I'd bring him notes,' he says. 'Little things I'd observed or ideas I had. At first, I was frightened about it, because, you know, who wants to criticize Michael Jackson? But he was not only receptive, he was so gracious and thankful. He said, "This is so nice. I can't believe you're taking the time to do this." '

By 23 February, the tour's opening night in Kansas City, Michael was raring to seize the Kemper Arena stage and display the true mettle of his talent. This, after all, was what earned him his fame, not the quirky tales that made him a headline sensation, and his fans wanted to recall that what he did best, probably better than anyone alive, was sing and dance. The moment of truth arrived with the subtlety of a sonic boom. A thunderous bass rumble shook the concert hall and a blinding bank of lights that slowly dropped into the bottom of the stage brought the packed house to its feet. Flanked by his dancers, backed by his hard driving musicians, echoed by his singers, Michael stood in the centre. 'What was remarkable,' said one critic, 'was that most people there seemed shocked that he was alive, right there in flesh and blood, and not some weird creation they only read about in tabloids.'

Indeed, onstage Michael was very real. Dressed in his silver-studded black leather, girdled in straps and buckles, a huge metallic belt buckle centred on his waist, Michael snapped out the lines to 'Wanna Be Startin' Somethin' ' in a way that barked to everyone he meant business. His rendition of syrupy ballads impressed hardcore rockers. 'With the possible exception of Frank Sinatra, there is no other male vocalist who can wring so much revelation out of sheer treacle,' wrote *Rolling Stone*.

Michael pulled out all stops. A fluff song like 'She's Out of My Life' was turned into a soul-filled lament of pain and emotion that packed both sweetness and rage. 'Jackson seemed to sing the song in two directions at once,' the review continued. ' "Why, why do you treat me this way?" he sang time and again, his voice full of honey, his face bursting with anger, as if the song conveyed all the hurt he may feel over the recent rupture in the public's love for him.'

His renditions of 'Thriller' and 'Beat It' were full-blown, gimmick-laden recreations of his popular theatrical videos. His performance of 'Billie Jean', a venom-spitting Michael dancing angry in the spotlight, showcased his spectacular grace and lighter-than-air prancing. But it was the poignant, raise-the-roof delivery of the gospel-tinged 'Man in the Mirror', which closed the show, that brought Michael to the centre of the stage by himself, no costumed foils to play off, and let him sing with the naked honesty that insured no one missed one iota of his overwhelming talent.

'That night at the Kemper Arena, one had the feeling the whole show had been building to this one performance,' said *Rolling Stone*. 'By the time it was over, what had seemed plain after his *Motown 25* appearance stood confirmed: in those moments when Michael Jackson chooses to give everything he has, there's probably not a more transfixing performer in pop music today.'

With the boldness of a championship fighter, Michael moved confidently from his tour opener directly into the centre of the showbusiness ring: New York City. Rather than iron out whatever wrinkles were in the show by playing secondary cities, where he could avoid major media coverage, his second stop was the media capital of the world, where his performance was certain to receive microscopic scrutiny. It was an audacious move that probably no other performer of Michael's stature would ever risk, simply because of how great a risk it truly was. However, there was method behind the madness.

The Grammy Awards were scheduled for live telecast from Manhattan on 2 March. Not only had Michael received four nominations, including Album of the Year, Best Male Pop Vocal, Best Male R&B Vocal Performance, and Producer of the Year. But he also agreed to perform on the show, his first live TV appearance since the 1983 Motown special that had impressed tens of millions of viewers. 'He wanted to prove that he was for real,' says Bob Jones, the former Motown publicist who'd been hired the week before by Michael as director of communications for MJJ Productions. 'Michael wanted to erase all the negative publicity that had been trailing him and replace it with a positive image of him doing what he does best.'

In addition, Michael's appearance on the broadcast was a terrific advertisement for his album. But it was also a gesture to the Academy, a notice, of sorts, of his competitive fire. That Michael was willing to risk his fabled perfectionism in the unpredictable conditions of live television signalled just how important it was to him that he win the awards for which he'd been nominated. He had already collected eleven Grammys, eight alone in 1984, which set a record.

Still, remarked an associate, 'you have to keep in mind what happened to Michael during the 1980 Grammy Awards. His album *Off the Wall* had sold over six million copies. In effect, Michael was the biggest black artist America had ever produced. He fully expected to be nominated for the Album of the Year and Record of the Year awards, and he deserved to. But instead he won only one award – best male R&B vocal.

'That experience hurt Michael, and it also taught him a lesson. You could be the biggest black entertainer in history, and yet to much of the music industry and media, you were an invisible man. That's why he aimed to make *Thriller* the biggest record of all time, and that's why he has aligned himself with Pepsi. Pepsi gave him the biggest commercial endorsement contract that anybody has ever received, and to Michael, the more accomplishments you have to your name, the more people have to recognize you. That's what an event like this is all about. Michael still wants the world to acknowledge him.'

His performance was a two-way street. With him on the

programme, the Grammy telecast was sure to receive high ratings. What did they have to offer him?

The morning of the telecast, Dileo, gnawing on one of his cigars, was clear about what he wanted. 'As far as I'm concerned, we need to win Album of the Year,' he said. 'That's the big one.'

Michael did his part. He opened his two-song showcase with his current single, 'The Way You Make Me Feel', which started slowly, allowing the singer to warm-up his animated gyrations, pumps, thrusts, and crotch-grabs, and then heated into a fast-paced boy-meets-girl chase, during which Michael caught fire, jumping, dancing, sliding and dashing across the stage in a flurry of smooth as silk moves that lit a fire in the audience filled with his peers.

When it was over the stage cleared and Michael, dripping sweat, moved front and centre and began the social-minded, gospel-inflected 'Man in the Mirror'. His fine, supple voice resonated with amazing clarity, then was joined by Andrew Crouch and the New Hope Baptist Church Choir, and the majesty of the spirited vocals carried the audience to a rapturous height, leaving no doubt of Michael's phenomenal ability. 'That was one helluva moving performance,' Liza Minnelli remarked several nights later. 'He just never lets you forget how good he really is.'

Awardwise, though, Michael was left disappointed. Sitting in the front row between Dileo and Jones, he watched sombrely as U2's *The Joshua Tree* claimed Album of the Year, and all the rest of the awards he was nominated for went to other performers. Dileo downplayed the losses and tried to salvage the other positives. 'Michael reminded everybody in the world what a great performer he is,' Dileo said. 'In effect, he told them to forget about all the trash they read about him. As far as I'm concerned, his performance hushed up a lot of critics. And as for a few of those academy voters, well, I hope they watched it, too.'

When the show concluded a very dejected Michael quickly returned to his hotel suite at the Helmsly Palace. 'I called him up and told him he was robbed,' says Marlon. 'He was really disappointed and hurt.' Dileo thought Michael took the shutout rather well – considering the obvious. 'He would've liked to have won,' says the manager. 'It always hurts to lose, and he's competitive. When I saw him later, it was like, wait a minute, forget we didn't win the damn Grammys. We gave the greatest performance of our life. If anybody didn't vote for you, they're sure sorry now. He then went to bed and woke up the next day and said, "Hey, what's the agenda? Let's do a show." '

'It was just wonderful,' said maestro Leonard Bernstein. 'Fabulous,' gushed bandleader Paul Schaffer. 'It was like the best of Broadway, the best of rock and roll and the best of Disneyland all on stage,' bubbled Christine Brinkley, the model-wife of superstar Billy Joel.

The three circus-like nights Michael performed at Madison Square Garden brought the biggest names in show business. Whitney Houston, U2, Brooke Shields, Bon Jovi, Hall and Oates, Madonna and New York mayor Ed Koch. Backstage, Brinkley complimented Michael's sister, Janet, on her hair. 'I just love it.' Miko Brando scurried to locate a block of seats so Janet and LaToya could sit together, and Madonna, waiting until the lights went off before taking her seat, talked about how excited she was to see the show. 'It's crazy out there,' noted the material girl.

Late at night, after the second show, Michael ensconced himself in his plush hotel suite with his A-list friends, including Minnelli, actress Amy Irving (Steven Spielberg's wife), Yoko Ono and her son, Sean, and went over a wave of glowing reviews. 'The notion that another pop singer and dancer could invest anything like the passion he stamps into every detail of the performance is practically inconceivable,' wrote Stephen Holden in the *New York Times*. Dance critic Anna Kisselgoff chimed in with her own opinion. 'Viewed specifically as a dancer, he is tops.'

But even this lionizing paled next to the tribute accorded that same week to Michael – who had little in the way of formal education – as he received an honorary doctorate from Nashville's esteemed Fisk University at the United Negro College Fund's forty-fourth anniversary dinner. Attended by two thousand friends and fans who paid $1,000 each to join in honouring Jackson, the four-hour dinner, like most events concerning Michael, cast the singer in the larger-than-life role he seems to prefer. Thankfully, it wasn't another example of that showbiz tradition, the roast. The worst thing anybody said about Michael all night was producer Quincy Jones revealing that Jackson's pals call him Smelly for his uncanny ability to 'smell out a good business deal'.

This was a testimony to the unpublicized charitable side of the young eccentric whose acts of generosity included a $600,000 contribution to the UNCF and a donation of all royalties from his single, 'Man in the Mirror', which went to number one two weeks later, to Camp Good Times, a charity for terminally ill children in Los Angeles. *The Wall Street Journal*, of all places, editorialized that he deserved wide praise for his often anonymous philanthropic activities. But not even the *Journal* could have forecast the bull market of praise that hit Michael as he sat on the dais with Liz Taylor, Minnelli, Whitney Houston and CBS chief Walter Yetnikoff.

'Michael is the only true entertainer who's happened in the last twenty years,' said Minnelli, adding that he is 'probably the most interesting person I know. His curiosity is boundless – art, literature, all the good stuff.' Taylor stood to say, 'I don't think a better person has ever hit this planet.' She also praised him for 'the things you have done that so few people know about, the things that you have done anonymously, alone, that not even the receiver knows about. That is true charity: asking nothing in return. At least it was all secret until I opened my big mouth.'

Even President Reagan checked in, via videotape, to pay homage to the man he called 'the new Dr J'.

This seemingly endless buffet of ego massage might have been just what Michael needed to make him feel loved and appreciated. But the only praise that brought real tears to his unshielded eyes came from Rust College honour student, Curressia McFarland, who said if it weren't for Michael, who had so far sponsored ninety-seven scholarships, she would not have been able to attend college. When the college senior noted that she had a 3.9 grade point average, the crowd gave her a standing ovation. 'I'm proof that something good can come out of the South,' she said.

Genuinely moved, Michael left his seat and gave her three kisses on the cheek, and as part of his brief thank-you speech, before which he laughed, 'I can't believe I'm nervous,' revealed the tender part of him that honestly believes he can make a difference in the world. 'To want to learn, to have the capacity to learn and not to be able to learn is a tragedy,' he said. 'I'm glad to be associated with an evening that says this will never happen.'

After all the ceremony, Dileo offered his own tribute to Michael, who had survived an emotional week filled with great highs and lows. 'I'm very proud of Mike,' he said. 'I think tonight people saw that the kid has turned into a man.'

16

Santa Ynez Valley, California. March 1988

Someone must've stopped and counted them, because one of the features listed in the mouth-watering description of the 2700-acre estate in the Santa Ynez Valley were the fifty thousand oak trees dotting the gorgeous property. Michael liked that. He also liked the twelve-bedroom house, the twenty-car garage, the crystal blue pond, the rock-lined brook that meandered sleepily and the endless maze of winding trails that led high into the green hills on the outer boundaries of the Sycamore Valley Ranch that was owned by developer William Bone.

For two years Michael had been searching for a home, the past year especially. With his family relations deteriorating as his success soared, he wanted a place of his own. His specifications were exact: the home was to be Tudor in style, the grounds had to be spacious enough to accommodate his existing menagerie as well as enable him to expand his collection, and it had to provide him with an overwhelming sense of serenity. A true getaway. Money was no problem.

Such a Shangri La he had once visited: the ranch where he stayed with Paul and Linda McCartney when they filmed the video for 'Say, Say, Say'. 'The only problem is that he couldn't remember where it was,' says a source. And he couldn't call and ask Paul: they weren't speaking because of the acrimonious bidding war over the ATV catalogue.

Beverly Hills realtor Gloria Berlin, a specialist in multimillion dollar estates, heard of Jackson's interest and set out to find him his Eden. 'It was common knowledge that he was having trouble keeping his animals in Encino,' says a source close to the deal. 'Michael had tried to buy a deer park in Malibu, but it fell through.'

As expected, dealing with Michael was made problematic because of his remoteness. Not only was he physically isolated from people, but in financial matters, he was strictly buffered by attorney Branca and accountant Marshall Gelfand. 'When Gloria tried to present properties, she was told she wasn't allowed to leave any packages with security outside his home,' confides the source. 'People were disturbing him all the time. She was told to mail her proposals or call, but they wouldn't give her a phone number or an address.'

Berlin was near to giving up when she encountered Michael's chief of security, Bill Bray, outside the Encino mansion, and was told that he would be her go-between. Over a period of several months, she showed Bray eight or nine properties. He previewed them, then told Michael about what he'd seen, and when the description seemed right, Michael himself ventured out to inspect the lots. But nothing came close to the image of the ranch he pictured in his mind. 'This place became his obsession,' says the source. 'It was all he talked about.'

Finally, after months of searching, Berlin came across the beautiful Sycamore Valley Ranch, the place Michael had been longing for, and when she showed it to him, he was overjoyed. 'He literally leaped four feet in the air, and then hugged and kissed her,' recalls the source.

The asking price was steep: $35 million furnished or $32.5 million unfurnished. Michael was unphased. He toured the grounds by the horse-drawn carriage provided by the owner, though he initially refused to meet Mr Bone, who had decided to sell to defray divorce costs. 'Bone had his feelings hurt when Michael didn't want to meet him,' says the source. 'He thought Michael didn't want to be his friend.' They met on Michael's second visit, and three more visits followed. 'He loved the place,' says the source. 'He was charmed from day one.'

In 1986 Michael's accountant submitted an offer of $15 million, which was turned down. At the end of March 1988, after more than a year and a half of negotiating, Bone accepted the superstar's final offer of $17 million. Michael was ecstatic. 'He talked on and on about the ranch's beauty, the spirituality, the fresh air,' recalls the source. 'He stood outside and imagined riding horses. He noted the quiet and the peace of the lake. He said he wanted to swim in the creek and build a Noah's Ark. To him, it was the grandest playground in the world. He said he wanted to put his Never-Never Land there.'

Almost immediately, tales began to circulate of Michael's exotic plans for his new home. In one part, he was going to plant authentic jungle vegetation and stock the grounds with leopards, tigers and zebras. Of course, he already owned Jabbar the giraffe. He was going to dig a moat and install a drawbridge. He was going to manufacture fake snow during the winter months. He planned to erect an aerial tramway and have robot-controlled cars zooming around a track. Even wilder plans called for him to have 100 foot-high crystal pyramids to recharge his psychic energy as well as a laboratory where he could hire scientists to research into longevity. 'That's all nonsense,' says Dileo. 'He just wanted a beautiful home and he's happy with what he purchased.'

Michael's new residence was news to his folks. 'I heard he purchased a ranch recently,' acknowledged Joe not too long afterwards. 'No one told me nothing about it. I heard about it on the television, same as his mother.' It wasn't likely that Michael would've told Joe in person. The two didn't speak, and even when he was in Los Angeles, Michael seldom visited the family's Encino spread. What was the beef? 'That's his problem, not mine,' snapped Joe.

Michael wasn't the only Jackson offspring to find moving away from home traumatic. About the same time as the family's biggest star was sewing up the deal for his new residence, LaToya also split from the Encino mansion and moved into a $800-a-day suite in New York's Waldorf Astoria Hotel. Her departure ignited a war of insults between her father and her new manager, Jack Gordon, a former carnival operator and Las Vegas casino worker with a shady background the Jacksons hadn't yet uncovered. 'I make 'em, they take 'em,' said Joe, who managed LaToya until Gordon swept her away. 'Gordon is a mooch.' Responded Gordon, 'I love Joe like I love poison.'

LaToya's circumstances had a familiar ring. In 1983 Michael had dumped his father and hired a new manager. The following year Janet manoeuvred around her father, moved temporarily to Minnesota and recorded *Control*, the smash LP that established her solo career. LaToya clearly envisioned similar results for herself. 'I want platinum albums,' said the singer, whose last LP in 1983 went nowhere. LaToya was more candid about the struggles with her stern papa than was her brother. 'My father would tell me what I should do and I'd just listen,' she said of Joe's management style. 'I didn't ever really voice my opinion. If I questioned him, he'd scream at me. So I wouldn't dare.'

Candour was not LaToya's strong suit, though. The 33-year-old singer, one year older than Marlon, claimed that she was actually twenty-four. She also denied reassembling her face with plastic surgery, though the influence of Michael's plastic surgeon is obvious. 'I don't know who she's trying to fool,' laughed Marlon.

However, in the Jackson family, reputations are as secure as a management contract. Joe's especially suffered with the publication of Michael's autobiography, *Moonwalk*, which accused him of beating his son with belts and wood switches. 'I don't remember spanking Michael,' said Joe. 'But if he got spanked for something, it was for a reason. I was especially tough on Michael because I had to make him the best. It was out of love. I really wanted him to be the best.' Michael subsequently withdrew these allegations. LaToya didn't accuse her father of physical abuse, but said he could be bluntly intimidating and emotionally cruel. 'He would have a look in his eye or a tone in his voice and you knew you had to do something,' she said. 'You wouldn't even question.'

When LaToya chose not to renew her father's contract, she elected to inform him by letter, even though they lived in the same house. 'I thought it would be the professional way,' she said. When he ignored her letters, she finally broached the subject in person. 'He'd say to me, "I will sit on you for five years before I ever let you go,"' she says. 'In other words, he was saying I'd never get anywhere and he'd make certain of that. And that made me feel awfully bad.'

LaToya's only confidante was her mother, who soothed her tears but refused to interfere. 'I don't want to get in the middle of it,' she'd say.

Outwardly, at least, each maintained there were no hard feelings. 'I'd see him fifteen minutes later and it was smiles like nothing ever happened,' said LaToya. 'I know it sounds strange that we live in the same house and all this was going on, but our parents always taught us to respect them. We try never to argue.' Joe waxed philosophic. 'If LaToya falls flat, I will then pick her up as a parent,' he said. 'She can always come back home and I'll treat her like I would the rest. When you have other people, all they're looking out for is the money. When she falls and can't make any money, they're gone to the next person.'

The way Joe saw it, greedy opportunists seduced each one of the children he'd nursed from obscurity into severing their contracts with him and pursuing individual careers, which broke up the family act. 'I found when you let one of them sing lead on most of the songs,' he grumbled, 'there's going to come a time when somebody comes along and says, "We don't need so-and-so. Why don't you do it yourself?" That's what happened to Michael.'

Despite his unprecedented success, contended his bitter father, Michael made a mistake by going solo. 'I've seen Michael's act a couple times, but it still wasn't like the brothers up there,' argued Joe. "Cause when you're brothers or sisters, there's a certain quality of tone in your voice that blends. It's family. Now, Michael's got a good show. But with the brothers, it's a better show.'

Joe, whose own career was reduced to managing several minor league singing acts and importing brandy from Cyprus, was attempting to angle a way back into the big money by ingratiating himself with his children. But they weren't buying it. As a matter of fact, the divisiveness ran so deep that Michael, LaToya and Janet had all conferred about offering their father a generous annuity if he would give up his delusions of managing them and retire from showbusiness. 'No figures were brought up,' LaToya says. 'But we discussed it and presented the plan to him.'

His answer? 'My father's a very difficult man sometimes,' said LaToya. 'He didn't understand.'

More than anything, Michael needed to distance himself from the family's nonstop squabbling and by the end of May he was pursuing the European leg of his world tour. The timing couldn't have been better. More than one million people, at an average price of $30 per ticket, had seen his concerts. *Moonwalk* was a runaway hit, topping the bestseller lists in both the U.S. and Britain, though it abruptly bottomed out after several weeks. 'Dirty Diana' was on its way to fulfilling his manager's promise by becoming the fifth straight number one single. And the press had finally quit focusing on his strange behaviour, writing instead about his music as if they'd just discovered that he could sing and dance. 'What Michael needed was to get away from his family,' says an associate. 'They put too much pressure on him, and he felt huge guilt when he ignored them. Besides, he put enough pressure on himself with just his career.'

The Jackson World Tour entourage checked into Rome on 19 May four days before his first concert. Typically, Michael was fêted in a manner usually reserved for dignitaries and heads of state. U.S. Ambassador Maxwell Rabb and his wife celebrated his arrival with a grand party at their formal home, Villa Taverna. The star-studded guest list included fashion designer Georgio Armani and screen sirens Sophia Loren and Gina Lollobrigida, whose presence indicated they'd called a truce to years of feuding to party with Michael. 'Michael had a lot of fun,' says a record executive. 'He didn't exactly mingle, but he enjoyed himself.'

Despite the accolades and achievements, there was still a disquieting sense of unhappiness in Michael's life. After his concert at the Stadio Flamino, he attended a fancy party thrown by the record company at the Palazzo Taverna, a historic sixteenth-century palace in the heart of Rome, and he took side trips to the Sistine Chapel, to Florence for a peek at Michaelangelo's David, and visited several hospitals. But for the most part, Michael confined himself to the only place where he felt comfortable: his hotel room.

What did he do there besides watch videotaped movies? When he checked out chambermaids discovered a neat, ten-inch-high ballpoint rendering of himself on the bed sheet. The table cloth bore a portrait of blonde bombshell Brigitte Nielsen, and there were additional self-portraits on the pillowcases and napkins. To the busy housekeeping staff, these introspective doodles of a bored superstar were nothing more than soiled linens that needed to be laundered.

The tour continued through Austria, Holland and Sweden, where Michael was greeted with pomp and circumstance. In Basel, Switzerland, pals Elizabeth Taylor and Sophia Loren showed up, along with Bob Dylan. The Paris shows were attended by thespians Rob Lowe, Yves Montand, and Grace Jones, along with Branford Marsalis, Ruth Pointer and Paris mayor Jacques Chirac. In Cologne, Michael visited Tina Turner, and when his magician friends Siegried and Roy invited him and his band to their amusement park, Phantasialand, he accepted, and the park closed down an hour early so Michael and his band could have free run of the place and watch the famous white tiger show in peace.

When he wasn't visiting celebrities, Michael sought companionship in Jimmy Safechuck, a ten-year-old Californian boy whom he had befriended while making his final Pepsi commercial. The superstar had a facsimile of his stage costume made for his playmate; they wanted to dress alike. He paid for the kid's plush hotel suite. He took the sixth-grader on

196

expensive shopping sprees to toy stores, like Hamley's in London, where he dropped thousands of dollars on toys and computer games. He even gave Jimmy's parents a brand new, $100,000 Rolls-Royce. 'That didn't go over well with some of his longtime associates,' says an insider on the tour. Several months later, Michael was forced to cancel two shows when he caught a cold from the boy. 'Who was going to tell him to keep away?' says the source.

While Michael played hide and seek in his hotel rooms, his hyperbole-spewing publicists mailed out five separate press releases heralding his touchdown in London, where he broke existing gate records by selling out the 72,000-seat Wembley Stadium seven nights in a row. Ava Gardner, Terence Trent D'Arby, Martin Scorsese, Harrison Ford, Penny Marshall, Peter Gabriel, Carly Simon, George Lucas, Dustin Hoffman, Robin Williams and Donna Summer were a few of the illustrious celebrities possessing backstage passes.

The third Wembley show was attended by Prince Charles and Princess Diana. 'This got Michael tremendously excited,' said chief publicist, Lee Solters, making no secret of Jackson's admiration for royalty. He presented the royal couple and their two children with tour jackets at a private meeting. Solters said, 'Michael couldn't stop smiling. He's a big fan of Diana.' But it was Prince Charles who got a laugh out of the superstar when he admitted he found rock and roll hard to dance to. 'Well, I can give you some dance lessons,' offered Michael.

Several nights later Michael dramatically stopped his performance twenty minutes into the show and stunned his British fans when he broke into tears and asked for a moment of silence for a close friend of his whom he had earlier learned had fallen ill. 'A very dear and close friend of mine, Elizabeth Taylor, is very sick right now,' he said in a quavering voice. 'I would like everyone in the stadium to bow their heads for five seconds as a mark of respect for her.'

Wiping tears from his eyes, Michael dedicated his next song, 'I Just Can't Stop Loving You', to Taylor, and then during the following tune, 'She's Out of My Life', again broke down and wept openly in his cupped hands.

When news of Michael's melodramatic reaction reached Taylor's overly-protective advisers in the U.S. a day later, they were livid. They hastily issued denials of her illness, saying that her only problem was her recurring back pain. However, Michael's info was correct. He'd inadvertently made public a personal matter that was strictly hush-hush. In reality Taylor was racked by excruciating back pain and was reportedly chewing Percodan pills like candy and washing them down with Bloody Marys. By autumn, she was hospitalized to treat her back, and soon after, she was transferred to the Betty Ford Center, where she fought her ongoing dependence on the painkillers. 'With all the drugs she's absorbed,' a staffer admitted, 'she's a female version of Elvis – and you know what happened to him.'

Yes, and so did Michael.

The blue van was speeding down a straight Nevada highway, its tinted windows rolled up against the desert heat. Inside, the air conditioning and the radio were both cranked up high. An overly excited DJ introduced 'Dirty Diana', the latest number one single from Michael Jackson, 'the world's biggest superstar', and the woman in the plush bucket seat switched her attention from the passing scenery outside. 'You can turn that one down,' she says to her husband. 'It's not really one of my favourites.'

But even if Katherine Jackson – the sweet-tempered matriarch of the pop dynasty that's produced one superstar Jackson after another – didn't care for that particular tune, she was fond of what it evoked. 'I feel good when I hear any of the children's music on the radio,' she sighed wistfully, as the big desert sky blushes ruby in the sunset. 'It takes me back to Gary, Indiana, when Joe was working hard and I was back home, struggling to make ends meet. My gosh, we've sure come a long way.'

Back in those hardscrabble times, when their nine kids were spilling out of the two-bedroomed house in Gary and Joe was supporting the crew as a welder and crane operator, the Jacksons undoubtedly would've been shocked to know how costly success could be. Almost twenty years later, with their net worth somewhere in the middle nine-figure neighbourhood, the closeknit clan was living out their dream of showbusiness fortune as a nightmare.

The Jackson Five had become ancient history, and the once-innocent boys – Jackie, Tito, Jermaine, Marlon and Michael – were now all strong-minded adults who found it difficult to cope with each other's varying levels of success. Sisters LaToya and Janet had spun off in separate directions, and the family itself had been torn by financial squabbles, professional disagreements, sibling jealousy and emotional discord.

'This isn't the way I planned it,' grumbled a dejected Joe. 'The fighting, the money . . . we were all supposed to share in the glory.'

By autumn 1988, the family's glory was owned by a single individual. Globe-trotting Michael was cutting a multimillion dollar path through Europe, winning crowds while becoming a virtual stranger to his family, whom he had last seen in February. LaToya, the family feared, was being held captive in New York by her less-than-reputable manager, Jack Gordon, whom Joe and Katherine had discovered was a convicted felon, which raised intense concern among the entire clan. Janet was in the midst of negotiating an end to her management contract with her father and getting ready for studio sessions for her next album. To top it off, Jackie and Jermaine were each trying to right their lives after failed marriages.

'The family situation is embarrassing,' admits Rebbie, the Jackson's eldest child, who set off on her own when the family still lived in Gary and making a record was an alluring mirage on the horizon.

Joe stood on the brink of desperation, a man of more pride than muscle. However, there were plenty of excuses. Over the years, he had been a ripe target for unscrupulous advisers – losing millions of dollars to dry oil wells, bankrupt office buildings and an accountant who, Joe maintained, pocketed hundreds of thousands earmarked for taxes. He couldn't admit that the family's complex financial empire had simply outgrown his capabilities. 'There's been an awful lot of money made, and there's been an awful lot of money taken,' he says. 'It's not pretty, not pretty at all.'

After Michael purchased his Xanadu near Santa Barbara, the Disneyesque Encino residence that was the family's headquarters for eighteen years took on the scent of a travelling carnival that was about to pack up and move on. 'When we built this house, we made it large enough for the whole family,' offers the patriarch plaintively, conveniently forgetting that it was Michael's money that enlarged the home while he was estranged from his wife. 'We honestly thought the kids would stay here till they got married, maybe longer. These kids seem more like kids now than when they were real small – at least they get into more trouble now.'

The kids didn't see things that way. 'A father will always feel he knows more than his kids,' says Marlon. 'It just got to the point where we were grown men and had our own lives. We couldn't always do what he wanted.'

Katherine tried to be objective but found her concerns too many and widespread. In May 1988, eight months into an international tour, Michael's strength had ebbed enough that a doctor ordered him to eat more protein. 'He had to choose between fish and chicken,' she says. 'The doctor made him choose one or the other.' Jermaine had recently moved back into the Encino home with his pregnant girlfriend, Margaret Maldonado, and their two-year-old son, Jeremy. 'Jermaine is such a nice young man,' she says. 'But I think it might've been hard for him having Michael be so successful.'

Katherine, the family's primary link with Michael, couldn't conceal a genuine blush when admitting that her most famous offspring regularly showered her with lavish gifts, like the very expensive diamond and emerald bracelet he'd recently presented to her. 'It embarrasses me,' she says. 'I'm always crying.' She tried to keep regular phone contact with him, occasionally venturing out on the road to allay her concern over what she read about him. 'I've heard that he's very lonely. I've never thought that. But I've heard it enough to be concerned about it like any mother would be.'

For a long time, she tried convincing Michael to speak out against the many nasty rumours in the press that were making his life miserable. 'Michael and I talked about this a lot,' she says. 'It really hurt him, all those stories about him being gay, about his voice being kept high artificially, that he had everything done to his face. It's all untrue. It not only hurt him, but it made me cry, too. I used to say to him, "Why don't you confront them, tell the truth?" And he'd say, "It wouldn't do any good. If I talked, they'd say even more."'

Katherine sat at the kitchen table, nibbling chocolate chip cookies and recalling bygone days with a tender smile. But her eyes were closed to the jealousies that strained the relationships of her sons. 'I don't think fame has affected us,' she says. 'I don't think any of my boys have changed. But as a mother, I guess, I might be looking at things a little differently.'

Ditto for her husband. He found it impossible to understand why his nearly thirty-year-old son never informed them about his new house. 'I was waiting for Michael to come and say something, but he never did,' Joe admits. 'That hurt us.' Michael obviously wanted to let his actions do his talking rather than risk an emotionally painful confrontation. He has been conspiciously generous with his parents, giving them more than a million dollars in cash, bailing them out of trouble with the Internal Revenue Service, sending them plane tickets and presenting them with wonderful gifts. Still, their relationship was poor, despite the outward portrait of familial bliss, and Joe was confused. 'We wonder why things have changed like they have, why he doesn't seem to care about his family,' he says. 'The few times we've spoken to him, Michael seems glad to hear from us. But when you talk to other people, they say he doesn't want to be involved with his family.'

The reason was simple, at least to Michael. 'Everyone always wants money,' says an associate. 'The family is broke or hurting for money – most of them, anyway – and all they want to do is get Michael involved in things he doesn't want to do.' He participated in the Victory Tour as a way of bailing out his siblings and filling their empty bank accounts. Tito, Marlon, Jermaine and Randy netted about $7 million each. 'If they've blown that,' says the associate, 'then that's tough. That's a lot of money to go through in a couple of years. And it's not Michael's problem.'

The brothers were tight-lipped when the subject was personal finances, but there was no question they longed to share Michael's spotlight. 'I feel I've contributed a major part to Michael's success,' explains Jermaine. 'Not only me but my other brothers, too. What's happened to Michael has a lot to do with what we all did as the Jackson Five. They didn't only scream Michael. It was Tito, Jermaine and so on. The world knew all of us. We feel a little bad when we can't be out there performing with him.'

Adds Marlon, who left the Jacksons in 1988 (after Michael personally called CBS chief Yetnikoff to get him released from the group's contract) to pursue a solo career, 'He's never come and directly said that he's purely a solo act and will never do another Jackson album. If he doesn't want to, fine. He's a grown man. But as a grown man, he shouldn't be afraid to explain himself, especially to his family.'

Disagreements aside, no one is giving up on Michael. 'I think the best thing for him would be to get closer to the family,' says Jermaine. 'Once you make so much money, it's just another dollar. At some point, you have to start looking at the important things like love, family and health. We're giving Michael his space now. But after he finishes the tour, we're all going to attack him – with love.' Even Joe still expects Michael

201

to one day return to the fold. 'But I may have to go get him and let him know that he has a family still,' he says. 'I can always go drag him out of there. He ain't never going to get too big for me to go get him. And he knows I'll come get him, too.'

Experience taught the family that old wounds heal – eventually. For many years, it was difficult to see what the Jackson elders had in common other than a trip to the divorce court. Joe, a swaggering sort with a marble-sized diamond pinkie ring, and Katherine, a gentle madonna with a benevolent glow, seemed to let success drag them in opposite directions. They made their peace, though, and they have kept it. 'We just let our troubles die out,' says Joe. 'We survived. We love each other and we have children. That's why we're together.'

Meanwhile, the Jackson parents had been bracing themselves for bad news ever since LaToya fell under the managerial spell of the fast-talking Gordon, the erstwhile carnival operator and casino worker, who, according to Joe, had designs on her bank account. In any case, they discovered he was hardly the stuff of a parent's dream: He had served two years in prison for trying to bribe the Nevada State Gaming Commission and was convicted of running a brothel. Says Jermaine, sounding very much the big brother, 'LaToya hasn't been out in the world and she's vulnerable to smooth talkers. If it was up to me, I'd run him off.' Katherine worried that her daughter was making decisions she was ill-prepared for. 'I hate to say it, but she was sheltered all her life,' says Mom. 'But it was her own choosing. She never wanted to get out in the world.'

But now that she was, LaToya was unwilling to venture back home, fearful of the repercussions that might result, though her family maintained that Gordon was keeping her prisoner in New York. From the Manhattan condo she purchased, in which Gordon decided to live, LaToya called her parents' worry 'nonsense'.

'Am I holding you hostage?' asked Gordon.

'Of course not,' said LaToya.

'Am I censoring your mail?'

'No, not at all.'

'These accusations could deter our goals here,' snapped Gordon. 'Everything is going to hit real soon. Real soon. We have the dates all lined up.'

'Actually, Jay,' ventured LaToya, 'we don't have any dates yet, right?'

The rest of the family was struggling to maintain whatever

good relations remained. When Janet went into the studio to begin recording her long-overdue followup to *Control*, this time without Dad's input, Joe simply shrugged. 'What can I do?' he says. 'I can't go after her like I would another artist. She's my baby daughter.' When Jackie's marriage crumbled and divorce left him broke, he moved into a condo Michael owned with his folks. 'You've got to help,' says Katherine. 'You feel bad and you help.'

No matter what occurred in their lives, the Jacksons, like all showbiz veterans, followed the cardinal rule of performing: the show must go on. And so the boys, minus Michael and Marlon, were getting set to deliver a new album that paid tribute to their Gary roots and served as a valuable reminder to the entire family, especially, they hoped, to Michael, who was still criss-crossing Europe. 'Even though we're two thousand miles away from there, it's still home,' says Jermaine. 'You can't forget where you came from and how you made it.'

17

Liverpool. September 1988.

Michael telephoned home. He was upset and disturbed. Reports of his family's displeasure with him had filtered back to his tour. What had been brewing for years was too difficult to ignore. It had finally become impossible for Michael to maintain a harmonious front and deny any difficulties.

Michael was close to securing a long-sought sense of independence and instinct told him that to keep moving forward, he had to confront his family directly. If he was ever going to free himself from his shackles, Michael needed to release himself from the old pressures to conform to family dictates.

He spoke to his mother first.

'I'm tired,' he said. 'I need a break. All this family stuff has gone too far. When I get home, we have to talk. All of us. I think it's important.'

She agreed. Then Michael asked to speak to his father, with whom he had exchanged so few words over the past year that their hellos echoed over transatlantic phone lines as if they'd nearly forgotten how each other sounded.

'I didn't mean for things to get like this,' said Michael. 'I didn't mean to imply that you were a bad man in my book'. It was the writer's fault.'

'Michael went on to explain that he was comfortable doing his own act and that he had no plans to rejoin the Jacksons,' says a source close to Joe. 'Then Joe told Michael that whatever he heard about his wanting some of Michael's money wasn't true. He didn't want to be involved with his business. He admitted he had some financial troubles. But most important, he wanted them to be a family.'

'I want to be a family, too,' said Michael. 'I don't like all the negative publicity.'

There was clearly a degree of change in Michael's persona. Less than two weeks earlier he had turned thirty, celebrating his milestone birthday by performing in Leeds, where the crowd of ninety thousand serenaded him with a rousing 'Happy Birthday' that left him standing centre stage, embarrassed and smiling. It wasn't a huge display of emotion, but the façade did crack a bit, revealing some genuine feelings. 'There's no question that Michael's grown up a lot on this tour,' says Dileo. 'I think he may be more secure in himself.'

But if Michael was maturing, he still clung to the outward signs of his success, perhaps not as desperately as before, but, like a weekend sailor who wears a life jacket on a sunny afternoon, he still enjoyed knowing they were there. His tour had already played to more than 3.5 million people (by the tour's end another million fans would turn out), a record. And he was downright giddy when he shattered all existing gate records by announcing in mid-September that his gate receipts had soared past the $133 million mark.

Still, he felt, there were setbacks. His five number one singles placated him temporarily. His sixth single, 'Another Part of Me', failed to reach number one, and then the next release, 'Smooth Criminal', stalled below the top ten, breaking his record of seventeen consecutive singles going top ten. More important, Michael still wanted *Bad* to sell more albums than *Thriller* had, but record sales had also slowed between the 15 million and 17 million mark, and he was frustrated. 'Michael was making life miserable for everyone,' says a record executive close to the situation. 'Everyone was getting telephone calls from him. "Do something," he'd say. He was on to Dileo to do something. He was on to his publicists to get him more magazine covers. Michael was very demanding, and he wasn't used to not getting his way.'

Dileo acted as the voice of reason. 'What are we going to do, say selling 17 million albums is a failure?'

No, not publicly, at least. But Dileo's pronouncement prior to the Liverpool concert, the last stop on the European tour, did come as a shock to the public. He had been hinting at it even before the *Bad* tour took off a year earlier, but now it was official: the Buckled One planned to quit live stage performances after this tour. 'Michael Jackson does not want to do concerts again, of any size,' said Dileo. 'Michael will instead be concentrating on film work and making records. He was exhausted by the grind of the tour.'

Returning to the U.S., Michael was followed by a new storm of rumours. One report claimed he had ordered purified mineral water pumped throughout his home so it would flow from every shower, faucet, dishwasher and bathtub. Another reported a cancer scare, an AIDS panic, and a life-threatening heart condition that was confining him to bed. A glaring three-inch-high headline screamed that 'Michael Jackson's Plastic Face Is Melting', claiming that his numerous operations were making his face fall apart and that the real reason he had decided to quit touring was fear that he'd soon be 'horribly deformed'. Yet another tale had Michael scheduling more plastic surgery on his face at the year's end to make it resemble Princess Diana's.

The truth is Michael barely had time for a rest, let alone surgery. He did take a brief respite from work at his ranch. But even this had proved troublesome. He went out shopping in a local mall one afternoon with a nine-year-old pal, disguised in muttonchop sideburns, a moustache and raggedy clothes. When they strolled into a pricy jewellery store and Michael began studying some of the more expensive trinkets, the shopkeeper panicked and called the cops, who apprehended Michael and his pal. They were quite embarrassed when he revealed his true identity.

But this wasn't the first time Michael had run up against the police. Several years before, while touring with his brothers, Michael had slipped into disguise and gone out shopping, wandering into a pricey antiques store in a predominantly white section of Atlanta. The store owner didn't recognize him, and grew suspicious, and then rude, when the seemingly downtrodden black man appeared disoriented and hid in an antique armoire.

'I thought of pushing the wardrobe over but it had a mirror on the front and it could have killed him,' said the store owner. 'I made a lot of noise, shouting that we were closing and that he had to come out. After ten seconds, he appeared. He looked so weird. He refused to move.'

The shopkeeper said he was going to call the police, but claims the mysterious intruder blocked his path, then reached his hand into his pocket as if he were drawing a knife. 'There was nothing to do but protect myself,' he says. 'I hit him in the face and he went down. As he got up, I grabbed him in a headlock.' A police officer was summoned. 'Jackson looked like a bum,' he recalled. 'I didn't know who he was and when he told me he was Michael Jackson, I didn't believe him.'

Charges were considered on both sides, but never pressed, though Michael never forgot the ugly incident. 'It was a disgusting incident of racism and bigotry,' says an associate. 'No matter what version the shopkeeper and the police officer tell, they were guilty of outright prejudice. Sure, Michael was in disguise, but he remembers being badgered and heckled and called horrible, demeaning names from the moment he walked in the store simply because of his skin colour. It's disgusting. They are lucky he didn't want to make a big deal out of it.'

After Michael's break he picked up the final leg of his tour in the U.S. The heartwarming memories spawned by his return to Detroit were highlighted by Michael's $125,000 donation to the rambling brick house at 2648 West Grand Boulevard, the past home of Hitsville, U.S.A. and original headquarters of Berry Gordy's Motown records, which was being turned into the Motown Museum. 'It's great to be here,' said Michael from behind sunglasses to the crowd that turned out for the opening. 'I'm happy and proud to give back to the soil from which I came. Berry Gordy made it all possible for me, and I want to say I love you, Berry, thank you.'

Who said you can't go home again – at least for the day? Michael and Gordy then disappeared inside the house that was the launching pad for greats like Diana Ross, Marvin Gaye and Stevie Wonder. As they stood beside the old baby grand piano the Jackson Five had used for their 1969 audition, the Motown founder didn't have any trouble dredging up memories of the first time he met Michael. 'He was a cute kid,' said Gordy. 'He could sing well and he danced like James Brown.' Michael's drive was evident from the beginning. 'He stared at me all the time,' he said. 'The other kids would play around, hit each other. He had nothing on his mind but learning.'

When Michael returned from nine straight sell-out dates at Tokyo's new 'Egg Dome' stadium in December, his second triumphant visit to Japan on the *Bad* tour, he could look over the past year and a half with some well-deserved satisfaction. His album sales were passed the 17 million mark. His overall grosses reached into the comfortable neighbourhood of $200 million. And he was reconciled with his family, even if they weren't comfortable with him. All in all, it looked like a pretty good outing.

Businesswise, what appeared to be the end of one sensational run was the beginning of another. Already in motion were a series of ambitious projects for television and film centring around the Beatles songs that he owned. In development was a pilot for a TV series and at least four movies using Beatles music, including *Strawberry Fields*, an animated feature well into production, and *Back in the USSR*, a film about real-life Soviet rockers. Movies based on 'Eleanor Rigby' and 'Fool on the Hill' were on the drawing board. There was also talk of using Beatles tunes for musical greeting cards and music boxes.

Despite appearances, Michael purportedly kept in mind the artistic value of the work. He 'is the world's number one Beatles fan, and he wanted to protect and cherish these songs just as the Beatles would,' said his attorney. 'We're in constant touch with the representatives of Paul McCartney and the estate of John Lennon, and nothing is done without their knowledge.'

If there was any summing up to do before he disappeared from the concert stage, Michael took charge of that with the end-of-year release of *Moonwalker*, the 94-minute feature that he had kept under top secret wraps for more than three years. Estimated to have cost upwards of $15 million to make, *Moonwalker* was a kaleidoscopic montage of live performance footage, special effects and insight into the way Michael perceived himself. Though Michael opened with 'Man in the Mirror', a message song about personal change, the rest of the film was merely a stunning display of high-tech moviemaking that showed Michael thought he was fine just the way he is.

A brief retrospective showed the hits that catapulted him to worldwide stardom. A segment titled 'Badder' featured children emulating their hero's tough-guy performance of 'Bad'. In 'Leave Me Alone', Michael chastized the press, portrayed as hound dogs in suits, and poked fun at numerous rumours by showing a shrine to Elizabeth Taylor, a dancing skeleton, and newspaper headlines that read 'Michael Weds Alien', and 'Michael Confides in Chimp'.

The forty-minute centrepiece of *Moonwalker*, 'Smooth Criminal', was standard comic book stuff, whose storyline starred Michael in the role of superhero foiling the evil Mr Big's dastardly attempt to take over the world by hooking children on drugs. Like so many times before, Michael was anointing himself the archangel of innocence and good, a messiah-like character working his darndest to lead his unspoiled flock of children to salvation.

One can almost imagine Michael weeping into his pillow at night, wishing, 'Oh, if only we didn't have to grow old and turn into those nasty adults.'

27 January 1989. The world's most popular entertainer stood at centre stage in the Los Angeles Sports Arena, bowed humbly and wiped away the tears. He hugged his band mates, then lingered awhile, not exactly sure what to do next but certain that he didn't want to let go of the adulation washing over him from a wildly cheering audience that included Elizabeth Taylor, Berry Gordy, Dionne Warwick, Princess Stephanie of Monaco and dozens of other celebrities. Then the triumphant star walked to the lip of the stage and accepted bouquets of roses, like laurels, from worshipful fans screaming for him not to leave.

Finally, after the final bars of the final number of his final encore, Michael Jackson made his final exit, skipping from the stage with one last wave and a fare-thee-well smile.

Fare-him-well, at least. After performing 123 concerts in fifteen countries on four continents Michael bid an end to his sixteen-month world tour on a note of triumph. 'It's been hard and exhausting,' said Frank Dileo, who was only too happy to relinquish the task of overseeing the marathon tour, launched on 12 September 1987 with a cast and crew of 137, a weekly payroll of $500,000 and enough equipment to fill twelve semi-trailer trucks. The grind, he said, caused Jackson to lose ten pounds and Dileo to gain forty.

So with an eye to his waistline as well as the bottom line, Dileo underscored all previous announcements that the Gloved, Clefted and Bobbed One was hanging up his tour taps for good. 'I don't think either Michael or I would like to go through something like this again,' he said. 'Mike's accomplished what he wanted. His goal was to establish himself as the world's biggest solo artist. He's done that.'

Not that Michael planned to disappear from sight. 'He'll do a live show every so often,' the rotund manager said. 'But he's not going to tour again. He didn't tour with *Thriller* and sold nearly 40 million copies. He didn't tour with *Off the Wall* and that did pretty well, too. I don't think Mike's going to have a problem. It's time to do something else.'

That something else is likely to be a movie. 'We've received lots of scripts, but we haven't looked at them,' Dileo explained. 'They're all piled up. We're looking to do a musical of some sort, but we'll start on that after some time off.' Industry types waged that whatever Michael chose to do, he would succeed. 'He's an extremely hard worker,' said producer and longtime Jackson friend David Geffen. 'He has a great track record. Michael's not the sort you'd bet against.'

Of course, some who knew Michael doubted whether movie-making would satisfy his hunger for audience approval. Ticket sales from a hit film are one thing, but there's little that can duplicate the intoxicating thrill of a packed stadium of wildly cheering fans. 'I can understand why Michael's decided not to tour any more,' said Marlon. 'We've toured since we were little, and it takes a lot out of you. But I think he's going to tour again. I mean, you say something like that and then three or four years pass and you get the urge again.'

In the meantime, the limousine carrying Michael motored from the Sports Arena, inching past throngs of fans who lined the driveway hoping for one last glimpse of the superstar. A shrill voice pierced the cool air. 'We love you, Michael!' While a police escort led the limousine forward, a tinted rear window slipped down a crack, enabling a long, thin hand to wave one last time. Then the cars were gone, disappearing into the night, ferrying Michael Jackson to his next destination.

The 13 February announcement startled everyone in the music industry. Michael Jackson and Frank Dileo were parting ways. The headlines made the split appear amicable. The tersely worded press release issued by Michael's publicist had him thanking Dileo '. . . for his contribution on my behalf during the past several years'.

Dileo, who was sequestered at a Duke University weight loss programme, was unavailable for comment. But those who spoke to the usually garrulous manager the day after the announcement was released said that he sounded 'depressed, removed, very tired, and angry.' There was no question that Dileo was as surprised by the decision as everyone else.

Speculation on what prompted Michael to fire the man who was virtually his only and clearly his most honest link to the outside world centred on several possible reasons. The first was that Michael was mad that Dileo wasn't able to sell *Moonwalker* to any motion picture distributors for a theatrical release in the United States. Instead, *Moonwalker* was put out as a home video, and though it immediately set sales records, Michael was said to be incensed that his ninety-minute movie wasn't given the due he thought it deserved.

The second reason, a few industry wags speculated, centred on Dileo's attraction to the spotlight. Michael, associates wondered, had perhaps grown jealous of the number of interviews his manager was granting and the credit he accepted for himself. However, Dileo had always been Michael's go-between to the outside world, which granted little credibility to this thesis.

The third possibility concerned Michael's future plans. Earlier on the *Bad* tour, Dileo had announced that Michael was going to leave the concert trail for good and concentrate on making films. If that was so, his needs were amply met by his attorney, accountant and his agent, CAA chief Mike Ovitz, who was widely regarded as the most powerful man in Hollywood. Michael, it seemed, just didn't need to be paying the commission Dileo commanded as a personal manager.

As the *Bad* tour wound down to its final dates in Los Angeles there were few signs that trouble was brewing. But a few tour insiders did notice something different. 'You could tell by the end of the tour that they weren't as close as they had been at the start,' one tour member says. 'Michael would be off doing one thing and Frank would be doing something else. Before, they would have been working together. They were still friendly, but there wasn't the closeness that had been so apparent.'

Another man who had dealings with both Michael and Dileo supposed that their parting had more to do with the singer's disappointment over *Bad*'s failure to surpass *Thriller* than anything else. 'The decision was all Michael's,' he says. 'And everyone who knows Michael is aware that he makes his decisions based on dollars and cents and record sales and success according to his overall business plan. Never mind that Frank had worked the album and given him five number one singles. He probably didn't think Frank was delivering and that was it, simple as that.'

Whatever the unknown reasons for Michael's decision one thing was absolutely certain. The end of the Dileo era marked a new beginning in the career of Michael Jackson.

Out of the bleak, industrial fringes of the American Dream he came, dancing and singing, a tyke bubbling with talent and personality. He leaped onto the twirling carousel and snatched

211

the golden ring, and then there was light. It was a game, it was fun, it was everything being a performer was supposed to be. Stardom beckoned and he skipped into the outstretched arms of an adoring public, an Afro-topped, dimpled cherub, smiling, laughing, turning difficult moves into an effortless flight, treating the spotlight as if it were an elementary school playground and he was enjoying a recess without end.

And then the fun disappeared . . .

When the music fades he is still there, much too visible for his own liking, ill-equipped for the journey that is life. Whether or not he wants to admit it, Michael Jackson is not that different from the people who gawk and grab at him, from the millions who've paid their money to see him and hear him perform and have made him wealthier than any individual has the good sense to imagine. Yet there he stands, bereft of camouflage no matter what costume he dons or how much makeup he applies or what changes he requests from his plastic surgeon.

Look at Michael. He is undeniably handsome, beautiful, his features moulded into the most exquisite shapes. And because of it, he is frightening, unsettling in his perfection. Listen to Michael. He is glorious of voice. The sounds he is able to hear in his mind and call up from his throat are clear and wonderful reminders of what glorious creations man is capable of producing. Watch Michael. He is eccentric and he is talented, and one helps the other, and if one were missing the other might not be possible.

Michael is the embodiment of everyone's dream. He lives the ultimate life and is trapped by it. He is rich beyond accounting and unhappy because of it. He is a lover too isolated to love. He is frightening because he is too scared to admit frailty. In some ways Michael is as perfect as he imagines himself. In other ways he fails miserably and he knows it. In all ways he is human, no different from anyone else.

212